5 March 1999

David —

I hope that you
find this book still
relevant useful.

best regards,

Tan

TECHNOLOGY IN BANKING
CREATING VALUE AND DESTROYING PROFITS

Thomas D. Steiner
Diogo B. Teixeira

McGraw-Hill
New York   San Francisco   Washington, D.C.   Auckland   Bogotá
Caracas   Lisbon   London   Madrid   Mexico City   Milan
Montreal   New Delhi   San Juan   Singapore
Sydney   Tokyo   Toronto

Irwin/McGraw-Hill

A Division of The McGraw-Hill Companies

Library of Congress Cataloging-in-Publication Data

Steiner, Thomas D.
   Technology in banking : creating value and destroying profits /
Thomas D. Steiner and Diogo B. Teixeira
     p.   cm.
   ISBN 1-55623-150-4
   1. Banks and banking–United States–Automation. 2. Bank
employees–United States–Effect of technological innovations on.
3. Bank employees–United States–Supply and demand. I. Teixeira,
Diogo B. II. Title.
HG1709.S757 1990
335.1'028–dc20   89–77170
                                            CIP

Printed in the United States of America

10 11   QPK/QPK   9 8

ACKNOWLEDGMENTS

This book represents the efforts of many people. It could not have been prepared without the collective client experience and resources of McKinsey & Company, Inc. Although this book is not based on confidential client studies or data, and does not involve any proprietary client information, our understanding of the issues is based on nearly fifteen years of work with financial institutions and with providers to financial institutions. More than 100 management consultants at McKinsey participated in developing the concepts, analyses, and ideas in this book.

The support of Don Waite, who leads McKinsey's Financial Institutions Group, was essential. Without his encouragement, the requisite time and resources to create this book could have never been found. Likewise, Fred Gluck, our Managing Director, created the management direction without which this book could not have happened. Carter Bales, Director of our Information Technology Practice, created a supportive climate for systems technology. Both Bill Matassoni and Brook Manville of McKinsey's communications staff contributed to the book's overall approach and have been staunch backers from the very beginning. Finally, our editor, Jim Childs, deserves our thanks. His cheerfulness and good will never lagged even as we missed first one deadline and then another.

Lowell Bryan, Director of our North American Banking Practice, deserves a special note. His intellectual leadership, recently published in *Breaking Up The Bank* — particularly his insights into the disaggregation of the credit markets — shaped our thinking about the forces at work in the industry.

This book really began with an effort several years ago to consolidate our thinking about how technology affects commercial banks. Despite years of effort, we had never clearly synthesized our thinking about the forces of change that are unleashed by substantial investments in information technology and what the ultimate financial impacts might be. This work was published as a research report in 1987 under the title *Systems Technology and the United States Commercial Banking Industry.* A preliminary version was originally co-funded with Salomon Brothers Inc. as part of their ongoing efforts to analyze major performance factors impacting the commercial banking industry. McKinsey staff who worked on the project included Roy Lowrance, Charles Kalmbach, and Julie Sakallariadis. Without their very substantial contributions and pioneering thought leadership this book would never have come to pass.

Virtually all of the specific ideas in the predecessor version and in this current book originated in our experiences serving financial institutions over the past fifteen years. While too extensive to list all McKinsey consultants who participated in this work, we must credit the principal thought leaders whose work is embodied in this book. In addition, other McKinsey consultants and partners reviewed the drafts of this document to assure that our facts and case examples were accurate.

Chapter 1 is based on an extensive analysis of industry data originally developed by Tim Boomer, Julie Sakallariadis, Charles Wendell, and Roy Lowrance. They contributed greatly to the laborious task of developing an accurate and high quality data base on financial performance and expenditures on systems technology. The data base has since then been improved and updated by Steve Runin, Randy Lewis, and Rolf Thrane.

Chapter 2 owes a debt to Maureen Ferguson and Ali Hanna. Together, in serving a technology provider nearly a decade ago, they first developed the initial theory of how automation proceeds in stages. John Mickel was also helpful and contributed particularly to the historical discussion.

Chapter 3 combines the concepts and thinking of several consultants. Lowell Bryan's ideas on industry disaggregation were extended to the entire banking business system by Toos Daruvala. Fred Gluck, Tom Woodward, Ennius Bergsma, and Toos all participated in a technology provider engagement in which, after extensive discussion, the highly simplified M1-M2-M3 framework was developed. Julie Sakallariadis and John Shuck participated in the original work on correspondent banking in which the Type I–IV competitive framework was created.

Chapter 4 draws on research and data developed by Tim Boomer and Glen Okun. Later, this data was expanded and updated, first by Steve Runin and Toos Daruvala, and then by Tom Tinsley, Randy Kelly, Amy Lister, and Sue Bostrom. Steve and Toos also collaborated on a payment systems workshop from which some of the case examples are drawn. Dick Foster, author of *Innovation: The Attackers Advantage*, helped with his concept of S-curves.

Chapter 4 also gained by a review for proper perspective and accuracy. Roger Kline read an early draft and clarified some case examples. Kevin Coyne suggested new ways to think about ATMs and about the long-run effect of home banking. Jim Bemowski helped us gain a better perspective on check processing and on POS systems. Finally, John Durrett reviewed an early draft for clarity.

Chapter 5 reflects the collective knowledge of several people. Toos Daruvala helped immeasurably with his knowledge of credit card economics and recent developments in competition. Barbara Park, Ennius Bergsma, and Jack Stephenson all contributed to our understanding of this industry. Rolf Thrane did many of the economic calculations. Andrew Power helped critique and improve the overall message. And, Richard Gridley deserves special thanks for his timely critique when our early drafts were bogged down in endless circles.

Chapter 6 also benefited from the assistance of several McKinsey consultants. Paul Allen used his experience in wholesale banking to review the entire chapter. Rainer Famulla helped us understand the relationship between payment systems economics and technology. Philip Langguth helped develop several early ideas on wholesale payments and cash management. Finally, Laura Daniels assisted in preparing the subsection on cash management.

Chapter 7 is based on work originally done by Julie Sakallariadis as part of the original Salomon Brothers Inc. report. This work was later updated and expanded by Rolf Thrane and Rainer Famulla, who used their knowledge of the securities businesses to provide fresh insights.

Chapter 8 was carefully reviewed by the McKinsey Cambridge Systems Center, headed by Will Riordan. Jeff Weiss read not only this chapter, but the entire book and made many useful comments. Other contributors included Arthur Chin and Peter Gaston. Peter Jessel and Chris Gardner, of our New York Office, contributed the data on trends and costs and reviewed the chapter for accuracy.

Special credit must go to those at the five banks illustrated in Chapter 9 who granted us interviews and gave us relatively free access to information. Their participation was entirely voluntary and is deeply appreciated. They include Peter Madden and Suzanne Clark at State Street Boston; Don McWhorter, John Fisher, and John Alexander, Sr. at Banc One; Mike Urkowitz, Phil Giaquinto, Jack Rosenstock, and Tom Kingston at Chase Manhattan Bank; Don Hollis at First Chicago; and Jim Brewer and Harrison Marks at First Wachovia. Bob O'Block, Jon Weiner, Dominic Casserley, Tom Tinsley, and Clay Deutsch all helped review and improve the illustrations of Chapter 9 by forcing us to be more straight-forward and clear in our thinking. Finally, Chip Chandler played a particularly vital role in our thinking in both Chapters 6 and 9 and deserves a special acknowledgment for his support.

Several people deserve special mention with regard to Chapter 10. Tom Peters and Bob Waterman created the original "tight-loose" concept in their book, *In Search of Excellence*. Marvin Bower, ex-Managing Director of McKinsey, provided a strong perspective and a clear understanding of the vital role of policy in the management process—which is illustrated extensively in his book *The Will to Manage*. Roger Ferguson adopted the "tight-loose" concept to management decision making in information technology and tested it in a banking client engagement. Mike Miron, assisted by Steve Runin, contributed very substantially by applying the "tight-loose" concept to management policies affecting information technology. These ideas and specific policies were rigorously tested in a significant client engagement.

No book could be prepared without the active aid of support personnel. Joanne Ferrari, Diogo's secretary, did a fantastic job of typing our documents and keeping track of the seemingly endless details involved in writing a book. Bill Porter also assisted in typing our many drafts. Gene Zelazny and John Donovan conspired to produce high-quality graphics from our initially illegible scribblings.

We also could not have prepared this book without the assistance of many people outside McKinsey who work at banks, vendors, or third-party providers. These include Merrill Burns of BankAmerica; Bob Hill, Jim Witkins and Ted Francavilla of MHC; Connie McCann of Chemical; Scott Gundaker of CoreStates; Don Long of IBM; Bill Walsh of CHIPS; and Carl Brickman of S.W.I.F.T. We appreciate their assistance.

Last, but certainly not least, we owe a debt of gratitude to our families. Without their support and understanding we could never have completed this book. Christine Halkiotis (Mrs. Diogo Teixeira) suffered through many late nights as Diogo kept calling to say he was not coming home yet. Maureen Ferguson (Mrs. Tom Steiner) also suffered as Tom called repeatedly to say he was about to leave for home—"in just a few minutes." It is to these supportive spouses that this book is really dedicated.

Thomas D. Steiner
Diogo B. Teixeira

CONTENTS

INTRODUCTION

In 1960, the commercial banks in the United States employed approximately 640,000 bankers. By 1975, that figure had approximately doubled to 1.26 million. Between 1975 and 1980 another 220,000 bankers were added, raising the total to approximately 1.48 million. During the turbulent first half of the 1980s the employment level remained steady, until 1987 when approximately 21,000 were fired! In 1988 the pattern continued and accelerated; approximately 33,000 more bankers were fired — bringing the total to nearly 55,000 in 2 years. If this pattern continues — and based on our client experience we think it will — then approximately 300,000 more bankers will leave the commerical banking system in the next 10 years, bringing the total number of workers down to approximately 1.2 million by the year 2000. In short, the United States banking industry reached its *point of maximum employment in 1986 and is now shrinking*. The same thing happened to the agricultural industry in the United States when it reached approximately 11 million employees in 1910. Today only approximately 2 million agricultural workers feed the 240 million people in our country. Peaking also happened to the steel industry in 1955 (700,000 employees) and the automobile industry in 1978 (1 million employees). This same phenomenon, now shrinking employment among banks, is due to a substitution of equipment — primarily systems technology — for employees. (See Figure Intro–1.)

Another perspective on this same phenomenon can be gained by viewing the increased expenditures made by commercial banks on systems technology. In 1988 the United States commercial banking industry's spending on systems technology (e.g., computers, software, and telecommunications) reached a total of $11.6 billion. This figure was almost 300 percent higher than it was in 1980. At the same time, the purchasing power of a dollar spent on systems technology has increased rapidly.

FIGURE INTRO-1

U.S. Commercial Banks' Employees and Systems Expense

1985 index = 100

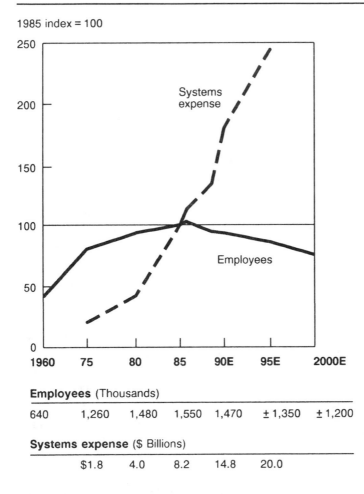

Employees (Thousands)

640	1,260	1,480	1,550	1,470	± 1,350	± 1,200

Systems expense ($ Billions)

	$1.8	4.0	8.2	14.8	20.0

Between 1980 and 1988, the price performance measures for basic components of data processing operations increased by ratios of 200 percent to 1,000 percent, depending on the type of equipment. The aggregate size of the industry's data centers have been growing at rates of 25 to 40 percent per year. All told, the industry has roughly 30 times more systems power available to it than it did a decade ago. Yet, banking is not a new industry; it is not experiencing tremendously high growth in the primary demand for its services. Rather, these systems expenditures represent a fundamental change in the way that banking services are being produced and delivered.

AUTOMATION OF BANK LABOR

Is there a connection between these two events – between the peaking of employment and the high levels of systems expense? Based on our experiences with clients, we believe that there is a very substantial – if lagged – relationship. Further, our experience in other industries makes us believe that it represents a fundamental, one-time change in the traditional, old-world activity of commercial banking. Banking jobs are being displaced by automation in a manner similar to that of the automation of the U.S. farm, a process which began in the last century. There, technology instigated a precipitous decline in farm employment that has now continued for almost a century.

Where were the 55,000 banking jobs eliminated? Some were from the ranks of lenders, managers, or customer service representatives. But most disappeared from the industry's 60,000 banking locations and from the back offices where banking services are processed. Put simply, automation in these areas has reduced the need for clerks who handle routine manual tasks. This can be seen quite clearly by looking at the percentage of noninterest operating costs which are devoted to systems technology. Depending upon the product line, this ratio, which we call "systems intensiveness," can be as high as 15 to 20 percent of total delivery costs. In comparison, only a decade ago this ratio was in the 5-to-10-percent range. Clearly, this is an economic transformation of fundamental importance.

Displacement of labor through the use of new technologies is an inherently slow process, especially when the technology deals with an intangible like information. Banks began investing in systems technology early in the 1960s, yet it has taken almost 30 years to produce the first fundamental decline in industry employment. The primary reason is that computer technology requires building a parallel electronic system beside the manual system. For a long period of time, duplication occurs as both paper and electronic systems exist. It is only when a paper system is dismantled that real head count reduction begins to occur. For a given product line, this process may take 10 years or more.

A second reason is that effective and complete automation of banking work requires changes in customer behavior. Ultimately, the customer determines how payments are made, and even today less than 10 percent

FIGURE INTRO–2
Technological Transformation

Payments made by paper

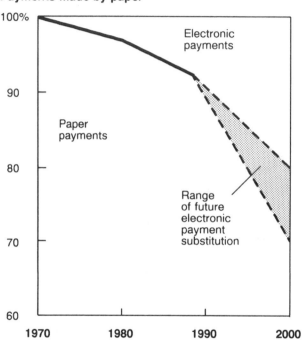

of the payments processed by banks are made electronically. (See Figure Intro-2.) The remaining 90 percent are still based on paper processing—a technology that tends to require high levels of manual labor. Because up to 75 percent of the industry's employees provide payment services, this initial decline in employment is extremely significant. As the percent of all payments, and therefore of the industry's workload, is gradually converted to electronics, we can foresee the potential for ongoing labor force reductions. In fact, we predict continuing declines well into the 1990s.

The types of technologies that are driving these declines are the electronic substitutes for labor. In the branches, automated teller machines are reducing the number of tellers. Sophisticated on-line systems are making the remaining branch employees more productive and more effective. In back offices, sophisticated computer programs are making customer service representatives, researchers, and collectors more efficient. New electronic payment technologies, such as the automated clearinghouse, point of sale networks, and wholesale electronic funds networks are gradually replacing paper-based payment methods such as checks, telex, or money orders. New computer models can control credit transactions better and extend credit faster. New applications software can process applications, track loans, and reconcile accounts quicker and more accurately than ever. The long awaited improvement in banking productivity looks as if it has finally arrived.

INDUSTRY FRAGMENTATION

To see this process clearly, it is necessary to look at individual lines of business. Banking is very far from being a homogenous activity. In fact, it is a collection of more than 150 specific product/market services. Lines of business differ by customer—whether retail, corporate, or other financial institution. They differ by distribution channel, whether by branch, by direct salesman, or by mail. They differ by product group, whether lending, deposit gathering, or payment product.

The degree to which systems technology has replaced labor in each line of business depends very much on the specific services offered as well as the economics of the line of business. For example, high value funds transfers between wholesale customers have become almost entirely automated over the course of the last decade. A $20 million payment between a manufacturer in Japan and a source of raw materials in Singapore, denominated in dollars, is usually handled electronically in New York by the Clearinghouse Interbank Payments System (CHIPS). Such a payment is processed almost instantly—it is completed within a single business day.

However, several of the most important banking lines of business have not yet reached the critical stage of automation where substantive labor displacement can occur. In particular, the retail payment system, which allows the United States' 88 million households to make payments, is still dominated far and away by the check. Also, United States corporations and businesses continue to write checks to pay employees, smaller vendors, and for miscellaneous services. In some manner, about 50 percent of all bank employees are involved in the checking system, which handled approximately 50 billion checks in 1988. In addition, banks still communicate with customers via paper-based statements and receive instructions through manual methods.

We believe that the potential to displace labor in the future through further automation of banking activities is very significant. The size and timing of these future displacements is what should concern bankers. As they occur, fundamental changes will occur in the economics, profitability, and competitive structure of these product lines.

COMPETITIVE IMPLICATIONS

As a line of business becomes highly automated it takes on the characteristics of a mature business. Fewer employees are needed because productivity is very high. The business begins to look like—and in fact becomes—an electronic network. Networks result in high fixed costs. This frequently forces competitors to begin to share the ownership, economics, and business risks of those fixed costs. Banking has several examples of such shared, or third-party, utilities. CHIPS makes large dollar payments, SWIFT transmits international payment messages, and Fedwire handles interbank electronic transfers.

Cost structures can become extremely low with full automation. For example, the cost of an electronic funds transfer is less than 10 percent of the cost of a paper-based check when full use of volume economies can be obtained. Pricing for mature products may also become very low as competitors seek to gain volume by grabbing market share. In turn, fewer competitors offer the product, and that line of business, if it was previously fragmented, becomes consolidated. This process can be clearly seen in the fewer number of banks that offer the more sophisticated electronic products (e.g., cash management, funds transfer, and immobilized securities safekeeping services) compared to a decade ago. In fact, as this process of labor displacement occurs, fewer profits may well be realized—instead of more—because of the competitive interplay. Specifically this means that fixed-cost competitors frequently get into price wars for marginal business volume.

For bankers, these developments have potentially enormous consequences. It is inevitable that systems technology will be employed to do banking work because it is more productive. Yet, it is relative efficiency that will dictate the survivors, not absolute efficiency. It is possible for most of the competitors to lose out when all competitors in a line of business automate—even though the production of the service becomes more efficient for each competitor. Thus, the bankers of today need to have a perspective on each line of business—all 150 of them—and how automation is affecting each one. This perspective needs to include the current structure and economics of that line of business, and the speed and sequence with which automation is changing those economics. This is a substantial amount of information. Yet without it, many banks may not become efficient fast enough to be real winners.

ABOUT THIS BOOK

This book is targeted at developing these ideas in more detail. It speaks to the need of bankers to understand the role that systems technology is playing in specific bank lines of business. We believe that every line of business is being influenced to some degree by systems technology. The level of influence ranges from very substantial for payment products to insubstantial for the type of banking work that does not involve many transactions. Understanding the scope of the technology and how that technology will work its way into the line of business is a critical element of competitive survival.

This book really began in 1985 when McKinsey & Company, Inc. began a jointly funded study with Salomon Brothers Inc. to study the influence that technology was having on the banking industry. Initial results from that study were published in a report entitled "Systems Technology in the United States Commercial Banking Industry," which was made available in late 1987. Throughout this book we have used two major information sources to support our perspective. First, aggregate industry data on revenues, costs, profitability, and production volumes has been drawn from a wide range of government and other publicly available sources which we maintain. Second, and most important, we have used our experience gained from more than 100 client engagements to understand the actual process of automation and labor displacement in dozens of lines of business.

A few caveats should be noted. First, the rate of technological change is high, for banks as well as other industries. As we indicated above, the computing power of the commercial banking industry is doubling approximately every 3 years. Although it is not difficult to foresee further substantial improvements in the price performance of computers, it is always much more difficult to foresee exactly how and when that improved technology will actually be applied. Because the banking industry may well have between 5 and 6 times as much computing power in 1995 as in 1990, it is difficult to predict the exact nature of the efficiencies. We need to be humble about both predicting that "a cashless society will arrive in 5 years," as well as that certain lines of business will become "totally efficient."

Second, the banking industry remains extremely fragmented and is therefore difficult to measure. Although there are reams of banking statistics, few address what we really need to know—namely how much technology exists in each line of business and how the economics have been affected. Likewise, industry structure is not easy to measure. Although consolidation is occurring and certain major banks are getting bigger, some lines of business remain highly fragmented. Different competitors occupy leadership positions in different lines of business. Product definitions in banking are difficult. Most banks maintain a high degree of shared costs across the lines of business they compete in and cannot easily break out operating costs or the underlying equity accurately across the lines of business. In short, it is never easy to be absolutely sure about the economics of banking lines of business.

Third, both external and transfer pricing determine profitability but are usually not explicit or consistent. Despite trends toward explicit pricing, banks still are paid for services primarily by accepting deposits. Although this is changing, there are enough of the old ways left so that a change in the level of interest rates can make one business look good and another bad. Determining banking economics remains a mercurial exercise.

For all these reasons, the conclusions we draw in this book about profitability, technology expenditures, and the relationship between the two have obvious limits. Only the internal proprietary financial structure of an individual bank can determine actual economics. Profits for a given activity may vary substantially between two banks, and especially between two lines of business. Furthermore, rapid changes can take place in market share—possibly superseding some of the specific analyses contained within this book.

Most of our comments are intended to be high-level. They should be used to provoke thought and to generate an interest in the concepts and trends outlined herein. We have not attempted to evaluate any specific institution's performance in a specific line of business. As a result, the references to institutions—and we have made more than 500 references to more than 100 institutions—are used as examples to illustrate our concepts, not as judgments on performance. We cannot give specific answers to competitive situations in specific lines of business. The best use of this book, therefore, is to generate a process of fundamental economic analysis within a bank and its relationship to technology. That is the best first step to future success in the new technological era.

PART 1

THE BANKING INDUSTRY: RESTRUCTURING, TRANSFORMATION, AND COMPETITION

The commercial banking industry in the United States is restructuring itself under the influence of deregulation as well as the transformative effects of systems technology. As part of this restructuring, information technology plays a strong enabling role and is influencing how banks compete with each other. Not surprisingly, commercial banks are suffering stagnant financial performance during this transition period. The first part of the book explores the interplay of these factors.

Chapter 1 contains an overview of industry economics. It describes the effects of deregulation, the trend toward concentration, and the growing power of the larger banks. It reveals the growing concentration of operating expenses and systems technology expenditures. Finally, it looks at line of business profitability.

Chapter 2 describes the historical and current technological infrastructure of the industry. It explains the purposes to which automation expenditures are put. Most of these deal with the automation of routine transactions created by operation of the payment system. This chapter also describes the stages by which lines of business reach complete automation.

Chapter 3 describes some frameworks for thinking about technological competition. It explains that the industry is disaggregating and that competition occurs on this disaggregated basis. It tells how banks compete with the application of their technology, not with the technology itself. Finally, it explores the role of shared networks.

CHAPTER 1

A STAGNANT INDUSTRY RESTRUCTURES: TECHNOLOGY PLAYS A KEY ROLE

The U.S. commercial banking industry turned in a stagnant financial performance during the 1980s. Return on equity dropped as net income failed to keep pace with expanding balance sheets. But this stagnant performance has not been distributed evenly throughout the industry. The large money center and particularly the large regional banks are now turning in better financial performances than the thousands of small banks that comprise the rest of the industry. In fact the small banks, as a class, are already on the decline.

The roots of this situation lie in the economic and competitive forces at work in the industry. The deregulation that began in 1979 is lessening the deep pattern of the industry's traditional protective framework and has enhanced the level and intensity of competition. Consolidation is slowly reducing the number of banks but rapidly increasing the size and power of the biggest competitors. The most successful of the large banks are changing their business mix and, in the process, are restructuring their business systems and their economics. Large banks are becoming the dominant players in the industry, spending by far the most on systems technology and positioning themselves to be the arbiters of competition in the future.

STAGNANT, DIFFERENTIATING FINANCIAL PERFORMANCE

From the perspective of financial performance, the U.S. commercial banking industry has not performed well since 1980. After-tax net income grew by approximately 4 percent annually from $13.9 billion in

FIGURE 1-1
U.S. Commercial Banks' Performance Measures

Net Income (After-tax, $ Billions)

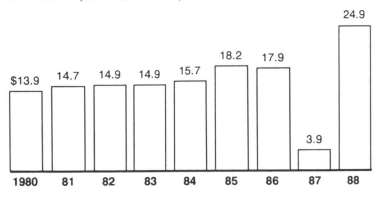

Return on Equity (After-tax, Percentage)

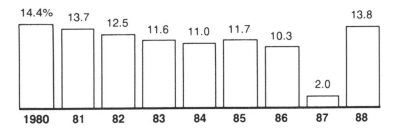

1980 to $17.9 billion in 1986, followed by the two anomalous years of
1987 and 1988. (See Figure 1-1.) The heavy loan loss provisions for less
developed country (LDC) and other debt problems reduced net income
severely in 1987 and were followed in 1988 by exceptionally positive and
certainly one-time events, such as sales of appreciated assets and real
estate as well as retroactive interest payments from some LDC debtors.
If these two years were averaged out, for example, industry performance
(i.e., total net income) would look essentially flat during the entire
decade. Even in the anomalous year of 1988 the industry had an after-tax
return on equity that was slightly lower than that of 1980.

Although the trend from 1986 through 1988 looks more positive, the fundamental factors contributing to this stagnancy have not yet run their course. One-time transactions to improve earnings on the order of those experienced in 1988 are not sustainable. The near-term indications are for continued stagnancy until the industry consolidates more and finishes its adjustment to the still evolving process of deregulation.

Differential Performance

However, these overall patterns at the industry level cloud significant differentials among banks. As we indicated above, the stagnant financial performance for the industry as a whole is the result of two different groups of banks that perform differently and are becoming increasingly divergent in their capabilities and characteristics. "Large banks" have done increasingly well during the 1980s while "small banks" have done increasingly poorly.

For analysis purposes, we have defined the large banks as the following group of 35 bank holding companies followed by Salomon Brothers Inc.:

The 35 Large Banks

BankAmerica Corp.	Fleet/Norstar Financial Group
Banc One Corp.	Manufacturers Hanover Corp.
Bank of Boston Corp.	Mellon Bank Corp.
Bank of New England Corp.	Midlantic Corp.
The Bank of New York Company, Inc.	J.P. Morgan & Co. Inc.
	National City Corp.
Bankers Trust New York Corp.	NDB Bancorp, Inc.
Barnett Banks, Inc.	NCNB Corp.
Chase Manhattan Corp.	Norwest Corp.
Chemical Banking Corp.	PNC Financial Corp.
Citicorp	Republic New York Corp.
The Citizens & Southern Corp.	Security Pacific Corp.
CoreStates Financial Corp.	Signet Banking Corp.
First Bank System, Inc.	Sovran Financial Corp.
First Chicago Corp.	SunTrust Banks, Inc.
First Interstate Bancorp	U.S. Bancorp
First Union Corp.	Valley National Corp.
First Wachovia Corp.	Wells Fargo & Co.

With few exceptions, these 35 are the largest U.S. commercial banks, including all of the money center banks, the super-regionals, and other banks with sizable market presence. This group is important not only because of its size but also because it sets the competitive agenda for the industry. It contains most of the aggressive competitors as well as industry leaders. Only a handful of institutions that will play a substantial role in reshaping the industry are not on this statistically representative list.

We have defined the small banks as the rest of the industry— approximately another 14,000 banks and bank holding companies. Most are quite small, although at the upper end a small bank may be large enough to be important. The dividing line between the two groups is somewhat arbitrary. Obviously not every small bank is doing poorly, and certainly not every large bank is setting the industry competitive agenda. But for the two statistical groups, our findings are easily supported by the data: the small banks are clearly falling behind the large banks.

Figure 1–2 shows how the performance levels of the two groups are diverging. Since 1980, most of the industry's net income growth has come from the large banks. If this group were a separate industry, it would look healthy and the word *stagnant* wouldn't be very applicable. Large banks are vibrant as a group, even though LDC write-offs have been concentrated in this group and a number of poor performers are present.

The small banks, however, are stagnating the most: Net income only grew at a 0.6 percent compound annual rate between 1980 and 1986. The return on equity (ROE) of the small banks was only 8.3 percent in 1986, for example, whereas that of the large banks was 13 percent. As the effects of deregulation continue, small banks should continue to perform poorly until the industry reaches a more stable level of concentration.

Changing Income Statements

This difference in the financial performance of large banks and small banks can be illustrated by analyzing how the two groups' income statements have changed during the 1980s. The large banks' profit sources changed significantly as they made efforts to adjust to a new, highly competitive era. The small banks' unfavorable financial performance reflected their inability to adjust to a less regulated and highly competitive environment.

Figure 1–3 shows the cause of changes in the large and small banks' return on assets (ROA) between 1980 and 1986. (The years 1987 and 1988 are excluded from the analysis because they are, respectively, negatively

FIGURE 1-2
U.S. Commercial Banks' Net Income

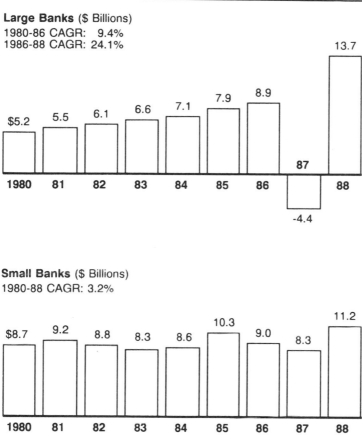

Large Banks ($ Billions)
1980-86 CAGR: 9.4%
1986-88 CAGR: 24.1%

13.7

8.9

7.9

7.1

6.6

6.1

$5.2   5.5

1980   81   82   83   84   85   86   87   88

-4.4

Small Banks ($ Billions)
1980-88 CAGR: 3.2%

11.2

10.3

9.2

$8.7   8.8   8.3   8.6   9.0   8.3

1980   81   82   83   84   85   86   87   88

and positively distorted.) For large banks, net interest income was up by 70 basis points resulting from a favorable shift in the balance sheet— particularly to credit card and other high-yielding consumer aspects. Non-interest income also increased very substantially (by 98 basis points!), reflecting new and aggressive explicit pricing, additional fee services, and new businesses. These two positive revenue developments (plus 168 basis points) were partially offset by non-interest expense increases of 111 basis points. This net benefit of 57 basis points was, however, virtually wiped out by the loan loss provision increase of 60 basis points. The

FIGURE 1-3

Sources of Change: Net Income as a Percent of Average Assets, 1980–1986

Large Banks

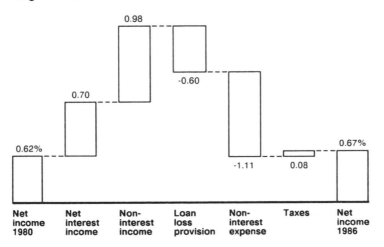

Small Banks

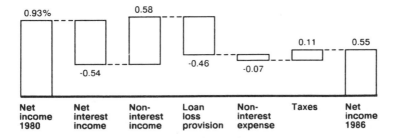

overall effect, including a small positive tax benefit, was to increase ROA very slightly from 0.62 percent to 0.67 percent. The net effect was that large banks roughly preserved their level of profitability while substantially repositioning their sources of revenue.

The anomalous situation of small banks outperforming large banks originally arose because of long-standing geographic, product, and interest rate protections that prevented the formation of a stable, market-based industry structure. When the process of degregulation finally began in an industry with far too many competitors, the irreversible process of consolidation was set in motion. To survive and succeed in this new era, the large banks have restructured their lines of business, which, as we have shown above, was reflected in both their balance sheets and their income statements. In doing so they are coming to dominate the industry's resources as measured by non-interest expense (and particularly expenditures on systems technology). The effect of consolidation is a permanent and natural transfer of power to this group of large banks.

DEREGULATION ARRIVES

Many of the laws that regulate the banking industry and determine banks' permitted activities are roughly 50 years old. They were passed in a time economically quite different from today and with essentially no foresight toward today's technological realities. The two key pieces of legislation were the Pepper–McFadden Act, passed in 1927, and the Banking Act of 1933, more popularly known as the Glass–Steagall Act. These laws established an enduring framework of geographical, product, and rate controls that began to be dismantled around 1980.

The Pepper–McFadden Act established geographic restrictions to prevent national banks (i.e., members of the Federal Reserve) from amassing too much power. National banks were prohibited from interstate branching, thus assuring a fragmented industry where there could be no undue concentration of deposits. In addition, this act also put national banks on an equal footing with state banks by stipulating that each state could control branching within its own borders.

The Glass–Steagall Act was passed as a result of the Great Depression. It was designed to stabilize banking, prevent failures, and prohibit activities that were viewed as having helped cause the Depression in the first place. Its essential scheme was to control excessive competition through rate and product restrictions. The Federal Deposit Insurance Corporation (FDIC) was created, along with the specification of a plan for deposit insurance. The investment activities of commercial banks were explicitly limited and were separated from those of investment banks. Finally, the era of deposit interest rate regulation was ushered in via Regulation Q. Payment of interest on demand deposits was prohibited, and ceilings were imposed for time and savings deposits.

This triple protective framework in rates, products, and geography stayed largely intact until the beginning of the 1980s. It helped make the financial performance of the banking industry attractive and relatively stable year after year—consistently across approximately 14,000 institutions varying in size more than 10,000 fold (ranging from $10 million to $100 billion in assets). This was a very, very rigid structure. Beginning in the 1970s, this ironclad structure began to spring leaks technologically, as banks lost deposits to money market funds and as corporate lending spreads shrunk under the pressure of commercial paper—both innovations that ended product, rate, and geographic barriers. Reacting to the market's ability to evade restrictions, the U.S. Congress removed the barriers with two pieces of deregulatory legislation: the Depository Institutions Deregulation and Monetary Control Act (DIDMCA) of 1980, and the Garn–St. Germain Act of 1982.

The DIDMCA authorized phased elimination of interest rate ceilings on deposits, thus beginning to unravel the locked-in profitability structure. It also allowed nationwide interest-bearing negotiable order of withdrawal (NOW) accounts and eliminated usury ceilings. The Garn–St. Germain Act authorized the development of the money market deposit account and the super-NOW account. The product and rate structure that guaranteed consistent profitability disappeared. It also expanded the powers granted to thrifts and authorized interstate and interindustry mergers in emergency situations.

The barriers against interstate branching have been lifted in stages. By 1988, 45 states had passed some type of legislation permitting regional or nationwide branching. Many states have allowed for the formation of regional compacts designed to give regional banks enough time to prevent themselves from being absorbed by the money center banks. Considerable merger activity has usually resulted. For example, the 25 largest bank holding companies in New England compacted to only 12 companies between 1983 and 1988. In the Southeast, there were 49 banks with market capitalizations of more than $100 million in June 1985; by 1988, these had consolidated to only 31 banks. By 1989, 17 states had adopted specific trigger dates for unrestricted nationwide branching. Most of these dates become effective in 1990 or 1991. By 1995, most banks will be legally allowed to gather deposits and perform other banking activities throughout the country. These legislative actions reflect a recognition that state-based geographic restrictions are not an effective or meaningful mechanism to limit size in an era of high technological communication and transportation.

In terms of financial performance, the removal of the regulatory structure has made the industry less stable even though it is changing to a more competitive structure. Even worse for financial performance, failing institutions have been artifically kept afloat, keeping too much capacity in the industry and failing to restrict the activities of the managers of weak performers soon enough. The resulting excess capacity has spurred certain less cautious bankers to accept too much credit risk without concomitant increase in spreads. As is well known, these factors resulted in the banking and thrift credit crisis of the late 1980s. The point of this brief review of deregulation and financial performance is simply to establish the complex backdrop of the current setting in which technology expenditures have accelerated.

CONSOLIDATION MOVES AHEAD

In an industry that fostered such an excessive number of competitors and maintained geographic restrictions until very recently, it is not surprising to see a pent-up consolidation process at work. Relative to that of other countries in the Organization for Economic Cooperation and Development (OECD), the U.S. banking industry is unique in its high degree of fragmentation. The geographically smaller European countries (and Japan) have never had our restrictions against interstate branching and, as a result, have substantially fewer numbers of banks. For example, the United Kingdom has only 7 clearing banks that dominate its commercial banking world. Japan has only 87 commercial banks, of which the 13 "city banks" control 56 percent of the assets. In Germany, 6 of 169 domestic commercial banks control 47 percent of that country's domestic commercial banking assets. Canada has only 10 banks of any size; Sweden has 14. Even in the bank haven of Switzerland, the 5 *Grossbanken* control 50 percent of all commercial and savings bank assets. Yet the United States has a multitude of deposit-accepting institutions:

1. Approximately 13,700 separate commercial banks, organized into approximately 10,000 corporate entities (banks or bank holding companies).
2. Approximately 16,000 credit unions.
3. Approximately 2,600 savings associations.

FIGURE 1-4
Large Banks' Share of Industry

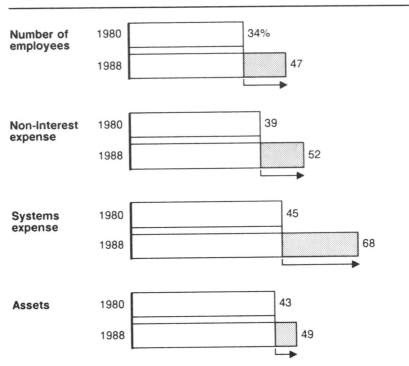

Increases in Consolidation

Although the United States today still has a great number of commercial banks, the process of consolidation made enormous progress during the 1980s. The status of this trend can be measured in dozens of ways, a few of which are shown in Figure 1–4. By all the measures, the large banks are increasing their share of the industry. Assets are the traditional measure of bank size, but they are no longer necessarily the most relevant. The large banks now have 49 percent of the assets, as opposed to only 43 percent in 1980.

Other measures that reflect the work of banking have concentrated more rapidly than balance sheets and are a better indication of the growing power of the large banks. For example, large banks now control 47 percent of the industry's employees and 52 percent of the non-interest expense. At the beginning of the decade, these measures were only 34 percent and 39 percent respectively. The dominance of the large banks is shown even more clearly in systems expense, where they control 68 percent of the industry total. This statistic is especially important because it is changing so rapidly and because it is setting the stage for the large banks' future control of the industry.

These trends toward consolidation should continue in the future for a number of sound reasons:

- The Federal Reserve Bank's higher capital requirements will require stronger balance sheets and will favor institutions that use capital more efficiently. Both effects will contribute to consolidation as institutions merge to spread capital more evenly and as large banks increasingly emphasize fee-based businesses that in turn require scale to operate efficiently.
- Securitization of financial assets, such as mortgages or consumer loans, will favor large players who can most efficiently generate hundreds of millions of dollars of loans at a time, giving them access to the capital markets and a potential advantage in their cost of funding.
- Weak banks and thrifts have capacity that will most likely be removed from the depository system in the next few years. By early 1989, there was about $1.5 trillion in deposits at undercapitalized banks and thrifts. This money must go somewhere as these weak institutions are shut down by regulators or forced to merge by market pressures.
- The continuing escalation of systems technology investments is spurring banks to spread their financial and managerial investments in technology resources over a greater base, inevitably leading to greater merger pressures.

These pressures are finally beginning to reduce the number of competitors. For example, the number of commercial banks dropped by 487 banks, from 14,209 to 13,722, between 1986 and 1987, the first time any noticeable decrease has occurred. In previous years, new banks were starting up almost as quickly as old banks were being merged. An even greater trend is evident in the thrift industry, where the total number of thrifts dropped by more than 1,200 institutions – approximately 25 percent of the industry – from 5,000 in 1980 to approximately 3,800 in 1988. Given the factors described above, the banking industry appears set to continue its trend toward consolidation for the next few years until a more concentrated and competitive industry structure results. Less fettered by

FIGURE 1-5
Growth of Selected Banks

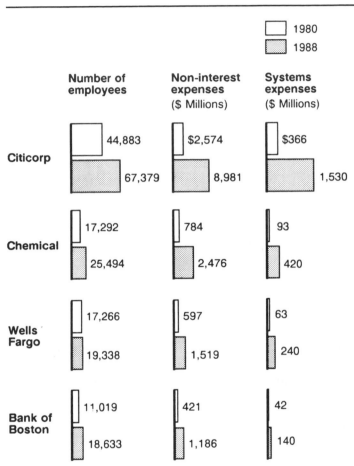

rate, product, and geographic shackles, the large banks should play an ever increasing role in the industry.

Players Become Larger

Reflecting this general trend, certain institutions in particular have become considerably larger during the 1980s. Figure 1–5 shows the changes in key measures of "work" (number of employees, non-interest expense, and systems expenses) for four major banks: Citicorp, Chemical, Wells Fargo, and

Bank of Boston. The growth at these banks has been very significant, resulting both from acquisition and merger and from internally generated growth.

For example, growth in the number of employees averaged 5.2 percent per year at Citicorp, 5.0 percent at Chemical, and 6.8 percent at Bank of Boston—substantially greater than the 1 percent per year increases that the industry as a whole incurred until 1987. The growing presence of these large players is influencing competition in the industry.

RESTRUCTURING OF THE BUSINESS MIX

Large banks have not been able to succeed in the deregulated competitive environment simply by growing and merging. On the contrary, the successful banks are growing by restructuring their business mix. They are changing their balance sheets to support higher yield businesses and are focusing on more fee-based businesses in order to diversify beyond lending and deposits. These changes have required the large banks to increase their spending dramatically on non-interest expense—especially systems expense. In the process, the large banks are irrevocably changing the balance of power in the industry.

Balance Sheet Changes

The major balance sheet change for the large banks has been their movement away from the less profitable—and often unprofitable—traditional large corporate and international loans and toward more profitable consumer lending. Many consumer loans, especially credit card loans, have very high spreads. Also, the average and aggregate levels of losses can usually be predicted more accurately than can the levels of losses among corporate or international customers, which are subject to less predictable macroeconomic trends.

This asset restructuring can be seen clearly at some of the industry's most aggressive banks. Citicorp, perhaps the leader in restructuring, increased its level of consumer loans from 22 percent of its loan portfolio in 1980 to 55 percent in 1988. Thus, its consumer loans now outweigh all other forms (international, corporate, and middle-market) combined. At Chase Manhattan, a similar but less dramatic story unfolded as consumer loans went from 11 percent to 30 percent of the balance sheet. Many of the best-performing regional banks are also following this trend. First Wachovia Corporation, for example, increased its consumer loans by 12.5 percent in 1987 while reducing its business loans by 6.5 percent.

Consumer lending and corporate lending require fundamentally different skills. Traditional corporate lending requires credit analysis skills (to avoid risk) and relationship management skills (to make the sale). The business system focuses on obtaining low-cost funding and providing enough "service" to get the business. The economics are driven by the spreads and have little to do with operating costs.

All this is different from consumer lending. The mass production and processssing of information required by consumer lending is more reminiscent of an industrial goods factory than a rarefied "big deal" atmosphere. Relationship management skills are not required because the lender typically has no face-to-face contact with, or knowledge of, the consumer. No traditional credit analysis or industry specific skills are needed. Instead, unique and highly dedicated resources are needed for operations: processing managers, computer facilities, distribution and communication channels, and systems technology are efficiently combined to make mass lending work properly. The phrase *back office*, once held in low esteem, has been replaced by *processing center*, and has come to be held in higher and higher regard as consumer lending has come more and more to the fore.

Due to the challenge of assembling these resources, this balance sheet restructuring trend is limited primarily to the large banks. Only they can operate at the scale required to make consumer lending really efficient. The constant improvement of systems technology has made many once-manual tasks, such as evaluating an installment loan application, cheaper to do with technology. Consumer lending utilizes more productive direct channels—such as automobile dealers (for auto loans), direct mail (for credit cards), and real estate brokers (for mortgages). Only the large banks have been able to afford these technological investments and to establish the required national, or at least regional, presence. A small bank whose only asset is a local branch simply cannot participate in this restructuring.

Fee-Based Businesses Grow

Not so long ago, non-interest income was viewed as strictly auxiliary to a banks' net interest earnings; this is no longer true. During the 1980s, the large banks went through a sea change in the way they generate revenues.

In 1980, for example, the large banks' non-interest income was only 23.9 percent of their total revenue (defined as the sum of net interest and non-interest income)—less than $1 in fees for every $3 of balance sheet income. By 1988, that figure had grown to 35.8 percent—more than $1 in fees for every $2 of balance sheet income. By the end of the 1990s, the ratio may even be $1 in fees for $1 in balance sheet income.

This sea change has been caused by a number of different developments:

1. Growth in trading of securities and foreign exchange (completely dominated by the large banks);
2. Growth in trust, custody, and agency fees, much of which results from technology-based processing businesses (again, dominated by the large banks);
3. Growth in fees on deposit accounts;
4. Growth in credit card fees, derived both from cardholders and from the merchant discount;
5. Entry into investment and merchant banking activities (again, largely confined to the large banks);
6. Entry into information-based businesses, such as Citicorp's acquisition of Quotron;
7. Sale of assets, such as mortgages, buildings, or subsidiaries, including venture capital gains; and
8. One-time nonrecurring gains, such as recapture of pension liabilities.

The trend toward non-interest income has been led by the money centers. Bankers Trust is the first bank to reap more revenue from non-interest sources than from net interest income—and several other large banks will cross that line very soon. (See Table 1-1.) But the small banks generally won't be able to do this. Too many of these non-interest revenue sources require huge investments in systems technology and require scale to achieve efficiencies. We believe that this trend is irreversible and is one of the strongest trends in the favor of the large banks. It is a welcome trend, fully in tune with the need for more focus, which will be outlined in Chapter 10. Non-interest income can more easily be identified with specific costs and output, and is one component of a more focused and manageable approach to banking.

TABLE 1-1
Leaders in Non-interest Income

| | Ratio of non-interest income to total revenue | | Driving force |
	1980	1988	
Bankers Trust New York Corp.	32%	64%	Trading, FX, Trust
Manufacturers Hanover Corp.	7	49	Trust, loan syndication
First Chicago Corp.	39	47	FX, credit cards, check processing, venture capital
J.P. Morgan & Co.	36	47	Merchant banking, trust, FX
Mellon Bank Corp.	24	46	Trust, cash management, data processing, mortgage servicing
Citicorp	32	42	Trust, information services, credit cards, one-time gains
BankAmerica Corp.	23	32	Credit cards, deposit fees, sale of assets
Chase Manhattan Corp.	27	29	Trust, investment banking, FX

Non-Interest Expense Rises

Non-interest expense is a critical variable in the story of how the large banks are getting ahead of the rest of the industry. *Non-interest expenses represent control of the industry's vital resources.* In turn, control of resources creates opportunities that are no longer rigidly controlled and evenly spread among all players. The large banks have rapidly increased their consumption of the people, the facilities, and, especially, the technology that produce banking products and services. This concentration of resources is an essential element of the restructuring that is setting the stage for the large banks to control the industry in the future.

Large banks have grown their non-interest expenses at a rate of 14 percent per year since 1980, whereas the small banks have increased theirs at only 6.6 percent, barely enough to match inflation. (See Figure 1–6.) And, as was demonstrated in Figure 1–3, the large banks have been able to cover their increased expenses with greater revenues from new or enhanced businesses. Thus, their expense growth has not become a negative factor, nor has it dragged down their income statements. On

FIGURE 1-6
U.S. Commercial Banks' Non-Interest Expense

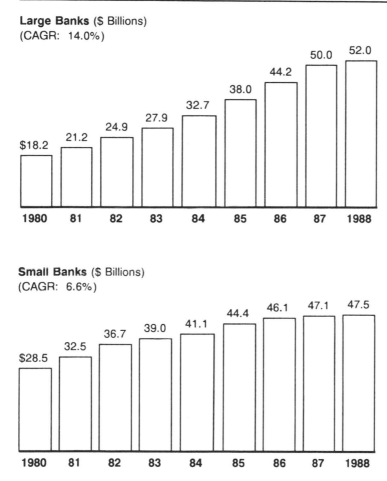

Large Banks ($ Billions)
(CAGR: 14.0%)

$18.2	21.2	24.9	27.9	32.7	38.0	44.2	50.0	52.0
1980	81	82	83	84	85	86	87	1988

Small Banks ($ Billions)
(CAGR: 6.6%)

$28.5	32.5	36.7	39.0	41.1	44.4	46.1	47.1	47.5
1980	81	82	83	84	85	86	87	1988

the contrary, this greater control of resources has been positive, helping to give the large banks a competitive advantage.

There are two major reasons for this growth in resources:

- The restructuring of the large banks involves many fee-based businesses that are resource-intensive. Thus, large banks have gone from being much less expense-intensive to being much more expense-intensive than small banks. For example, the large bank spread of non-interest expense to assets went from 230 basis points in 1980 to 349 in 1987. The equivalent spread at the small banks is now only about 300 basis points.

- Substantial vestiges of geographic, product, and rate regulation still exist, retarding resources and capacity from leaving the industry. In effect, the industry structure still has a regulatory "revenue subsidy" element to it. This subsidy enables less efficient competitors to survive and to pass cost increases on to customers. It also retards the process of putting real competitive pressures on the stronger survivors. As a result, this means that many banks (both weak and strong) do not place enough consideration on cost control — a situation further exacerbated by the lack of penalties.

Recent evidence suggests that cost consciousness is rising rapidly at the large banks. In effect, the growth trend in non-interest expense is being curbed as the large banks get more efficient. In 1988, this seemed to happen. Banks controlled increases in non-interest expense much more rigorously than they ever had before. Industry non-interest expense only increased by $2.77 billion, or 2.8 percent, over the year before. This was the smallest increase in a decade. Whether or not these reduced levels of expense increase can be maintained, a gap has already been opened between what the large banks control and what the rest of the pack controls. It is very likely to stay that way.

Rapid Growth in Systems Expenses

Of all non-interest expense categories, systems expense is the one that ultimately offers the most leverage to dominate lines of business. In fact, because using technology to process information has continually gotten more cost-effective, banks have relied on systems expense as an engine of growth. They have increased their spending on systems technology even more dramatically than on non-interest expense. Between 1980 and 1988, the large banks increased their systems investments from $1.8 billion to $7.9 billion — a 20.3 percent compound annual growth rate (CAGR). For the small banks, the story was again one of not keeping pace: only a 6.7 percent CAGR. (See Figure 1–7.)

Because systems technology investments are now so concentrated, the few largest of the large banks dominate the industry in terms of technology resources. Figure 1–8 illustrates that there is an emerging group of

FIGURE 1-7
U.S. Commercial Banks' Systems Expense

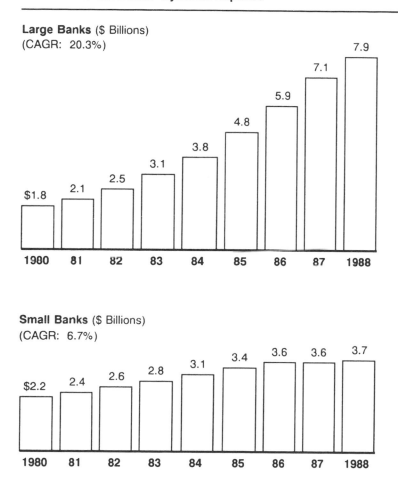

Large Banks ($ Billions)
(CAGR: 20.3%)

1980	81	82	83	84	85	86	87	1988
$1.8	2.1	2.5	3.1	3.8	4.8	5.9	7.1	7.9

Small Banks ($ Billions)
(CAGR: 6.7%)

1980	81	82	83	84	85	86	87	1988
$2.2	2.4	2.6	2.8	3.1	3.4	3.6	3.6	3.7

seven "superplayers," whose continued investments in technology each exceeded $300 million in 1988. They are building a formidable base in technological skills and resources that is in turn contributing to the industry's concentration and the competitive advantage of the large banks. Citicorp is the leader and may be making 20 percent of the industry's systems expenses by 1995 — and in the process is threatening to establish a unique and unassailable position. A group of seven "big players" is right behind — with investments of more than $100 million in 1988.

FIGURE 1-8
Large Commercial Banks' Systems Expense, 1988

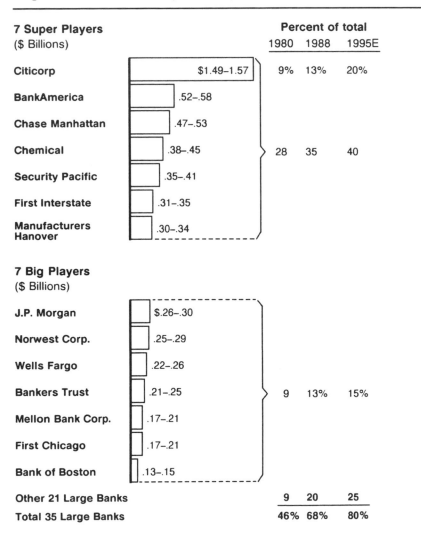

7 Super Players ($ Billions)		Percent of total		
		1980	1988	1995E
Citicorp	$1.49–1.57	9%	13%	20%
BankAmerica	.52–.58			
Chase Manhattan	.47–.53			
Chemical	.38–.45	28	35	40
Security Pacific	.35–.41			
First Interstate	.31–.35			
Manufacturers Hanover	.30–.34			

7 Big Players ($ Billions)				
J.P. Morgan	$.26–.30			
Norwest Corp.	.25–.29			
Wells Fargo	.22–.26			
Bankers Trust	.21–.25	9	13%	15%
Mellon Bank Corp.	.17–.21			
First Chicago	.17–.21			
Bank of Boston	.13–.15			
Other 21 Large Banks		9	20	25
Total 35 Large Banks		46%	68%	80%

Of course not all systems expenditures are wisely used. Indiscriminate increases in expenditures do not necessarily equate with increased systems effectiveness. Nevertheless, our client experience suggests that consistently larger commitment of resources to technology tends to signal (1) a broader range of technology-based businesses, (2) deeper reservoirs of skilled technical personnel making a career with an institution, and (3) increasing sophistication in evolving the business impact of systems expenditures.

For the past decade, in virtually every institution we have observed — and certainly in the industry as a whole — systems technology expenses have increased faster than all of the other types of non-interest expense. In the long run (i.e., 5 to 10 years) systems expenses result in a continual improvement in the cost-value equation. Information technology is particularly effective at streamlining manually repetitive data-intensive tasks — exactly the kind of tasks found at banks. To summarize our experience, a substitution phenomena is going on as clerical processes and procedures are replaced with automated ones. In the process, productivity has been improved, and banks may react by either reducing their absolute level of costs, or, more often, increasing the absolute level of output of their goods and services.

As a consequence, "systems-intensiveness," or the fraction of all expenses represented by systems expenses, has increased steadily in the 1980s. From an approximate level of 10 percent for the large banks in 1980, this measure reached 15.2 percent by 1988 and may well hit 20 percent or more in the mid-1990s. In many cases we have found that banks have perhaps not been effective enough at reaping the full economic benefits of this substitution. Opportunities exist for large banks' non-systems expenses (e.g., manual labor) to be substantially better controlled because of these technological investments. Yet, non-systems expenses increased at a 13.3 percent CAGR during the 1980s — perhaps faster than they should have.

Banks have also focused on creating value from their systems investments. Much of this value is in new products or services that are "systems-dependent." These services, such as 15-minute reporting of a corporate customer's global cash position, are only possible because of technology and are often *more expensive* to produce, in total, than were the previous level of products, such as "next-day" reporting of positions. Additionally, systems-dependent products are fundamentally different from older, traditional products. For example, passbook checking, invented in precomputer days, bears little resemblance to demand deposit account (DDA) services that include automated teller machine (ATM) access, the ability to shift between multiple accounts, and overdraft privileges — all vitally linked to systems technology. Thus, traditional products may be modernized and made more efficient through technology, but they also contain enormous increases in value.

This concentration of systems expenditures has had — and is having — a significant impact on industry competitive structure. As banking products reach a stage of relatively sophisticated automation, only those players with the most efficient technological infrastructures are going to be capable of surviving. Systems generally display certain aspects of economies of scale. Highly automated lines of business can support far fewer than the existing 10,000 commercial banking competitors—possibly fewer than a dozen in certain lines of business. Based on our experience in certain mature or more highly automated businesses, we can say that many of the evolving lines of business in banking will have competitive structures with relatively few competitors. The current decisions that banks—particularly the large banks—are making in allocating their systems investments are thus important long-term choices.

LINE OF BUSINESS PROFITABILITY

Banking is not one highly integrated business; it is a collection of as many as 150 substantially different and independent lines of business. Increasingly, competition is focused on a "line of business" basis. Banks select which businesses to focus on, which to ignore, and which to devote new resources to. In fact, businesses vary widely in attractiveness based on each bank's set of skills, customer base, location, related businesses, and other factors. The attractiveness of these businesses has been substantially affected by the economic forces described at the beginning of the chapter.

Our estimate of how the industry's 1988 net after-tax income breaks down into seven related groups of businesses is given in Figure 1–9. These estimates are for the entire commercial banking industry and for the large banks as a group. They include a consideration of assets, deposits, transfer rates, and allocation of operating expenses. The striking feature is the unevenness of where the industry is making its money. In working with individual institutions—with full access to critical internal data—we have seen this phenomenon of unevenness over and over. No "hidden hand" has yet made all banking lines of business uniformly profitable.

Consumer lending, the most profitable line of business, generated $7.5 billion in net income. ROAs within this group ranged from 0.76 percent on residential mortgages to 3.1 percent on credit cards. Domestic wholesale lending was profitable and international wholesale lending was break-even, but as mentioned earlier, 1988 was a very atypical year. Following the heavy losses of 1987, banks took the lowest loan loss provision

FIGURE 1-9
Profitability by Line of Business, 1988

		Operating expense allocation (Percent)
U.S. Commercial Banks ($ Billions)		
Consumer lending	$7.5	17.9%
Domestic wholesale lending	7.0	7.5
International wholesale lending	0.1	5.9
Consumer deposits	2.0	40.0
Wholesale deposits	1.0	14.5
Fee-based processing businesses	2.0	9.9
Other fee-based businesses	2.2	4.2
Extraordinary items	3.1	0.1
Total	**$24.9**	

Large Banks Only ($ Billions)	
Consumer lending	$3.3
Domestic wholesale lending	3.6
International wholesale lending	0.1
Consumer deposits	0.7
Wholesale deposits	0.8
Fee-based processing businesses	1.5
Other fee-based businesses	1.8
Extraordinary items	1.9
Total	**$13.7**

in five years—only 54 basis points, as opposed to 127 basis points in 1987 and 78 basis points in 1986. Further, the October 1988 agreement with Brazil to restructure $86 billion dollars of debt allowed banks to recognize two years' worth of interest payments in just the final quarter of 1988. These interest revenues contributed more than $1 billion in incremental net income for the industry. Thus, a normalized line of business breakout would show wholesale lending to be significantly less profitable than the 1988 snapshot shows.

In our view, consumer deposit-gathering was a marginal business in 1988. It earned only $2 billion on total liabilities of $1.6 trillion—or an ROA of 12 basis points. The reason for this low return is that, in our analysis, we assigned a large share of the industry's cost structure—some $40 billion—to this product. While endless arguments could be heard about the fairness of the allocation (and *all costs* need to be paid for by *gross revenue*), the fact is that substantially more efficient means of deposit gathering exist. The industry's branches and back offices are quite costly and exist primarily to raise and service consumer deposits — particularly as consumer lending has become branch-independent. Wholesale deposits did better, earning $1 billion or an ROA of 0.79 percent. Nevertheless, corporate customers have become extremely sophisticated at negotiating adequate value for their deposits—generally in the form of payment services.

Fee-based processing businesses, such as trust, cash management, and letter of credit, are profitable, as are other fee-based businesses that do not involve processing (trading and merchant banking, for example). Trading—especially foreign exchange trading—has proven to be very profitable in recent years. Finally, the industry profited by more than $3 billion in extraordinary dispositions, such as asset sales, in 1988. Again, these are anomalous events and help confirm that the industry's underlying core earnings obviously are not as robust as the bottom-line 1988 figures would suggest.

Many things influence profits in specific lines of business. *Technology plays a role but is not the only factor in profitability*—particularly in the very short run. The level of interest rates, credit experience, and the availability of nonbanking substitutes all have powerful influences on the determination of profitability. In later chapters, we will often mention that the profitability of one or another line of business is being influenced by technology. For any particular year, for any particular institution, and for any particular line of business these influences must always be measured against these caveats.

SUMMARY

Technology is playing a key role in helping the large banks to restructure their lines of business—and especially in determining the relative importance of each of them. The group of 35 large banks includes many of tomorrow's eventual winners. They are pulling ahead as they focus their balance sheets on more profitable balance sheet activities, such as consumer lending, and on more fee-based businesses. This restructuring has enabled them to increase their net income and even to improve their ROA in the face of both industry overcapacity and a declining performance on the part of the rest of the industry.

The result of the large banks' pulling ahead in this period of deregulation is a trend toward consolidation. Large banks now control much more of the industry's resources than they did in 1980. Non-interest expenses (the measurement of future resources) are more concentrated than are assets (the measurement of the past), and systems expenses (the "leading edge" measurement) are in turn much more concentrated than even non-interest expenses. Until the industry reaches a stable structure, these trends should continue and even increase. The large banks have, and should maintain, a significant competitive advantage against the small banks.

Yet this is not the end of the story. As the consolidation continues, large banks must compete among themselves, not just with the small banks or the thrifts. Already this is the case in many banking lines of business. More than a few of the large banks had severe performance problems in the 1980s. No guarantee exists that all of the current 35 large banks will survive. In fact, only 22 of the existing 35 have been on the list since 1982. Making the most of the possibilities and learning to perform better in the new technological era is what the rest of this book is about.

CHAPTER 2

THE TRANSFORMATION OF AN INDUSTRY: FROM PAPER TO ELECTRONICS

The restructuring efforts of the banking industry have been driven primarily by economic and competitive forces. Banks are using systems technology as a key element in that restructuring process. But there is a second major force at work in the industry. Banks are undergoing a fundamental operational transformation as advances in systems technology gradually make it possible to replace paper—used to effect transactions or to store and manipulate data—with electronics.

Although systems technology often seems to be penetrating every nook and cranny of the banking world, there is a pattern to how it is used. The bulk of banks' work is in establishing accounts (or customer relationships) and handling transactions within those accounts. Many of these transactions are payments. The volume of transactions is roughly 100 billion per year, so most systems technology expenditures support the automation of these transactions. By their very nature, payment transactions are standardized and not proprietary, meaning that the systems expenses behind them cannot easily become competitively distinctive.

Not only is there a pattern to the functions performed by systems technology, but there is also an observable three-stage sequence by which the business system for performing transactions becomes automated. The three stages occur at different times for different banking products, but the economic effects are consistent enough to be predictable. The first two stages—back office and front office automation—usually do not substantially change the economics nor are they particularly visible to customers. It is in the third stage—when the direct customer interface becomes automated—that economics change the most and competition usually reaches a critical juncture.

Although this paper-to-electronics transformative process is affecting *how* banking gets its work done, information technology, as an "enabling force," is affecting *what* the industry does. New products spawned by technology are the most visible (and most beneficial) result. These new electronic transactions and products are the world of the future for the banking industry.

THE LONG EVOLUTION OF SYSTEMS TECHNOLOGY

Although the commercially available computer is only about 40 years old, mechanical counting machines have been used for more than 350 years. There has always been a need for scientific or engineering calculations, and for endless amounts of number crunching in commerce and trade. The abacus, the first counting aid, dates from prehistoric times, long before most people were literate or even numerate. It is still in use today. Another calculating aid, the slide rule, was developed in 1622 by the mathematician John Napier shortly after the invention of logarithms. It survived in essentially the same form until it was replaced by the electronic calculator in the 1960s.

Mechanical Calculating Machines

The first mechanical calculator was invented in 1623 by Wilhelm Schickard, a student of the astronomer Johannes Kepler. Schickard's "Calculating Clock" used mutilated gears to do limited addition or subtraction, and could automatically carry or borrow tens from one column to the next. Other inventors of the 17th century, including Blaise Pascal and Gottfried Wilhelm Leibniz, built refined mechanical calculators that could do more elaborate addition and subtraction. Leibniz's "Stepped Reckoner" could even multiply. But practical usage and adoption did not come about until 1820, when the Industrial Revolution allowed production of mechanical calculators that were easier to use and more reliable than those of previous centuries. The first commercially produced mechanical calculator, the "Arithmometer," was invented by a Frenchman, Charles de Colmar. He sold approximately 1,500 models, primarily to banks and insurance companies!

Charles Babbage (1791–1871) devoted his life to developing a machine accurate enough to calculate the nautical tables that the world so depended upon at that time. Previously done by hand, these tables always contained errors, which could lead to a miscalculated position – and potentially a shipwreck. Babbage's crowning achievement, the "Analytic Engine," was designed to calculate any mathematical series. Designed to be as big as a steam engine, the Analytic Engine had some surprisingly modern features. It could add two 40-digit numbers in three seconds. External programming was provided by punch cards. But the Analytic Engine was never completed, and Babbage was the last to attempt a mechanical calculating machine. The difficulties of performing arithmetic with gears and wheels were overwhelming, and were bypassed only with the development of electricity.

By the 1880s, banks and other bureaucratic organizations had begun to use machinery to handle information processing. The Industrial Revolution was in full swing, with vast increases in the array of raw materials available, the amount of goods produced, and the speed of transportation and communications. The demands upon banks escalated as the volume of monetary transactions grew and as their lending and financial decisions became more complex.

As a result, banks began installing office machinery whose purpose was to speed the flow of information and automate manual work. The modern office calculating machine, the "Comptometer," was introduced in 1887. The "Burroughs Adding–Subtracting Machine with Printer" arrived in 1892, followed in the next year by the four-function calculator. A card punch and sorter was available in 1894.

Early Data Processing Technology

The needs of banks, however, were heavily data-intensive and banks could not make use of technological advances targeted at solving complex calculations. For example, early analog computers that could solve differential equations appeared in the mid-1890s, but they were useless for the major data processing needs of banks: to keep records of transactions in extremely high volumes.

The solution appeared in the person of Herman Hollerith, a Columbia-trained engineer who was a patent examiner and an expert on railroad technology. He began inventing electrical tabulating systems in the early 1880s. His system stored data on punch cards, with the position of the holes serving as the information. His systems did not really calculate but rather added, sorted, and collated. A card puncher was used to put the data on the card. Then the electric tabulator could count the cards at high speed – up to 19,000 per day.

Hollerith's invention revolutionized the census of 1890, which had promised to get out of hand. The previous census, in 1880, had been done entirely by hand, but had taken nine years to complete. With considerably more people to count in 1890, the Census Bureau was afraid the 1890 census would not be completed before the next census, so it sponsored a technological competition to develop better methods. The Hollerith machine was a great success, yielding a preliminary count in just six weeks. Significantly, the overall 1890 census cost *more* to complete when it was all done, because it did a more careful job and produced more reports. *Thus, the principle of greater output from automation-engendered productivity improvement has a long history.*

Hollerith's machine and its descendants were widely adopted by government and business. Prudential Insurance Company had two of Hollerith's systems running by 1891, although it later shifted to a proprietary technology. Foreign governments bought the equipment for their censuses. By 1894, more than 100 million cards had been sold by Hollerith to support his systems. His company, the Tabulating Machine Company, was the root from which IBM eventually sprang. Tabulating machines were widely employed by banks in the decades before World War II. For example, First Wachovia first installed tabulating machinery in its trust department during the 1930s. IBM first introduced an electric keypunch for coding data on 80-column cards in 1923.

Other technologies were used early in banking. For example, an electric funds transfer system that eventually became Fedwire began in 1918. Check photographing began in 1925 with a machine called the "Recordak," which used 16mm film from Kodak. But until World War II, there was no technology able to replace paper information with electronic information. All that the technology up to that time could do was to speed up certain steps in the flow of information processing. Once any step (such as a calculation) was over, all of the information reverted to its previous paper-based existence. And information stayed on paper because no electronic storage device had yet been developed.

Rise of the Programmable Computer

A computer offers great flexibility. It is *programmable*, meaning that its instruction sequences can be determined by the user in order to solve a wide variety of problems easily. One of the early computers was the famous ENIAC, developed at the University of Pennsylvania by J. Presper Eckert and John Mauchly, with help from the mathematical John von

Neumann. The ENIAC was huge, with 17,468 vacuum tubes, 30 tons of weight, and 174,000 watts of power. It required two days to set thousands of cables and switches for each separate problem. Like so many previous efforts, its purpose was to develop tables, in this case for artillery.

The EDIAC, also by Eckert and Mauchly, was the first computer with the ability to store a program in memory. Eckert and Mauchly also developed the idea of one memory, for both data and programs, and one arithmetic unit—the so-called von Neumann architecture, still standard today. Eckert and Mauchly eventually developed the Univac, which even had one of its first contracts with a financial institution—Prudential Insurance Company. The Univac helped form the public's first impression of the computer when it and Walter Cronkite predicted the 1952 election on television. The Univac was never commercially successful, however, and its ultimate manufacturer, Remington Rand, lost the race for commercialization to IBM.

The earliest computers used vacuum tubes to perform calculations and used electrostatic memory devices for storage. This severely curtailed reliability and performance. Magnetic core memories did not appear commercially until 1955, when they were used in the IBM model 704. The early computers were also designed for scientific and engineering use. They had virtually no systems software, and as a consequence had no applications programs. Users had to be experts—everything was done by hand. Even when punch cards could be used for programming, the user had to input a long sequence of 1s and 0s. The first compiler, a device to convert a programmer's instructions into machine instructions, was not developed until 1951. The first relatively easy high-level language, FORTRAN, was not available until 1957.

In fact, computers might still be stuck in the laboratory if three key inventions in materials science had not occurred after World War II. The *transistor*, invented at Bell Labs in 1948, was smaller, faster, and more reliable than the vacuum tube. It required considerably less power to operate. Production of transistor radios began in 1954, and more important, replacement of vacuum tubes in computers began by 1957. Transistors started the trend toward miniaturization, which was essential then (and now) in speeding up the computing process and enhancing reliability. This trend was hastened with the invention in 1958 of the first *integrated chip* by a Texas Instruments engineer, Jack Kilby. Computers with chips first appeared in the mid-1960s and the use of magnetic core memory, which has a very low capacity for data storage, began declining. Rotating magnetic storage began about this time, first on drums and then on disk.

Finally, the *microprocessor*, developed in 1971 by Intel Corporation, led to the development of a general-purpose logic chip that could be programmed. Microprocessors allowed the development of the personal computer and the placing of intelligence in objects such as autos and microwave ovens.

What Banks Were Doing

Banks were key commercial customers throughout the period of computer development. They had employed electromechanical equipment, from IBM and NCR, for many years. Generally, this equipment used punch cards and relays and was employed mainly in keeping account records. Beginning in 1948, banks began purchasing the IBM 604, an electronic multiplier that could perform arithmetic operations on 100 cards per minute. Again, usage was restricted to keeping accounts, primarily checking accounts, and had little impact on the front office or on what products and services were offered.

It is instructive that banks first used programmable computers to process checks. Prior to 1960, checks were sorted by hand, usually at the branch level. They were stored at the payer's bank in giant filing cabinets, each one of which had a ledger card on its front showing a current balance. The only way to ascertain an account's balance was to call the bookkeeping department and ask someone to look it up. A popular machine at the time was the NCR Postronics machine, which would encode and read a magnetic strip on each ledger card. The Postronics machine was used to post debits and credits to each ledger card. As late as the early 1970s, some small country banks still used these types of ledger card systems.

Magnetic Ink Character Recognition (MICR) began in 1960 and allowed the first automated handling of checks. Bank of America developed the first MICR technology based on a study by Stanford Research Institute. Early computers of the 1960s (NCR 315s and 316s) could then sort checks and capture the check data automatically. However, the real rush to computerize began with the introduction of IBM's System/360 in April, 1964. This was the first family of compatible computers, spanning a wide range of performance. It was $5-billion gamble by IBM that turned out to be enormously successful. Realizing that much more extensive automation would become possible, banks lined up at IBM's door. This was roughly the beginning of the three stages of automation, discussed later in this chapter, when affordable and practical computer technology became generally available to the banking industry.

TODAY'S BANKING SYSTEMS LANDSCAPE

As a result of this 350-year progression, banks today support much of their operations and products with information technology. This "landscape," or collective accumulation of both hardware and software, is not only pervasive, but it is also in constant danger of becoming obsolete. As price performance improves, the only constant in the future may be constant change.

Budgets Are Divided

Year to year, banks usually split their systems budgets into about one-third for hardware, one-third for software development and maintenance, and one-third for everything else. These ratios vary only moderately from bank to bank. The splits also appear to be relatively constant over time, as the decreasing cost of hardware is offset by ever increasing demands for more capacity. Usually, most software development goes into maintenance, leaving no more than approximately 10 percent per year for truly new initiatives.

One major change in recent years has been the significant investment in microcomputers; they now constitute 19 percent of all hardware expense. (See Figure 2–1.) By 1989, banks had bought an estimated 250,000 microcomputers, or one for every six employees. Including "dumb" terminals (those without microprocessors or memory), virtually every bank employee now has, or soon will have, a workstation device on his or her desk. And, over the next five years, many banks will be replacing dumb terminals with microcomputers. Processing will be shared between the mainframe and the local machine, giving users more capability and more user-friendly features.

Resources Are Centralized

The heart of most bank's systems landscapes is a large mainframe computer, which tends to be oriented toward transaction processing applications. This is true for the standard machines that may run many batch programs as well as for the newer fault-tolerant machines used to drive real-time networks. Banks rarely use supercomputers, which do engineering or scientific calculations. Bank mainframes do simple calculations, repeated over and over again on very large quantities of data. Banks' processing requirements are *input–output intensive*, and the architectures

FIGURE 2-1
Distribution of Systems Expense, 1988

100% = $11.6 billion

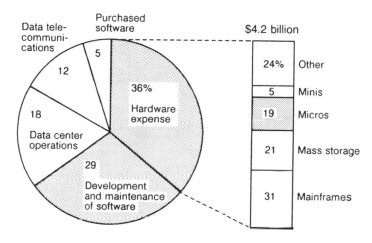

are thus configured to maximize the speed of access to the data. In turn, huge databases arise from the operation of transaction-type accounts.

As a result, a bank typically has one or more very large data centers with several high-capacity mainframes, a disk storage farm, and a large network of on-line terminals. Usually, the data center runs thousands of jobs for the bank's different divisions, businesses, and products. Usually, batch programs run at night to do account updates and on-line programs predominate during the day to provide information. In the largest banks, there is some evolving decentralization. For example, a very large division may have its own data center. But because economies of scale are still very strong for high throughput applications, and for security and control reasons, most banks continue to centralize the bulk of their systems investments.

Applications Software Is Critical

Application programs are really the heart of every bank's technology infrastructure. They convert computing capability into specific products and services. Any major bank needs a portfolio of thousands of applications to get each day's work done. Development of these applications is usually centralized along with the data center, with one group of programmers serving the needs of many users. Other central core groups maintain the bank-wide network, support decentralized equipment (check encoding equipment, for example), and perform systems planning work and technical research and development (R&D). Some large banks have decentralized their applications development groups to enhance flexibility and user responsiveness. The credit card operation or the securities processing division, for example, might have its own applications development groups even if it uses the centralized data center to run the applications.

The costs that banks incur for applications development are high and show few signs of coming down. Programmer productivity does not increase at the same rate that hardware capability increases. Once built, however, most applications programs are used for years. We estimate that more than 50 percent of the typical bank's programs are over 6 years old. Of the typical applications budget, between 50 percent and 80 percent goes for maintenance of old programs—a situation that seems unlikely to change soon.

Because of the difficulty of building applications, the relative standardization of the banking functions, and the large number of potential buyers, entrepreneurial vendors have invested millions of dollars to develop packages that carry out core functions, such as deposit and installment loan accounting. Yet purchased software still represents only 5 percent of overall bank systems expense. Some of this is the cost of systems software, so only about 3 percent is the cost of applications packages. About 55 percent of the top 50 banks have "home-grown" proprietary demand deposit account (DDA) and installment loan systems, and even among the banks ranked from 100 to 150 (by assets), 40 percent still have proprietary systems.

Special Equipment Is Pervasive

Data centers are the hub, but not the totality, of banks' investments in systems technology. There is a large body of special-purpose banking machines whose main purpose is to process paper items in high volumes. It is truly ironic that so much systems technology has been used to handle paper so efficiently. As will be discussed in Chapter 4, banks' paper-processing equipment has gotten very efficient, slowing the development of electronic payment technologies. MICR is the chief culprit. Common types of MICR equipment include reader/sorters (such as the industry standard IBM 3890), check encoders, reject reentry equipment, proof machines, and so on. Today, most of this machinery uses microprocessor technology to allow direct capture and transmission of data from these machines to the host data centers. This equipment is widely available.

Other types of special-purpose equipment include automated teller machines (ATMs), data capture and authorization terminals at retailers, plastic card production equipment, statement stuffing and mailing equipment, optical character reading (OCR) equipment (for scanning sales drafts), microfiche readers, remittance processing systems, lockbox processing systems, and magnetic stripe encoder/readers. Even though some of these machines are specialized, they are all manufactured by vendors, sometimes with the active involvement of banks. Little, if any, competitive differentiation occurs as a result.

Price Performance Improvements Are Continuous

Price performance defines how much equivalent computer power or capacity can be bought for each dollar. Improvements for IBM mainframe central processing units (CPUs) have historically averaged about 15 percent CAGR. Today, an IBM 3090-300E, a typical bank mainframe, has a processing power of approximately 45 MIPS.* Price performance may improve another 50 percent by 1992. Beyond that, processors employing parallel processing architectures may allow a 500 MIPS-equivalent machine by 1995. By then, 1 MIPS on a mainframe may cost between $10,000 and $20,000 — one-third of today's cost.

Only 10 years ago, a large mainframe (e.g., an IBM 360 series machine) might have had a power of 2 to 5 MIPS — roughly equal to a 1989 personal computer (PC). But the PCs of 1998 will probably have 50 to 60 MIPS — equal to today's high-end mainframe. Another advance will be more powerful minicomputers. They will perform a wide variety of general-purpose computational tasks. In addition, banks make great use of specialized computers, such as the Tandem or Stratus fault-tolerant machines, which process high volumes of transactions in a real-time environment — particularly where they serve as communications links for incoming transactions.

---

*MIPS = Million Instructions (Executed) Per Second. MIPS is the most commonly used off-the-cuff measure of processor performance, even though its use can be misleading, especially when comparing different types of computers.

The same story of improvements in price performance can be found in mass storage devices. One key criterion is the amount of data that can be held on-line in direct access storage devices (DASDs) and is, therefore, available to the now ubiquitous on-line terminals. For example, the cost of magnetic disk storage dropped from $500 per megabyte in 1970 to $10 per megabyte in 1988. Nonerasable optical storage currently costs 5 cents per megabyte and continues to decrease in cost. A second key criterion is access time, which has shown similar dramatic improvement.

In fact, this story can be repeated for virtually every piece of hardware found in any bank's data center. There are continuous increases in capacity, power, and raw underlying capability for each dollar spent. When combined with the fact that banks are spending more total dollars on technology, the result is an even more spectacular increase in the amount of processing power available to them. *The banking technology infrastructure should continue to grow until the underlying physical limits of the technology are reached.*

Infrastructure Metrics Are Large and Growing

The industry as a whole is increasing both its computer processing power and its volume of on-line storage between 25 and 40 percent per year. The industry now has approximately 250 data centers containing at least one IBM mainframe class 3000 CPU or the equivalent. These centers average approximately 80 MIPS apiece. Roughly another 1,750 banks have small data centers outfitted with at least one IBM 4381 low-end mainframe or IBM AS/400 minicomputer or the equivalent. A large data center may have on-line storage capacity of 200 billion characters, equivalent to 60 million pages of text. Because a piece of data (e.g., a balance amount or a name), contains multiple characters, the total pieces of information at a typical large bank might be 5 to 10 billion. All this adds to a weighty, and growing, sum. By 1988, the industry's data centers had an estimated 30,000 MIPS of processing power and approximately 85 trillion characters of on-line data. (See Figure 2-2.) Although these numbers are only estimates—because of definitional problems and a lack of published data—they should illustrate the main point. The computer power, capacity, and resources available to the industry continue to grow at remarkable speed.

This increase in processing power serves as the driver for other changes. Decision support systems can now handle more data and do more complex analyses. Prompted on-line systems have grown in the

FIGURE 2-2
Banking Industry Data Center Metrics (Estimate)

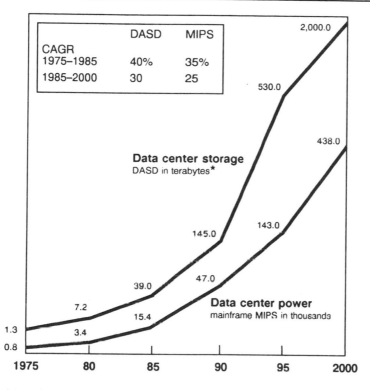

	DASD	MIPS
CAGR		
1975–1985	40%	35%
1985–2000	30	25

Data center storage
DASD in terabytes*

Data center power
mainframe MIPS in thousands

2,000.0
530.0
438.0
145.0
143.0
39.0
47.0
7.2
15.4
1.3
3.4
0.8

1975   80   85   90   95   2000

* 1 terabyte = 1 trillion characters

credit and customer service areas. Much of the growth in MIPS goes to support more sophisticated operating systems and greater operational overhead in the data centers. In turn, more transactions are handled, networks grow, and new high-level technologies become possible. For example, one of the "hot" new technologies bankers discuss is *expert systems*, which have the potential to solve judgmental decisions, such as commercial lending decisions, that are not amenable to exact algorithms. Expert systems were not affordable until recently because they are resource "hogs." (The Lending Advisor, a middle-market expert system package from Syntelligence, Inc., may require 25 million CPU instructions to execute one terminal transaction. A typical banking transaction using conventional technology might only require 300,000 CPU instructions.) But, as the cost of one MIPS has dropped, the cost of expert systems has come down from the stratosphere.

The same process is stimulating initial adoption of *image processing*. American Express has already used it to simplify and clean up its charge card statement, and Citibank has used it to process customer correspondence. High-volume lockbox and remittance-processing operations use it to assist with data entry. Like a fax machine, this technology can be used to store and transmit images of paper documents. It is, however, is a resource hog, requiring an extensive amount of storage. A compressed image of an $8\frac{1}{2} \times 11$-inch piece of paper requires approximately 50,000 bytes — up to 100 times more storage than a text file of the same information. Even a check requires approximately 20,000 bytes. But the drops in the cost of storage have propelled *some* image processing applications into commercial feasibility.

The major implication of the overall growth in processing power is that more change is inevitable. As the cost of power and storage continually drop, more and more functions become financially feasible. The scope of automated functions will continually expand into areas where automation was formerly not possible. Partly as a result, systems technology is a leapfrog game. New systems are always going to be at least a little outdated as soon as they are built. Obsolescence is a constant threat. Some new approach, feature, or value-added extra that utilizes the continual advances will come along. In fact, as we said earlier, the constant in today's technological world is change.

HOW AUTOMATION SUPPORTS TRANSACTIONS

The work of banking consists largely of processing transactions. A transaction can be defined as any change to an account (like a debit/credit) or any customer event, such as an inquiry, credit application, statement, or phone/mail contact. Whatever it is, a transaction requires expense to process and an infrastructure, with its fixed costs, to assure that the transaction can reach its destination. The vast majority of these transactions occur within the funds-movement segment of the banking business system. Most are either payments or are supporting transactions, such as credit card authorizations, that occur within payment products. For this reason, payments and transactions have been the major target of banks' investments in technology. Payments and transactions are where the costs are and where the paper is. Yet at the same time, payments by their very nature must be standardized and capable of distribution throughout the banking industry. Systems investments that support funds-movement functions are therefore routine and not distinctive. This fact goes a long way toward explaining why profits do not automatically flow from systems investments.

Although there are many kinds of transactions, more than 90 percent of them are payments or related to payment products. To illustrate this, the following transaction statistics revealed by Bank of America in its 1988 annual report show that on an average day, Bank of America processes:

12,100,100	checks
3,600,000	travelers check redemptions
1,112,000	pieces of mail
995,000	credit/debit card transactions
650,000	consumer deposits
598,000	ATM transactions
539,000	statements
220,000	business deposits
77,000	customer inquiries
49,700	wholesale funds transfers

This litany is revealing for two reasons. First, it illustrates the predominance of payment transactions. Checks, deposits, card transactions, ATM transactions, and transfers are direct forms of payment. Statements and inquiries are very likely about payment products. Even the majority of the undefined 1.1 million pieces of mail probably involve payments to a large degree. Some common types of transactions not listed, such as loan applications or IRA openings, are not repetitive events and do not occur in enough volume to make the list. The bottom line at Bank of America, as elsewhere, is that well over 90 percent of the transactions are related to the payment system. Second, this litany shows that the overwhelming majority of these transactions are still paper-based. Only Bank of America's ATM, wholesale funds, and (some) card transactions are electronic. There is still a vast amount of paper in the U.S. banking system—paper that will be the target of systems investments for years to come.

Non-Interest Expense Is the Target of Automation

Systems investments are usually targeted at reducing non-interest expense, and that expense is, in turn, generated by the volume and type of transactions. Yet the expense of the industry, when distributed across the business system, is not strictly congruent with the distribution of transactions. Some transactions, such as mortgage loan applications, are substantially more expensive to process than are simple deposits or checks for cash. Customer service, or exception-event, transactions (e.g., returned checks) are often 10 or 20 times more costly than payments because manual intervention is required.

Thus, the distribution of non-interest expense incorporates, but does not exactly mirror, the distribution of transactions. Based on McKinsey's experience in working with clients, it has been shown that the two highest cost functions are funds movement and marketing/distribution, accounting for approximately 49 percent and 19 percent of all expenses, respectively. (See Figure 2–3.)

The funds-movement function includes much of the cost of banks' back offices, where the operations occur. But even more important is an allocation of the cost of the industry's branch network. The nation's approximately 60,000 banking locations (including 46,000 branches and 14,000 bank home offices) make up about one-half of all industry expense. Much of it should be allocated to funds movement, because accepting deposits and allowing withdrawals is such a high percentage of the activity that goes on within branches. Some of the branch cost, however, should be allocated to distribution, because deposit accounts, personal trust, and some loan accounts are opened in branches. Some branch expense is also allocated to the customer service function, because tellers and platform people answer questions and adjust for problems.

Distribution involves calling officers for corporate and middle-market customers as well as branches and direct channels for retail customers. Credit approval requires credit officers for wholesale loans and a combination of credit scoring models and officers for retail lending. Both customer service and collections involve telephone service for retail, as well as a combination of branches and calling/workout officers.

Given these distributions, it is not surprising that so much attention has been paid to automating the movement of funds. If it were possible to make *all* funds movements entirely automated, up to one-half of the industry's existing cost base, (approximately $50 billion) and one-half of

FIGURE 2-3
Distribution of Non-Interest Expense

	Marketing and distribution	Credit approval	Funds movement (debits and credits)	Customer service	Collections	Investments and trading	MIS
Major elements	Calling officers Direct mail Branches	Credit officers Scoring models Data bases	Check processing Operations Cash management Branches (tellers) Networks	800 numbers Correspondence Branches Calling officers Statements	Workout Retail collections Legal	Trading Foreign exchange Treasury	Accounting Management reporting
Percent of non-interest expense	19%	5	49	13	8	3	3

its labor force might be displaced. This significant goal will continue to influence the pattern of the industry's systems investments.

Many Systems Expenses Are Routine

The transactions within funds movement are the most logical ones to be automated. Funds-movement transactions are usually very simple, with only a minimum amount of data to be communicated, and they occur in high volumes. But systems expenditures have been devoted to automating many other types of transactions as well. Consumer credit functions, once made manually, are now usually automated. Most installment loan or credit card collectors of any tenure can remember when their first automated collection system was installed. Elaborate files for tracking and following up their case loads were replaced with on-line note taking and work scheduling. The same goes for seasoned customer service personnel, whose store of information has moved from paper to microfiche to on-line terminals. We estimate that *65 percent of the industry's systems expense goes to support just this one function of funds movement.* Most of the rest occurs either in distribution (e.g., branches) or in customer service (e.g., inquiries and adjustments).

One reason why systems expenses are going up so fast is that most of the expenditures do not go toward anything that might be viewed as offering distinctive competitive advantage. Banks are making the same systems investments and not seeing any disadvantage to themselves in doing so. *Although the movement of funds can be complicated, it is relatively mechanical and is not the source of competitive differentiation in a bank product, if there is one.* Funds-movement products, almost by definition, must be able to reach a wide range of potential destinations (e.g., other individuals, corporations, governments, or other banks). In turn, this requires cooperation and standardization. Funds movements are not the place for a unique transaction simply because no one else could then receive it.

As a result, we estimate that a very high proportion (more than 95 percent) of all of the systems expenses going into funds movement are routine. They are not capable of creating a sustainable competitive advantage in and of themselves. In most of the other functions, we believe, routine expenses similarly make up the lion's share (more than 80 percent) of all systems expenses.

The areas where real value can be added in banking—the key success factors, if you will—are in credit (where avoiding loss still has the biggest differentiating impact on the bottom line), in marketing (where retail product innovation and wholesale customer control count for a lot), and in distribution (where service distinctions are noticeable to the customer). Trading and investments can make a difference as well. Yet systems expenses are not concentrated in these high impact areas. We estimate that, at most, in the aggregate *only around 10 percent of the industry's systems expense goes into functions that are even potentially distinctive.* Of course, routine functions are necessary to gather the data upon which higher value-added applications can be placed. Yet, in our experience, the task of distinguishing between value-added and routine investments is frequently not accomplished.

These types of calculations merely mirror industry experience. Most banks are aware that systems investments support transaction-processing applications. The usual justification is not that the end product is unique. Rather, justification is expressed as "cost control" (displacement of labor and/or paper) or "better service" (doing more for the customer). *In fact, the vast bulk of systems investments support products or services that are commodities throughout the industry.*

STAGES OF AUTOMATION

Banking transactions have become automated in an observable sequence. As the sequence occurs, it affects the economics of the business line, particularly in the third and final stage, when competition really tightens. To explain this, we must look at the steps required to process a transaction. The first step is almost always initiation by a customer, for example, when a customer writes a check or makes an inquiry about a wire transfer. The second step is an internal initiation that occurs within the bank's network. Data may be captured from a document or a request made for information or records. The third step is that accounts are processed and accounting entries are computed. The sequence of automation is illustrated in Figure 2–4.

Stage A: Back Office Automation

The back office had to be the first part of the overall transaction business system to become automated. Building off the computer's ability to make calculations rapidly, banks began automating core record-keeping in the

FIGURE 2-4
Transactions Transformed by Automation

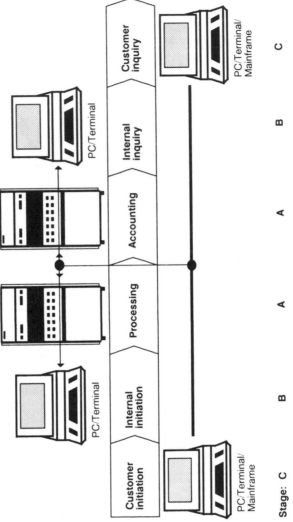

early 1960s. Depending on the product, this process went on well into the 1980s. Typical automated functions were nightly account updates, monthly cycling of accounts, statement preparation, and general ledger maintenance. In the 1960s, of course, batch processing was used and many of these functions are still carried out through the use of giant batch-processing routines. The customer typically saw little change in the product, however, because most of the benefits were absorbed in back-office cost reductions.

Stage B: Front Office Automation

With the development of on-line terminals in the early 1970s, portions of the front office could be automated, and bank employees could use automation in their interactions with customers. Transactions could be entered on-line and customer service could be improved. For example, a balance inquiry could be made against the previous night's transactions instead of against a month-old microfiche copy of the last statement.

To implement Stage B, banks built networks to connect their centralized data centers with many scattered access devices. These networks now link a variety of devices: teller terminals, 3270-type terminals, terminal controllers, laser printers, and so forth. Off-line devices, such as check reader/sorters, also became part of the network. For large banks with dozens (or hundreds) of locations, expensive investments in telecommunications networks were (and still are) required.

The effect of these on-line systems has been to make inquiry and data base changes near and immediate instead of remote and slow. As bank networks grow, many things change: Programs are developed to control the workflow of customer service representatives, credit analysts, and collectors; some substitution of internal paper documents takes place; better control of credit and fraud becomes possible; and more information can be passed around the bank, and between the branches and the data centers. Nevertheless, there is a limit to the economic effects of Stage B because bank employees are not totally displaced by technology but merely assisted and made more efficient by it. Most transactions are still originated by customers in paper form and a complete transformation to electronics cannot occur.

Stage C: Customer Interface

Stage C is reached when the actual customer interface is automated — eliminating the bank employee between the customer and the bank. When customers begin the transaction in electronic form, paper is eliminated right from the start. To do this, electronic networks reach outside the bank to corporate treasurers' offices, retailers, brokers, insurance companies, and correspondent banks. Also, ATMs are a Stage C development. A transaction can begin at a customer's terminal, proceed to his or her bank, go to a correspondent bank, be switched through a utility (such as CHIPS or MasterCard), and finish up with the receiving bank and the recipient — entirely without paper.

Stage C is very complicated because of the different methods for achieving interface automation. Corporate customers, for example, may ship magnetic tape to their banks for high-volume items that are not time-sensitive, such as direct deposits of payroll amounts. Direct transmission between a customer's personal computer and a bank mainframe is good for high-value, time-sensitive transactions, such as large dollar payments. CPU to CPU transmissions are the most efficient and are used in many interbank situations.

Depending on the specifics, Stage C has the potential to create significant economic change. For one thing, the costs of extending networks to reach customers' premises are quite high. Also, the backoffice systems, built during Stage A, usually need modification to provide adequate security, to enhance user-friendliness, and to add functionality targeted at customers. Thus, the fixed costs rise and the product or business becomes more of a volume game. Competition becomes fierce and profits may evaporate if too many competitors build too much capacity.

This scenario has been observed in international funds transfer, credit card merchant banking, and corporate cash management, to mention just a few. (See Chapters 5 and 6 for a detailed discussion of these specific examples.) Many other banking lines, especially retail lines, have not yet reached Stage C. ATMs are just the beginning of an automated customer interface for the retail branch network, for example. The specifics of the business dictate when Stage C will occur. By making this projection, banks can estimate when competition may heighten and margins begin to erode. However, the process may not totally stop at Stage C. Other evolving technological developments, such as image processing and expert systems will be part of newer, as-yet-undefined stages of technological evolution. We do not pretend that today's automated customer interfaces are the end of technical evolution. No one can be completely sure what the next stage will be.

NEW PRODUCTS

A final characteristic of the technological landscape is product proliferation. Bank products are simply information combined in new ways, so with hundredfold increases in the amount of information available, it is not surprising that there are a lot of new products. Most are "systems-dependent" and literally could not be produced in a manual environment, for example: (1) variable rate consumer loans (either mortgage loans, installment loans, or revolving credit) that depend upon computer-generated indexes and programmable interest-calculating algorithms, and (2) funds concentration services that allow corporate customers to pull funds from different accounts in different places and to send them to one central location for maximum overnight investing. To give a specific case, Bank of America's retail deposit division only introduced five new products in the five years between 1977 and 1982. Yet in response to the lifting of rate barriers, they were able to introduce 18 new products in 1982 and 1983 because they had the flexibility information technology provides.

The total number of bank products, while obviously on the rise, is undefinable. We estimate that banking contains approximately 150 lines of business, but each may contain numerous products, services, and product features. Furthermore, corporate customers get many of their products tailor-made based on options in timing, interest rates, geography, handling and many, many other factors. For example, wholesale lockbox customers dictate what data gets collected when, and how fast it gets communicated. When Wall Street invents a new derivative security, which itself requires computerization, banks in the securities processing business must modify existing (or invent new) computer application systems to handle each derivative security. Each pension fund customer gets a slightly different segmented and performance-driven report from the banks that offer master trust accounting systems. No two asset securitization deals have been the same.

This product proliferation trend is entirely logical and is likely to continue. *There is no reason that information products cannot be segmented substantially more than they already are, driving systems costs even higher than they already are.* Who are the beneficiaries of product proliferation? The customers, who have more choices than ever before, tailored more closely to their needs. For the banks, however, product proliferation is a two-edged sword. Popular new products can be a salvation, but only if they're distinctive. Too many banking products are still commodities even when they offer new features. Chapter 10 will discuss the need to focus more on a limited set of products and businesses—a natural reaction to the product proliferation trend.

SUMMARY

There has been a lot of evolution in the technology that banks use. But the potential to truly change the economics and the structure of the banking industry did not arrive until the programmable computer first became available about 1960. This is because technological developments prior to the computer did not offer the potential to displace labor completely. The process of integrating systems technology is a lengthy one. Just to convert one function with one line of business may take 10 years or more. So the impact on employment and on productivity has been slow to be felt. Moreover, the rapid evolution of core technology is continuing—ensuring that much of the ultimate evolution that will occur in the industry is yet to come.

CHAPTER 3

COMPETING WITH TECHNOLOGY

The banking industry is restructuring itself in response to the economic and competitive pressures brought on by deregulation. Most banks are using systems technology as a key element of that restructuring. Moreover, the way the industry performs its work is changing radically as electronic technology increasingly substitutes for paper. All of these factors have stimulated many banks to think of systems technology as a competitive weapon and to explore ways to get ahead of their peers through the aid of technology.

These desires have often led to a race to be the first with the latest, most advanced, or largest investment in technology. In other words, being on the leading edge with technology has been linked with the *hope* that better financial performance would result. Based on our experience with clients, we believe that in reality the situation is frequently far more complex than that. Owning equipment vendors' leading-edge products only makes sense in certain selected situations and for some players. As a result, in many lines of business, especially those in which a bank cannot easily offer truly distinctive products, technology investment can be viewed as a defensive requirement instead of as an offensive weapon. Management emphasis, in our experience, should be focused on cost control and avoiding mistakes, not on making leading-edge investments.

With today's expanding and increasingly independent lines of business, competition does not occur across the board; rather, it occurs on a product-by-product basis. This pattern is reinforced by a disaggregation among product lines. For example, new nonbank players, such as FDR (First Data Resources) in credit cards, are splintering off key elements of the business system. Specialized players are focusing on just part of either funds gathering or transaction processing. Thus, competition increasingly occurs on a disaggregated basis, especially that which involves technology or businesses based on technology. Moreover, the technological infrastructure itself can be disaggregated. As a result, the most effective competitors in core technology (e.g., platform/hardware) are not always the most effective in applied technology (e.g., application programs).

As we have seen our clients restructure and transform their product lines, we have also observed changes in economics. For example, fixed costs are displacing variable costs in many product lines, and competitors are being driven toward a more volume-oriented game than ever before. The result is that consolidations and profit pressures are occurring in the most automated lines of business. *We have found that this economic shift is making attractive returns more difficult to achieve, even though actual productivity is substantially improving.*

We have also found that technological leadership can be quite effective in extending a competitive advantage when a unique line of business with high market share has a large technological content. In these cases, the technological investments are not just defensive and can and should be aggressively maintained. State Street Bank, for example, has attained this advantageous position in its mutual funds processing business. However, most players have not been able to achieve such a distinctive advantage. To compensate, they often band together to create shared solutions. By using these shared solutions, they can present formidable competition to proprietary investors. Examples of shared solutions include the banking application packages from vendors or the services of third-party processors. Other examples include shared networks—such as Cirrus, Visa, or even Fedwire—that act as utilities and help maintain a fragmented industry structure despite the pace of automation. Many shared networks have become quite powerful. Only a few large players with distinctive investments can run the risk of competing against them.

The overall effect, then, is that competition with a high technology component involves a rich mixture of business position and technological innovation. Competitive strategies based on information technology advantages may succeed, but in our experience, leading-edge investment without a distinctive business strategy will probably backfire. Given the industry's current consolidation trend, there may well be both big winners and big losers ahead.

COMPETITION ON A DISAGGREGATED BASIS

We have found that the pattern of banking competition increasingly occurs on a disaggregated basis. Banking is following the general pattern of mature industries, which separate their functions and selectively focus

FIGURE 3-1
Financial Services Disaggregation

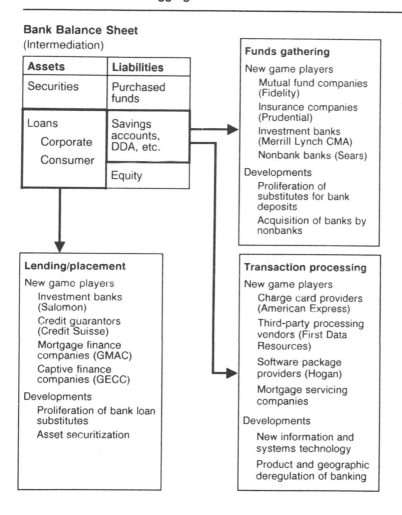

Bank Balance Sheet
(Intermediation)

Assets	Liabilities
Securities	Purchased funds
Loans Corporate Consumer	Savings accounts, DDA, etc.
	Equity

Funds gathering

New game players
  Mutual fund companies (Fidelity)
  Insurance companies (Prudential)
  Investment banks (Merrill Lynch CMA)
  Nonbank banks (Sears)

Developments
  Proliferation of substitutes for bank deposits
  Acquisition of banks by nonbanks

Lending/placement

New game players
  Investment banks (Salomon)
  Credit guarantors (Credit Suisse)
  Mortgage finance companies (GMAC)
  Captive finance companies (GECC)

Developments
  Proliferation of bank loan substitutes
  Asset securitization

Transaction processing

New game players
  Charge card providers (American Express)
  Third-party processing vendors (First Data Resources)
  Software package providers (Hogan)
  Mortgage servicing companies

Developments
  New information and systems technology
  Product and geographic deregulation of banking

on areas with distinctive effectiveness. We can see this happening today in banking in two ways, both related to information technology:

1. *Balance sheet* disaggregation, as new game players (i.e., non-banks) enter the province of the banks—by making loans, gathering deposits, and processing parts of the payment system. (See Figure 3–1.)

2. *Functional* disaggregation, as third-party providers (that are not banks) increasingly provide bank services themselves – often the parts that involve technology.

Balance Sheet Disaggregation

Historically, the traditional banking system was highly integrated. As reviewed in Chapter 1, regulation tended to reinforce this. Each bank effectively made all of its product itself. It raised its own funds, lent its own funds, made its own credit evaluations, kept those funds on its own books over the life of the loans, and did all of the required back-office processing. This "make-make-make" approach was the result of regulation, protection, and a unique franchise. Importantly, this integrated structure guaranteed an attractive profit margin to virtually every bank, large or small. The unfortunate corollary was that this profit subsidy enabled banks to spend resources inefficiently without incurring any penalty.

With time, and with increasing levels of investment in technology, this old world gave way to a new one. Other competitors that were not banks began to invade the banks' turf. These new competitors were not subject to banks' restrictions and could cherry-pick the profitable customers and product lines. The increasingly easier and cheaper transmission of information (caused by technology) was fundamental in creating this opportunity. Now, large corporations, many of whom have better credit ratings than the banks themselves, can borrow in the commercial paper market and bypass banks completely. Other nonbanks have simply gone straight into lending. Finance companies such as GMAC, Ford Credit, and GECC would rank as some of the country's largest banks – if they were banks. In fact, the only U.S. bank that has more assets than GMAC is Citicorp. Because of the tax laws, there is virtually no substantive (and profitable) industrial corporation without a leasing subsidiary – and a lease is just another form of loan. Finally, deposits can now be gathered by many players in addition to banks. Even if they are not legally considered deposits, the funds are still being drawn out of the banking system. Mutual fund companies are the most obvious example, followed by brokerage accounts that allow check writing privileges.

Another good example of disaggregation is found in American Express, whose green, gold, and platinum charge cards and Optima credit card have drawn off transactions (and balances) that could be viewed as bank turf.

American Express has been very successful. Many things have contributed to its success, but the one that stands out is its *focus on one disaggregated product* rather than the full-service product line offered by most banks.

Functional Disaggregation

Functional disaggregation arises when banking production functions are separated and performed only by those best able to perform them. The bank moves away from a make-make-make philosophy toward a more rational and economical rethinking of the buy-versus-build decision. For example, small banks could become local "retailers," buying bank services from another company that is the "wholesaler." Large banks could become manufacturers and wholesalers, and nonbanks could become production subcontractors. Greater efficiency results in a consequent lowering of overall costs; Figure 3–2 lists some examples.

The mortgage banking business illustrates the functional disaggregation process. Most new mortgages are now securitized and sold off in the secondary market. This trend has revolutionized how the business is conducted. In the past, of course, mortgage lenders raised funds via deposits and kept the mortgage on their books over the (extended) life of the loan. This resulted in a lack of liquidity and periodic shortages of credit.

But, the mortgage-backed security (about $600 billion issued) has changed all this. Different organizations now carry out each different function: origination, servicing, credit enhancement, placement, and investment. Competition has been changed in a fundamental way as new competitors have begun specializing in a particular function. Investment banks have done the structuring, placing, and trading of the securities, and selected banks have entered the processing end. Investors, of course, got a new option, with different risk/reward characteristics. Although the forces pushing mortgage securitizations were primarily economic, the enabler, once again, was technology. Mortgages could not be pooled and variable amounts of principal could not be paid down each month without computer programs to track the payments and calculate the constantly changing values.

Functional disaggregation is now evident in many businesses. Part 2 of this book will mention many nonbanks that now play essential roles in the payment system. The work of banks is no longer restricted to banks themselves. *It is more accurate, in fact, to speak of an overall payments industry that includes, but is not limited to, banks.*

FIGURE 3-2
Functional Disaggregation

Marketing and distribution	Credit	Funds movement	Customer service	Collections	MIS
Direct mail firms	Credit bureaus	Service bureaus EDS Citicorp Systematics		Collection agencies	
List vendors	Scoring model developers (Fair Isaacs)	Credit card processors FDR Total Systems			
Telemarketing firms	D&B reports	Merchant bank processors NaBanco National Data			
Indirect auto loan/lease (dealers)	Application processing (Varidyne)	Cash management reporters			
New home builders		Value-added networks			
Deposit brokers					
Product enhancement vendors					

Transaction Processing

Functional disaggregation can be seen in how new nonbank players, often with data processing skills, are now providing substantial parts of the transaction-processing business system. A good example is the action undertaken by Manufacturers Hanover Corporation (MHC) with respect to its credit card portfolio. The fifth largest bankcard issuer, MHC had 3.4 million accounts and a portfolio of $2.5 billion at year-end 1987. It also processed $2.5 billion yearly in credit card sales drafts for merchants. During 1988, MHC made three major efforts to improve its financial performance:

- MHC sold its entire merchant bank business to Fort Lauderdale's NaBanco, a leading third-party merchant processor. NaBanco is a low-cost specialized data processing company, handling 12 to 15 percent of all credit card transactions, which total some $12.5 billion per year in sales. MIIC could not equal NaBanco's high volume approach, and probably concluded that exiting this business did not necessarily threaten other relationships it might have with the same merchants. (Security Pacific did the same thing in 1988, selling its merchant business to NaBanco.)
- MHC participated actively in the sale of the credit card processing cooperative, Eastern States Bankcard Association, to First Data Resources, a subsidiary of the American Express Corporation and the leading third-party processor of credit cards. Again, MHC probably made this sale, which covered the account processing and other back-office functions, because it recognized that customers would be unaware of the processor and believed that no substantial competitive disadvantage would accrue.
- Finally, MHC securitized and sold off $475 million of its credit card receivables in 1988, giving itself better liquidity, reduced capital requirements, and protection from future raises in the cost of funds.

The result has been to create credit card transactions that are captured by others, routed to MHC via others, processed by others, and the balances of which may ultimately belong to others. MHC retains the customer servicing, collections responsibility, and authority over all credit decisions. Perhaps one-half of the overall cost of processing each transaction is incurred by nonbank third parties, on a card that ostensibly belongs to MHC.

Of course, banks can sell transaction processing services as well as buy them. First Wachovia is a good example of a bank benefiting from that trend. It is the country's second largest processor of student loans, serving more than 900 colleges, banks, and state guarantor agencies. Other major competitors are Citibank and Fleet Financial. Student lending is extremely complex, because each state has different rules for each type of student. A medical education loan is different from a liberal arts education loan, which is different from a truck driving school loan. Even worse, the guarantor agencies require processors to be extremely accurate. For example, a graduating student must be billed within so many days of graduation, regardless of when it occurs or whether the student was diligent enough to notify the processor of last minute changes. Delinquent student loans, of which there are many, have to be collected against precise standards. Failure to perform actions properly may jeopardize state or federal guarantees.

Thus, a few vendors dominate the market for processing these loans. First Wachovia has developed proprietary software to track student loans and deliver the required servicing. The software is, of course, unique and serves as a substantial entry barrier. It accommodates thousands of different capabilities, parameters, and features. The price tag for duplication might be around $20 million. As a result, First Wachovia has a nice annuity, with estimated revenues of $23 million per year and net profit of about $5 million. We estimate that the ROE is 100 percent or more because virtually no equity is required.

Two points are worth noting about the overall process of functional disaggregation:

- First, *functional disaggregation is being caused by the increasing power of systems technology.* Technology has speeded up the flow of information and destroyed the old local concept of banking. It has created economies of scale that require outsourcing by banks. It has destroyed the brick and mortar distribution channel (branches) in favor of other channels that banks do not own or control.
- Second, *functional disaggregation is most obvious in the technology itself.* Whether a bank is buying technology to support a banking product (e.g., deposit account processing), or developing new ways to reach the customer (e.g., direct mail channels), a specialized vendor of the technology is almost always available. In short, the function for which disaggregated suppliers are most evident is the systems technology function itself.

The concept of disaggregation is useful because it breaks down what otherwise appears as a monolithic whole and allows us to distinguish the individual workings of parts of the whole. By using the concept to think about competition, we see that the nature of banking competition is changing dramatically.

The same concept can be applied to the technological infrastructure created within each bank to support the bank's work. It, too, is not a monolithic whole and can be broken into individual parts. By focusing on these individual parts, we can better see how each of them might (or might not) contribute to the bank's overall competitive agenda. There are key parts where competitive leverage is potentially significant and others where it is less so. Making this distinction is helpful in developing a more sophisticated understanding of how to compete with technology.

THE M1, M2, M3 FRAMEWORK

We call our individual parts (or levels) of technological infrastructure M1, M2, and M3, which refer to first level, second level, and third level management. These three levels categorize what goes on within a bank to manage (and compete with) systems technology. Each level represents quite a different part of the overall systems infrastructure. (See Figure 3-3.)

M1: The Core Technology Level

M1 is the core technology level, which in effect supports the two higher levels of M2 and M3. The technology level includes the hardware, systems software, and generally accepted technical knowledge so prevalent today. M1 is generic: It is not specific to a bank, or to any business. All hardware in banking—from mainframes and personal computers to printers, disk drives, and modems—is bought from vendors. Systems software—such as operating systems, database management systems, or telecommunications monitors—also comes from vendors.

Because M1 is largely obtained on the open market and embraces no proprietary expertise, it has fundamental characteristics: It provides no competitive advantage and is defensive in nature. Everyone else already has the technology or will soon get it. A limited competitive advantage can be gained over some of the players by seeking economies of scale in M1 or by executing M1 skills well. For example, large data centers have

FIGURE 3-3
The M1–M2–M3 Framework

	M1 Management–1 **Core Technology** hardware oriented	**M2** Management–2 **Applied Technology** software oriented	**M3** Management–3 **Business Needs** end-user oriented
Key elements	Data center Distributed minis and micros Telecommunications network Systems software Knowledge and techniques	Applications portfolio Processing work flow Product and feature know-how Clerical staff	Business strategy Marketing effort Sales force Customer service Trademark
Source of advantage	Economies of scale Timing and execution	Depth of skills Proprietary processes	Identification of needs Market franchise
Time dimension	Short term (less than 5 years)	Long term (more than 5 years)	Short and long term

very definite economies of scale. A large bank with its own data center has approximately a 1 percent overall operating cost advantage over a small bank. But most banks attain reasonable size in M1 through consolidation. To give an example, Bank of New England collapsed nine data centers, gained through acquisition, into three during 1987. Most other banks have done or are doing the same.

Much of the popular PC software, such as Lotus 1-2-3, should also be considered part of M1 because it is widely available and not business-specific. No one gains advantage from owning it. Banks' specialized equipment (e.g., check reader/sorters) is part of M1. Although essential and custom-designed for banking, this equipment is standard from bank to bank and its possession conveys no particular advantage. M1 includes knowledge, too. Technical staff members must know languages, protocols, and programming techniques to do their job. This type of knowledge advances constantly as technical people learn new tricks, such as using reusable codes or adopting CASE tools. But these generic technical skills, useful as they are, do not yield any *competitive* advantage.

Even though it provides no competitive advantage, we cannot ask: "Why invest heavily in M1 technology?" It is obviously necessary, just totally defensive. It is a "ticket to play," and must be done right for the bank to work at all.

Losers who do not measure up in M1 may fall far behind. For example:

- One major United States bank with more than 20,000 teller terminals, ATMs, and personal computers faced a need to deal with retail customers on a total relationship basis. These 20,000+ devices were tied to on-line IMS database applications through front-end minicomputers. The bank decided to link TPF transaction processing systems capability with their IMS databases to achieve three-second response time, higher flexibility, and support more devices. This feat had never been accomplished before, and the bank misjudged both the complexity of the task and the range and depth of the skills required. It was forced to abandon the project, purchase solutions that were less satisfactory, and use CICS/IMS to achieve its goals instead. This process took three years, during which time management's attention was diverted from other needed activities. Direct losses were estimated at about $150 million.
- An international bank chose one of the lesser known hardware vendors to supply its worldwide branches. As the volume of transac-

tions grew, however, even the vendor's top-of-the-line product could not provide sufficient capacity. The bank was forced into an expensive migration to IBM equipment, where it ran the previous vendor's software in emulation mode. This kludge-like arrangement made it permanently more difficult for the bank to work with the software and develop new features.

- Finally, another bank acted poorly in making a strategic migration from IBM's old OS operating system to the newer MVS system. This change was needed to allow use of larger mainframes and to develop applications that could handle more sophisticated accounts. However, it was unable to accomplish this task for over two years, meanwhile delaying all new applications development and missing most of a critical market window. For example, it was unable to offer an equity account until long after its competitors had done so. The opportunity costs, although not directly measurable, were considered very significant.

Aside from problem cases like these, M1 does not do much to winnow the pack. Too many banks can get the help they need from vendors; or they can buy shared solutions. Thus, most pass the screening. Some aspects of M1, such as knowing when to adopt a new technology, can be very critical. And M1 management must constantly select from a multitude of hardware and software components. *Yet the impact, as long as it is done right, is just to set the stage for the more important decisions in M2 and M3.*

M2: The Applications and Processing Activities Level

We define M2 as the set of processing activities and resources that get built onto the M1 level. M2 is the work, in industrial engineering terms, that each bank does. It consists of two parts: application programs (which we label M2–A) that run on the M1 hardware and the ever present manual processing operations (which we label M2–B) that interact with the application programs. Virtually everything in the back office still requires this complex mixture of both automated and manual effort. For example, a worker in an installment loan credit department will use an on-line terminal to input application data, determine a credit score, do other tasks manually, and then go back to the terminal. It takes extensive interaction between worker and machine to complete most banking activities.

Even eliminating the paper does not eliminate the mixture of automated and manual processes. The bank of the future may be paperless, but it will not be workerless. Every terminal requires a brain and two hands. Futurists sometimes equate *automation* with *automatic* or *predetermined* operations that do not need any labor. In banking, at least, this is not true. People are an absolutely essential part of M2, even if the total labor force in the industry will be reduced in the 1990s.

Every bank needs a mammoth M2 infrastructure to process the information for every type of product. Completing an international funds transfer, purchasing or selling a security, or evaluating an auto loan application requires dozens, even hundreds, of separate steps within the processor's M2 infrastructure. Marketing functions require software to manipulate computerized customer lists and analyze product/market data. Even customer service requires an on-line system for account inquiry and tracking of complaints or disputes. In short, M2's importance can hardly be overestimated.

Competition Within M2
Banks compete within the M2 level. The competition is in the application of the technology, not in the technology itself. Banks are betting that their business ideas, expressed through an M2 infrastructure, will get to the market first, capture it, and maintain high margins. Many banks that have been successful with technology have followed such a path. Examples include CoreStates Financial, with its MAC ATM transaction processing business, and Banc One Corporation (to be described in Chapter 9), which sells its back-office functions to brokers, credit unions, and the like.

Most banks, however, have not been particularly successful with technology. As discussed in Chapter 2, 90 percent of all systems investments support a commodity product or service. But with commodities, even the best technology will not make any competitive difference, which points up the essential difficulty with M2. Traditionally built in-house, most M2 investments do not, in fact, result in any competitive advantage, precisely because there is nothing unique about the functions or products provided by the M2 investment.

For example, of the 150 largest banks, roughly one-half have proprietary deposit systems. Yet, the products — CDs, savings accounts, and checking accounts — are mostly perceived as commodities, with little differentiation beyond branch location and interest rate. In other words, too many banks have an indistinguished proprietary M2. This situation has caused enormous problems as M2 has been extensively *overbuilt*. A myriad of details and complexities have been added, all in the name of service competition. Outsiders (including senior bank executives) typically have no comprehension or appreciation for the degree of complexity built into M2. They wonder why a system whose only job is to track and help resolve customer inquiries takes 1 million lines of computer code— yet it does at one major bank.

Because of all this proprietary M2, the skills to run it are not easy or cheap. They are learned at each bank, are specific to that bank, and are not available on the open market. Only the tenured programmers have any idea what the codes and flags buried in the software mean. (For example, a *20* in Field 14 of a transaction account master file could mean one thing if the account was opened before 1975, but something else otherwise. This information is rarely documented, but is carried in the heads of the maintenance programmers. It is the inevitable result of twisting an old architecture to meet constantly changing user needs.) The question is: Does a bank really benefit from a throwback to the medieval concept of handmade goods? Should a bank depend on its programmers' individualistic field/code conventions to get its work done?

How Automation Changes the Costs

The systems costs that were quantified in Chapter 1 thus consist of M1 (for core technology) and M2–A (for applications software). Looking at the amount of money spent on these two levels within a specific line of business is a good way to judge how far the process of automation has gone.

In Figure 3–4, we estimate how the costs of selected lines of business can be disaggregated. Each selected line of business shows the costs of M1 and M2–A. For example, 55 percent of the costs of the cash management business consist of M1 core technology and M2–A applications technology. The lines with a high degree of automation are precisely the lines in which margin pressures are worst and competitors are being squeezed the most.

At the other end of the spectrum are businesses, such as personal trust, that are still labor intensive and where consolidation is not taking place. Overall, wholesale lines of business involving payments (i.e., most nonlending lines) are more automated than their retail counterparts. Given equal volumes, higher value transactions have tended to become automated first, thus putting the squeeze first on wholesale lines.

FIGURE 3-4
Non-Interest Expense Distribution: Selected Lines of Business, 1988

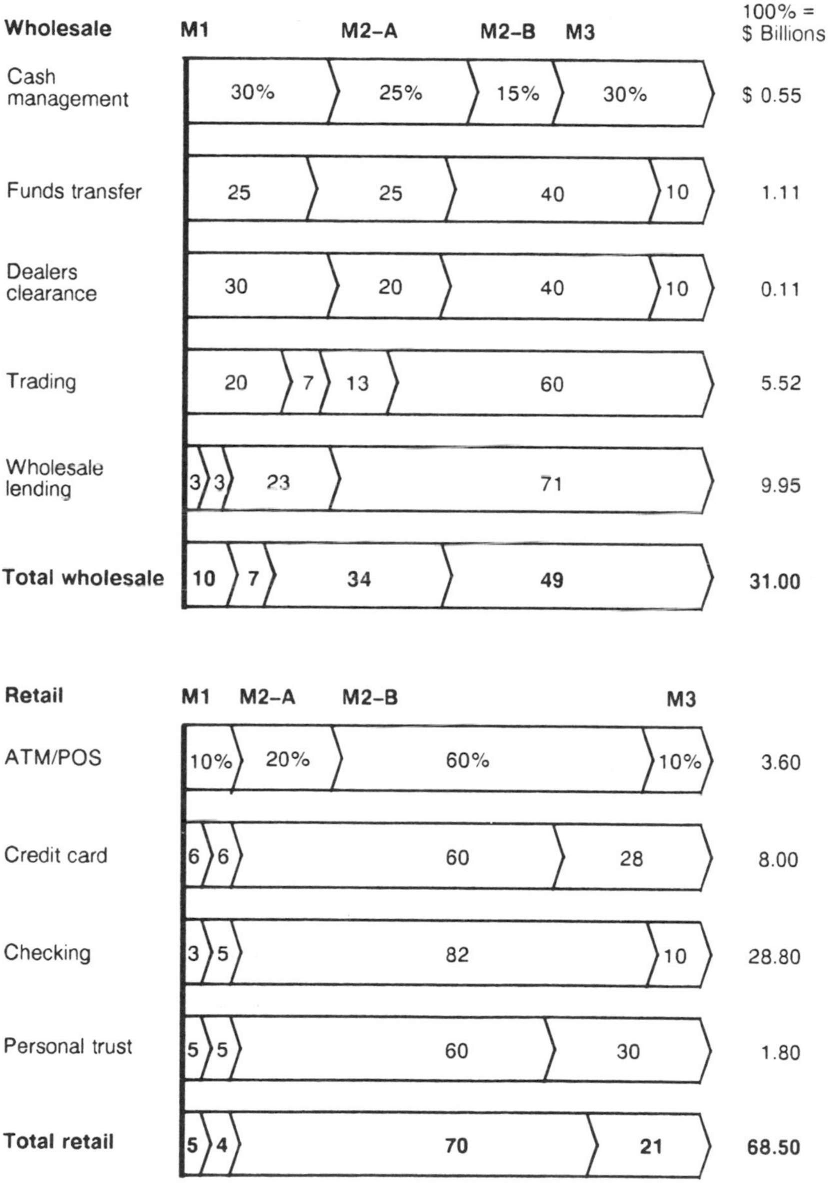

Wholesale	M1	M2–A	M2–B	M3	100% = $ Billions
Cash management	30%	25%	15%	30%	$ 0.55
Funds transfer	25	25	40	10	1.11
Dealers clearance	30	20	40	10	0.11
Trading	20	7	13	60	5.52
Wholesale lending	3	3	23	71	9.95
Total wholesale	10	7	34	49	31.00

Retail	M1	M2–A	M2–B		M3	
ATM/POS	10%	20%	60%		10%	3.60
Credit card	6	6	60		28	8.00
Checking	3	5	82		10	28.80
Personal trust	5	5	60		30	1.80
Total retail	5	4	70		21	68.50

The bottom line on M2 is whether it is unique enough to justify its costs. If so, its uniqueness can act as an entry barrier to a nonparticipant desiring to enter a new business. If the competitors have something to protect, this barrier is terrific. But if the product is a commodity, it may be no more than a lot of wasted effort. The result is that M2 represents either a threat or an opportunity based on what products or services it produces.

M3: The Business Needs Level

M3 is the business needs level of our framework. It is not a technology per se but is the set of business needs that drive the requirements for technology. For example, such questions as What business is the bank in?, What products does it offer?, or What support features are needed?, must be answered. Many factors contribute to a successful business strategy. The sum total of a bank's needs for technology is what constitutes M3.

A simple example in a trading environment illustrates the three levels of M1–M2–M3. Bank traders spend their days staring intently at an array of computer screens and barking out orders on the phone. The trader or the support staff analyzes the prices and their movements. Periodically, the trader scribbles a completed deal on a ticket that is then sent off to be processed. All three levels of our framework are present. The screens the trader looks at, the networks in back of the screens, and the distant computers supporting the screens are all M1. The code that supports the trader's decision-making analysis and the back-office clearing and settlement factories are all M2. The trader and what he or she wants the technology to do are M3.

In sum, these three levels allow us to understand better what goes on inside a bank as it reinvests in more technology. Actions that make sense in one level may not make sense in another. As the overall level of systems intensiveness grows, the cost of M1 and M2-A grow and, in turn, increase the level of fixed costs. These economic changes help to explain why banks have such a hard time making profits out of technology.

HOW INCREASED TECHNOLOGICAL CONTENT CHANGES INDUSTRY STRUCTURE AND PROFITABILITY

As the conversion from paper to electronics proceeds, and as the share of all costs in a business line that are devoted to technology (M1 and M2-A) grows, the economics of the business change. The relative proportion of fixed costs rise and the minimum efficient scale for a producer goes up. These changing economics should, in turn, compel a new industry structure that is more consolidated. Profits may well be destroyed during the transition period when the automation is actually occurring and the industry structure is changing.

To understand this process more closely, let us consider the situation of the U.S. banks prior to the advent of systems technology. Banking (at least in the United States) is a highly fragmented business. There are thousands of competitors for the more common activities. The largest competitor will typically have only a small market share. Even in specialized lines of business, there may well be hundreds of competitors.

Manual processing has few economies of scale because of the high labor component. In other words, the minimum efficient scale is low. This situation is exacerbated by the fact that many processing activities serve only as product support. For instance, check processing is support for the deposit gathering product. Because every bank raises deposits, they all come to believe they must process their own checks. This makes banks much more willing to continue their processing activities, even if they are not capable of reaching a minimum efficient scale. The tendency of even very small banks to process their own checks will be documented in Chapter 4.

In any event, systems technology enters a specific line of business by automating these processing activities. As the three stages of automation described in Chapter 2 occur, the fraction of all costs devoted to M1 and M2–A rises. There are more economies of scale with systems technology than with manual processing. Data centers and telecommunication networks are more efficient if they are large, and application portfolios only need to be purchased or built once.

As the conversion occurs, each competitor may only see that its unit costs will decrease if it makes the technological investment. It will appear almost as a mandatory step—unless the bank is willing to keep processing by paper and incur a competitive disadvantage. So most competitors—too many—make the investment. They will frequently increase industry capacity so much that overcapacity results. Each competitor will try to build in more transaction processing capacity than it had in the past because of the economics and because of a desire to accommodate future growth. The leaders, which make the investment first, may be especially aggressive in this regard, viewing low-cost processing capacity as a way of gaining market share.

Investments in support facilities usually make the overcapacity situation worse. Not only are they considered mandatory, but they also tend to be invisible. There are no easily defined and agreed upon measures of capacity, for example, expressing exactly how many funds transfers can be made. Management is usually unfamiliar with capacity concepts such as "throughput rates," "peak load," or "queuing time." What is readily observable to management, however, is a noticeable drop in industry price levels signifying overcapacity. In our experience, pricing pressure is "sensed" relatively early in the game by virtually all competitors. However, this perspective does not usually deter development plans. Ultimately, competitors recognize that until the overcapacity leaves the business, there will always be continuing pressures on profits.

We have lived through this chain of events several times with our clients in automating businesses. The sequence tends to occur in a very fragmented business (or function) where processing is a significant part of overall cost. New businesses, such as mutual fund processing, which developed relatively late (i.e., in the 1970s) and never had a fragmented industry structure, would not be so affected. This product emerged in a stable industry structure. Other examples of profitable automated lines include student loan processing, mortgage processing, master trust, and global custody. Another exception is the lending businesses, where the cost of processing activities is typically quite small. Even if the requisite back-office tasks become automated (creating overcapacity), not enough of the operations cost structure is transformed to hurt profits or force consolidation.

Finally, several major banking businesses have not yet been completely converted to electronic technology. Checking is the classic example—and involves literally thousands of banks. One reason banks may not see profits in point-of-sale (POS)/debit systems, for example, is simply that banks foresee this process of overcapacity, price pressure, and consolidation. They recognize the great difficulties in sustaining profits as the retail payment system automates despite the generally recognized advantages in productivity.

From these thoughts come the second half of this book's title. Profits do get destroyed by technology, but only because of this adjustment in industry structure caused by changed economics. Once the adjustment period is over, this particular influence on the level of profitability should end. How and where this transition takes place is what competitors must keep in mind.

TECHNOLOGICAL LEADERSHIP

Bankers are often concerned about whether they are up-to-date technologically and about how they compare with their competitors. Because developments in the underlying technology (i.e., the M1 platform) move so quickly, many executives fear being left behind in the race. Some banks have reputations for leading technologically and are successful performers; examples are Citibank, Banc One, and Security Pacific. The reputations of such banks cause other bankers to ask, "Should my bank become a leader too?"

We believe that technological leadership within M1 confers no advantage at all by itself. The M1 profile should be driven by the technical needs of M2. *Appropriate* technology is more often the watchword at these successful firms. For example, Total Systems Inc., a large credit card processor partially owned by Columbus Bank & Trust, uses Assembler language for most of its code—a technology that is more than 20 years old. Both Citibank and MHC use the 15-year-old TPF/ACP operating system for their high-volume transaction-processing applications. Many banks use the 15-year-old MVS operating system; even the instruction set of the IBM 3090 is about 20 years old. Although these systems are constantly being updated, they do face underlying limits to their development, limits that in some cases have been reached.

This "if it ain't broke, don't fix it" attitude saves resources for other purposes. Technological leaders get their reputation by being first when it makes a real difference. For instance, Citicorp is using image processing technology to implement the first major folder management system for handling credit card correspondence. Why is Citicorp the first? Image processing is most efficient with high volumes, and with more than 15 million accounts, Citicorp leads the bankcard industry.

Conversely, the first adapters of a new technology may face trouble. For example, two banks that were involved with experimental expert systems that made lending decisions found themselves using the technology only for training. It still needed a substantial amount of development work. *The lesson: Do not lead in M1; be a fast follower instead.*

Leadership with M2 technology, however, is a different story. Here it often pays to be the first if the business need (M3) is unique and successful. State Street Bank and Bank of New York were the first to develop the mutual fund processing business and have prospered with it. Their success rests upon proprietary M2 applications and a knowledgeable work force. Merrill Lynch continues to dominate the market for broker cash management accounts because it was the first to develop the product and the software. In fact, virtually every success story in information technology can be traced to early entry with a new product or new business approach, backed up by an appropriate M2 investment in both software and people.

Laggards in M2 often have a difficult time. They may never catch up once the leader gets a dominant market share. Twenty years ago, Barclays Bank introduced the United Kingdom's first Visa card and had to make the first systems investments to support it. The other U.K. banks took six years to follow suit, and they have never regained the lost market share. In fact, the last competitors to build an M2 system may suffer higher per-unit development expenses because the customers often cannot be convinced to switch back from the leader.

Yet, attaining technological leadership in M2 is not a one-time event. M2 is never static. It requires constant changes and enhancements as more manual support functions are automated and as new customer features are added. Yet, processing capacity, especially the software, can only be built so fast, no matter how many people or resources are thrown at the job. The competitor who builds the first M2 capability and who keeps adding new features will frequently not allow the laggards to catch up.

THE BUY-VERSUS-BUILD DECISION

It is a rare bank that has never been burned on the buy-versus-build decision. Tales of unhappy experiences with vendors are all too common. Other banks have refused to use a vendor, mounted elaborate development projects, and turned out equally unhappy. There does not seem to be a single right choice. But the presence of so many banking industry vendors, from manufacturers and turnkey vendors to third-party processors, makes the choices tough. The right way to think about the issue is to focus on the business purpose of the investment.

M1 Issues

Almost all M1 technology is purchased from the outside. IBM plays a leading role, not only as a hardware supplier, but also as a source of systems software that becomes the de facto industry standard. IBM has 95 percent of the mainframe market at larger banks, although it shares the mainframe market with Unisys and NCR in the smaller bank market. IBM also owns the teleprocessing market—most banks use its CICS systems, and those that do not use its IMS system instead. IBM also dominates the large check reader/sorter market and the PC market. On the other hand, Unisys and NCR have a lock on the proof and unit encoder markets. Several other markets are very competitive, including the markets for teller terminals and large laser printers. Thus, choosing a hardware vendor can be a major decision, and *changing* a vendor can be even worse, as witnessed by the difficulties encountered by many data processing shops that converted from something else to IBM.

Another critical decision banks face is whether to use the data processing facilities of a third-party processor or facilities manager. Currently, thousands of small banks do this. Vendors such as EDS, Systematics, and Citicorp Information Services Inc. offer reasonable transaction costs, because their high volumes afford great economies of scale. But for the bigger banks, the situation is more complex. Traditionally, large banks have relied almost exclusively on in-house operations. But recently the third-party processors have begun making inroads in serving the large banks. The real issue for a large bank considering third-party servicing has less to do with pure scale considerations than with overall business objectives, financial condition, comfort with existing data processing capabilities, and the economics of alternatives.

The market that is emerging for third-party processors in the larger banking institutions is intensely competitive. In addition to traditional competitors such as FiServe, Systematics, or EDS, one new entrant has joined the competition: IBM. Some of the most sophisticated large banks have begun to recognize that these emerging competitive vendors can be a source of cost effectiveness in certain activities—particularly those that require less strategic distinctiveness and more low-cost delivery. The one clear implication for large banks is that scale advantage alone is increasingly unlikely to yield a competitive edge for a proprietary competitor.

M2 Issues

It is in the M2–A level of management that buy-versus-build decisions become truly difficult. There is often a strategic argument that favors the build option and a cost argument that favors the buy option. The standard M1 environments and the high number of banks (i.e., potential customers) have spurred many small vendors to develop business-specific M2 application packages. However, the traditional approach of large banks is to do M2 in-house. Small and medium-size banks usually use outside vendors—for example, service bureaus such as First Financial Management Corporation—to do their processing until the product volume gets too high. Then such banks might want to bring processing in-house as a sort of strategic move against vendor dependence. Merrill Lynch, for example, went through several years of agonizing conversions (and great expense) to bring its check and credit card processing in-house (from Banc One), once its CMA product became so successful.

Yet the issues discussed earlier make it extremely difficult economically and technically for every competitor in a business line to build and maintain its own M2 software. Application solution providers now offer everything from low-cost PC-based packages to multimillion-dollar integrated packages. Banking has more than 240 industry-specific vendors that sell application packages or turnkey solutions. Also, many banks are increasingly serious about installing an integrated package. For example, MHC recently decided to install the Systematics retail deposit package, ending 20 years of proprietary software.

Making a decision to buy a major M2 application software package is not easy. Sacrifices and trade-offs are always involved because no package, even with customizing, can meet every bank's needs. The ongoing stability of the vendor must be considered, as must the potential loss of technological advantage. Each line of business tends to have only a few integrated packages that, if successful, become standards. Those who use these packages must focus on some other aspect of the business system to achieve distinctiveness.

The hardest part comes last—installing the vendor's software and integrating it with the clerical work force. The interaction between desk and computer is frequently so tight in M2 that clerical operations may be in a state of substantial upheaval during and after a major conversion. As a result, adopting a package may take almost as long as proprietary development. Even when a new system is successfully implemented, the conversion cost is usually greater than the purchase cost, and these migration costs may largely offset assumed economic benefits.

Still, it makes sense for every bank to keep a sharp eye on vendor activity. When banks begin buying more shared solutions in particular areas—either functional (such as general ledger systems) or product (such as credit card processing)—competition can change. Smaller players may be able to start buying the software and their processing costs start to go down. For proprietary players, it is time to reexamine their own M2: Does it really offer enough unique features to compete with the shared solution?

The bottom line is that technological competitiveness within M2 is a moving target. Functions or products that have been automated for a long time tend to become commodities because packages become available. Then the value goes out of them. To keep ahead of the game, competitors need to keep adding features. Most banks, for example, have thought about a combined billing statement to reinforce their customer relationships, but they cannot get it from a vendor. Likewise, Citicorp Mortgage recently introduced an escrow analysis statement to tell its mortgagees how much of their money it holds; this most likely did not come from a vendor, either. Adding unique value within M2 is frequently the best way to compete and is the best place for proprietary approaches.

SHARED NETWORKS

A shared network is a utility; it includes both a consortium that switches transactions as well as a third-party that does processing for a multitude of competing players. Shared networks have arisen subsequent to the arrival of technology in most of the major banking lines of business. It is usually a cooperative owned by its competing members. (See Table 3–1.)

The issue is whether a bank can compete in a newly automated line of business in a proprietary way and establish a defensible position. The competitive battle usually begins when the shared utility enters the business and competes directly with banks. Because it gets so much volume, the shared utility can usually get the upper hand and achieve a significant cost advantage. Small banks will not be willing to switch transactions via a proprietary network when given the option of using a less expensive shared utility.

A good example of this competitive pressure comes from the experience of the money center banks when the SWIFT utility was established. SWIFT is a Type 2 cooperative. (See Figure 3–5.) Its establishment diffused the power of the money center banks that were Type 1 competitors with worldwide proprietary networks. Much of the profit left the international correspondent banking business as the banks lost volume to SWIFT. In turn, SWIFT allowed smaller competitors (Type 4 firms) to

TABLE 3-1.
Shared Networks

Shared Network	Line of Business	Type of Transaction
Society for World-wide Financial Telecommunication (SWIFT)	International funds transfer	Messages transferring funds between banks or intrabank; settlement through other avenues; 1,600 member banks
Visa, MasterCard	Bankcard	Authorizations, purchase/cash advance transactions, and card standards for all bankcard issuers
Plus, Cirrus, NYCE, other regionals	ATM & POS switching	Cash withdrawals, balances, and other eligible transactions switched between participants
CHIPS (NYCHA)	Large dollar payments	139 U.S. and international banks make large U.S. dollar payments
Fedwire	Domestic dollar payments	Payment and settlement via Fed Funds
NACHA (42 regional ACHs)	Automated clearinghouse	Transfer of recurring debits and credits between thousands of banks
Depository Trust Company (DTC)	Securities trading	Switch-of-ownership messages for immobilized equities and bonds

achieve a low-cost alternative in sending messages and so helped prevent an overwhelming accumulation of power on the part of the big banks.

A similar story can be told at the other Type 2 shared networks. The shared ATM networks, such as Most or Star (see Chapter 4), allow very small banks to issue ATM cards and attract deposits, even if they do not own a single ATM. Citicorp, by not sharing its ATMs in New York City, runs a distinctive yet so far successful Type 1 strategy. Some data indicates that Citicorp's ATMs are frequently more desirable to the average account holder than are those of NYCE, the local shared competition. Between 50 and 60 percent of Citicorp's account holders are designated as frequent ATM users—a noticeably higher percentage than at some of the NYCE banks. Citibank's proprietary approach may not work forever, but currently it is highly competitive.

FIGURE 3-5

Competitive Position Following Full Impact of Technology

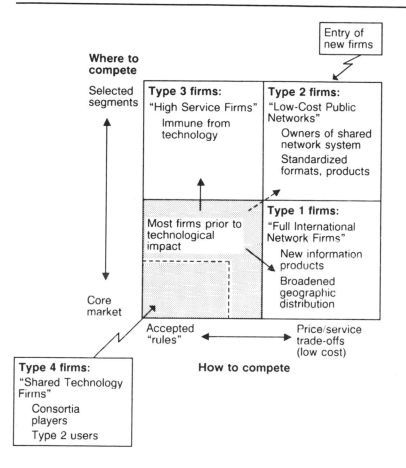

Most of the shared networks are owned by their members. But one, the MAC system, is owned outright by CoreStates, with consequent advantage to them. Usually, Type 4 players dislike having their shared networks owned by one competitor, so CoreStates's position is quite unusual. This unique business probably contributes above-average profits to CoreStates.

Visa and MasterCard both play the Type 2 role in the credit card world. They allow many banks—some quite small—to issue cards and not worry at all about the merchant side. The proprietary competitors — including American Express, Sears' Discover Card, Diner's Club, and Carte Blanche (all Type 3) — are all high-risk, high-reward cards. American Express is reaping substantial rewards, as will be documented in Chapter 5. Diner's Club and Carte Blanche are taking the risk, and the jury is still out on Discover. (Note that Citibank recently folded its regional stand-alone card, Choice, into the Visa network.)

This competition between shared and proprietary networks is caused by the arrival of technology. Each major electronic product needs its own switching network, whereas when all transactions were paper-based, the major shared network was the check-clearing one. A reason for this need might simply be that technology allows so much more information to be added to transactions. An electronic transfer contains many fields and so needs to be isolated from other transfers with radically different characteristics. In addition, Type 2 firms usually do much more than simply transport transactions from place to place. Transactions are stored, converted, summarized, reversed, and so forth — all of which requires sophisticated and highly specific software that is part of the switch. In fact, it is reasonable to predict that new shared networks will come into being; point of sale (POS) systems, corporate EDI, and home banking are just a few possibilities.

To make sure that it does not run afoul of these shared networks, any bank that wants to invest in a proprietary network should insure that it is very knowledgeable about the emerging industry structure. If the small players band together, they will not be very good customers. Success can have excess rewards, but the risks are high. Our client experience indicates that those that can establish a sustainable position *early*, before the shared network comes into being, have by far the best chance of success. And, a differentiable product is almost a necessity.

SUMMARY

Competing with technology is a complicated undertaking. It is quite different from simply trying to improve productivity through automation or keeping up-to-date with new computers. In a fragmented industry such as banking, with so many competitors and so much of the technology available from outside vendors, the competitive positioning of *what is done with the technology is all-important*.

Unfortunately, the nature of the business (and its regulation) has created overcapacity, oligopolistic tendencies, and a propensity to compete through service. We estimate that more than 90 percent of the current expenditures on technology go into essentially routine tasks, which provide few opportunities for distinctive performance and profits. The only approach that really makes sense in such defensive situations is to minimize the technological cost, use (where appropriate) less expensive shared resources, and (again where appropriate) not even attempt to be a technological leader.

The other 10 percent or less of the technological expenditures goes to support truly differentiable business approaches, where early entry, better products, and an aggressive approach can really pay off. Here the technology should be as proprietary as possible in order to set up barriers and maximize market share.

In Part 2 of this book we will explore specific lines of business, focusing on those that comprise the bulk of the industry's costs and constitute the target of most systems investments. The economics, competition, and technology of each line of business will be analyzed as it converts from paper to electronics. The reader will note how difficult it is, given some of the pending developments, for banks to make profits on these conversions. What banks might do differently will then be discussed in Part 3.

PART 2

SPECIFIC LINES OF BUSINESS: PAYMENT SYSTEMS AND TRUST

This part of the book explores how systems technology has impacted some specific lines of business. We have chosen two broad categories of product where the role of automation is most important: payment products and trust. The overall payment system is the heart of the banking industry. Processing about 63 billion noncash payments in 1988 cost U.S. banks over one-half of all non-interest expense (i.e., $50 billion). Because of this, payments have been the major target of the industry's investment in automation; 68 percent of all system expenses (i.e., $8.12 billion) was so targeted in 1988. (See Figure P2–1.) Although trust is smaller (about 8 percent of costs), it contains some of the industry's most automated businesses.

Chapter 4 will discuss the retail payment business (e.g., consumers' transaction accounts), Chapter 5 discusses the credit/charge card businesses, and Chapter 6 discusses the wholesale payment systems. Chapter 7 will cover the trust and securities businesses. Each chapter will look at the current state of development of these products, the technology used to produce them, how the economics have changed, and what these economic changes are doing to competition and industry structure.

The retail payment system is still largely based on the paper-based check. (See Figure P2–2, which describes the overall payment system volumes.) The transformation to electronics has not proceeded very far

FIGURE P2-1

U.S. Commercial Banks' Systems Expenses by Line of Business, 1988

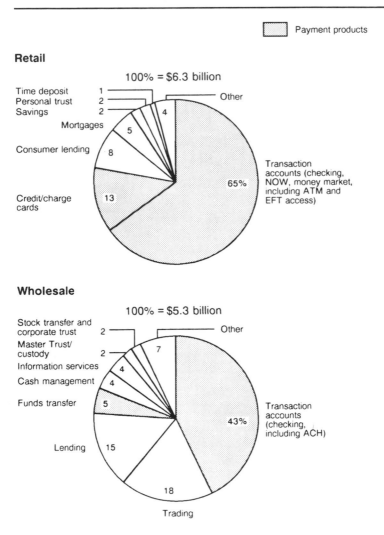

□ Payment products

Retail

100% = $6.3 billion

Time deposit 1 — Other
Personal trust 2
Savings 2
Mortgages 4
5
Consumer lending 8

Transaction accounts (checking, NOW, money market, including ATM and EFT access) — 65%

Credit/charge cards 13

Wholesale

100% = $5.3 billion

Stock transfer and corporate trust 2 — Other
Master Trust/ custody 2
Information services 4
Cash management 4
Funds transfer 5
7

Transaction accounts (checking, including ACH) — 43%

Lending 15

18

Trading

yet, although the potential benefits of the retail electronic payment technologies (ATMs, POS/debit, and home banking) are high. Partly because the payment habits of 88 million U.S. households are involved, change in the retail payments system always takes a long time. As a result, the retail payment system is still in Stage B of the automation process, where

FIGURE P2-2
U.S. Payment System Volumes, 1988
(billions of transactions)

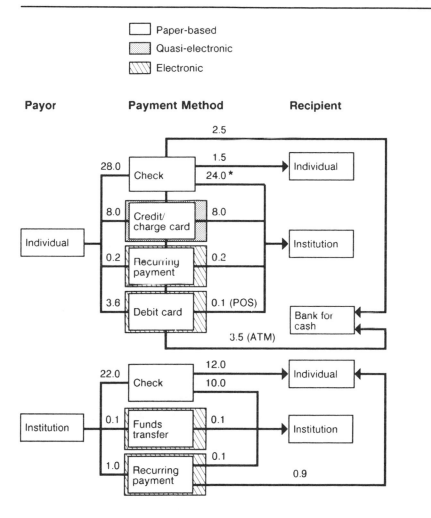

☐ Paper-based
▨ Quasi-electronic
▧ Electronic

* 9.0 in store, 15.0 via mail

technology has aided but not eliminated the clerical function. The customer interface has not yet become automated, and the economics and competitive structure of retail payment business lines have not yet shown any significant degree of change.

The credit/charge card business is one of the bright spots in U.S. banking because its profitability is so high. Systems technology has been employed throughout the cardholder business system, not only to process transactions, but also to create extra features and value. Competition within the business has been very disaggregated since nonbank competitors have come to play significant roles. On the merchant side of the business, however, Stage C (automation of the customer interface) has been reached and the margins have been squeezed.

Wholesale payments are more automated than other payments because of their higher values and greater per-customer volumes. The customer interface is extensively automated in many cases, and several of the lines of business have become quite systems-intensive. The effect of this has been to fundamentally change the economics. Fixed costs have risen, excess balances have declined, and margins have been squeezed. Competition has gotten much harder and consolidative pressures are strong.

Trust and securities businesses are important endeavors for some banks, especially for the large banks where they make up approximately 10 percent of all operating expenses. Systems technology is used heavily in some but not all of the businesses, making competition generally strong.

The degree of automation in any particular business is a "moving target." Overall, the competitive structure of the payments business is still highly fragmented but is becoming less so—particularly as technology expenditures change the economics of certain lines of business. Many of the trust businesses are at a more advanced stage of consolidation. As a result, our experience indicates that advantages accrue to those who compete successfully with market-oriented distinctive offerings—and in certain cases with scale. These should be the objectives of banks' systems investments in the critical areas of the payment system.

CHAPTER 4

RETAIL PAYMENT SYSTEMS

Deposit-based transaction accounts (e.g., checking accounts) are the heart of the retail payment system. However, the cost to operate transaction accounts constitutes roughly one-half of all banking industry expense. Thus, the use of systems investments to reduce costs by replacing paper is of paramount interest. Substantial amounts of money have already been spent on ATMs and may well be spent in the future on POS/debit card systems and on methods to conduct banking transactions from the home. The three electronic transaction methods can all be described as Stage C developments because they are extensions of automation that directly reach customers. ATMs automate customers' interactions at the branch, POS/debit card systems automate customers' interactions in a store, and home banking automates and facilitates customers' activities at home. But none of these has progressed enough in consumer acceptance to reduce the volume of checks, and so the retail payments business is still very largely paper-based. Substantial transformation of the business system and industry concentration have not yet occurred, and the economics of the business — particularly the cost side — have not yet fundamentally changed.

We believe that because of the high growth rates and lower costs of electronic payments, the retail payment system will eventually enter Stage C. However, all payment system changes have traditionally taken place quite slowly. The retail system, which involves the payment habits of 88 million American households, changes extremely slowly. Thus, substantial changes in the economics and competitive structure of the retail payment system have not and, we believe, will not occur rapidly. But as changes do occur, they may be similar to the changes that have already occurred in the wholesale payment system, as will be described in Chapter 6. Margins may be squeezed and the thousands of banks that currently participate in the retail payments system may find their ability to remain competitive curtailed.

In the remainder of this chapter, we will discuss the current development and technology of the four major retail payment methods: checks, ATMs, POS/debit, and home banking. Then, the economic and competitive impacts of each will be assessed.

THE CHECKING SYSTEM

American households are highly dependent on checking accounts, as each household writes approximately 320 checks per year. Furthermore, the volumes continue to increase each year, even though electronic substitutes for checks are now available. POS/debit can replace checks at a point of sale, ATMs can replace checks cashed over a bank counter, and the Automated Clearinghouse (ACH) can replace both retail and wholesale checks for recurring payments. Although the transactional base of each electronic alternative is small relative to the check volume, the growth rates of each are high. (See Figure 4–1.) However, to date, probably less than 5 percent of all retail payments has been displaced by electronics.

The Technology of Checking Accounts

Although checks are not electronic transactions, a substantial amount of information technology is used in their processing. In fact, so much technology has been applied so effectively that real per-unit processing costs dropped by approximately 70 percent between 1960 and 1988. Most functions needed to process checks have been extensively automated, except for the initial step (encoding) and the handling of exception items (e.g., rejects and returns).

Checks are handled on a variety of high-speed equipment. IBM 3890 reader/sorters—the workhorses of the industry—capture the MICR data, endorse the checks, microfilm them, and sort them at a rate of 33 per second in bursts. For low-volume operations, reader/sorters of slower speed are available. Statement-stuffing machines and bulk files are available. Also, vendors provide a wide variety of mechanical and electronic check-handling equipment. Transit cases, MICR trays and trucks, joggers, sorter racks, and bulk filing cabinets are the prosaic but essential furniture of every bank's basement.

FIGURE 4-1
Payment System Changes

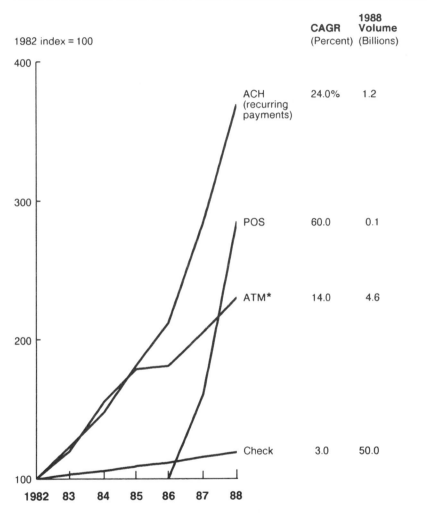

1982 index = 100

	CAGR (Percent)	1988 Volume (Billions)
ACH (recurring payments)	24.0%	1.2
POS	60.0	0.1
ATM*	14.0	4.6
Check	3.0	50.0

1982 83   84   85   86   87   88

* All transactions, of which approximately 75 percent are withdrawals

Because of such equipment investments, it is not as easy as it might otherwise be to switch to the electronic payment technologies. In his book *Innovation: The Attacker's Advantage*, McKinsey Director Richard Foster describes how technologies progress up an S-curve, performing better as

FIGURE 4-2

Mature Check Technology Versus Emerging Electronic Payments Technology

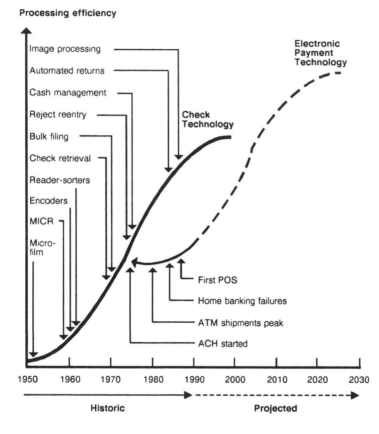

more effort is put into them. Check processing technology has improved steadily for more than 40 years. (See Figure 4–2.) Incremental improvements, such as automated return processing (beta-tested in 1989 by BankAmerica), are still possible, and image processing may soon be speeding the data entry process. But, as if to prove the checks are near the top of their technological S-curve, the important measure of encoding productivity ceased improving in 1983.

In *Innovation*, Foster describes how returns eventually diminish from further investment in the old technology and people begin casting about for new technologies. A period of discontinuity may occur between the S-curve of the old technology and that of the new. Because competitors have such big investments in the old technology, many cannot (or will not) make an immediate leap to the new technology. This is what has happened in banking. The electronic payments technologies are still in their infancy, and an immediate leap is not supportable. Despite their high potential in the future, their current performance is still on the lower part of their S-curve. For example, the ACH still processes returns by paper and only recently stopped receiving entries by magnetic tape. ATMs have not yet been productive enough to reduce the number of bank branches. Both home banking and POS/debit face development issues. This discontinuity is maintaining the checking system longer than many observers thought possible only a few years ago.

The Economics of Checking

The cost of the checking business and all of its related services was approximately $45 billion in 1988 — a fully loaded cost of 90 cents per check. Much of this is an allocation of the part of the banking industry's branch network that goes into servicing checking accounts and providing deposit account-related services. The incremental cost of a check for only the back-office processing is at most between 10 and 15 cents. Efforts to improve checking productivity are usually focused on this relatively small back-office component.

The most labor-intensive part of check processing is encoding, the first step after a check is deposited. Encoding alone accounts for 32 percent of all check-processing labor. Each check must be individually observed and the amount encoded on the MICR line. There are few economies of scale. Our data indicates that encoding productivity is approximately 5,200 checks per day per machine for all banks over $100 million in size and does not increase with size of bank. Another costly aspect of the checking system is the approximately 1 percent of all checks (i.e, 500 million per year) that are returned from the payee's bank to the bank of first deposit. The process today is slow and inefficient. Some returns are sent back through each bank that handled the check during the forward presentment process. It currently takes an average of 5.6 days to return a check, even though forward collection averages 1.2 days.

Thus, check economics are not changing rapidly. But three developments of note in the check clearing business are related to the above-mentioned economic issues: increasing the availability of deposited checks, check truncation efforts, and check safekeeping.

Check Clearing Developments

The Expedited Funds Availability Act of 1987 and Federal Reserve Regulation CC are targeted at giving consumers faster availability of deposited funds. They narrow the window within which the bank of first deposit is required to make funds available from a deposited check. Because availability depends on processing speed, these developments are putting a lot of pressure on the industry to speed up processing and clearing of checks.

From an information technology perspective, the response has been a series of exploratory efforts to truncate the movement of the check and replace it with electronic movement of the MICR line information. For example, in 1988 the Minneapolis Federal Reserve Bank sponsored a regional electronic clearinghouse (ECH) in which participating banks store interbank checks where they are deposited and only clear the MICR information. This procedure produces one-day-earlier availability and, potentially, less paper-processing cost. However, a nationally mandated ECH is unlikely. A Fed study required by the 1987 legislation recommended against such a project, and predicted that only 10 to 20 percent of forward presentments and 40 percent of return presentments would be accelerated by an ECH.

In check safekeeping, checks are truncated at the paying bank. This option is already offered by all credit unions, by approximately 67 percent of all thrifts, and approximately 20 percent of all commercial banks—and is growing in popularity. At Bank of America, for example, only one-half of all customers receive checks back in their statements. Nationally, it is estimated that 10 percent of all checks are not returned to the writers. The benefits to the bank are reduced postage expense, because fewer of the statement envelopes will exceed one ounce; less sorting expense; and less paper filing. Some of these benefits, of course, are offset by archiving and retrieval costs. Normally, the checks are filed for 90 days, then destroyed and kept on microfilm for seven years. But check retrieval request costs have proved to be acceptable. The unforunate part is that check safekeeping, while sensible, does not influence the speed or efficiency of interbank check clearing. As a result, it is also not an event that will substantially meet the public's demand for faster funds availability. Thus, in our opinion, check safekeeping will not change the industry's economics in any major way.

Incidentally, it is entirely consistent with this book's major themes that faster availability—not necessarily lower costs—is the primary factor behind a future shift to electronic payments. Faster availability benefits bank customers, of course. In the age of the telephone, television, and worldwide on-line terminals, why should the public be satisfied with seven days to get availability on a check drawn on an adjacent Federal Reserve District? The "double whammy" companion issue is that banks will not necessarily see a boost to their profitability. In fact, faster availability will probably reduce the average balances in retail transaction accounts and cut this low-cost funding source.

In improving the check clearing system, banks may well spend *more* money than before, not less. Productivity improvements engendered by technology often do not reduce the absolute level of costs. Instead, they go into creating value. Here we see that the need for value, in the form of faster availability, could be what helps push banks toward electronic payment technology in the first place. Cutting costs really is not the primary agenda item at all. The net result is that the economics of the checking business, although stable today, could be impacted negatively in the future.

Competition in Check Processing

Check processing per se is not viewed by banks as a distinctively competitive area. Rather, it is a highly fragmented, vertically integrated support activity performed by thousands of banks. Although the checks are essential, what customers buy from the bank is not the check processing activity, but the array of services that surround the deposit account. The mechanical processing of checks themselves is traditionally viewed as just routine support.

The competitive situation is quite different in the check clearing business, that is, the function performed by banks that collect checks for other banks. A few dominant correspondent banks are in this business, as is the highly competitive Federal Reserve Bank. In terms of size, the check collection business is relatively small; approximately 9 percent of all checks are cleared by third-party banks, and revenues are only $300 to 400 million per year.

The largest processor of checks is Bank of America, which, because of its large branch system, handles some 3 billion per year. Other major processors are those with big branch systems, extensive corporate operations, or well-developed clearing operations. (See Figure 4–3.) But there are only six banks beside Bank of America with more than a 0.5 percent

FIGURE 4-3
Fragmented Check Processing Market, 1988

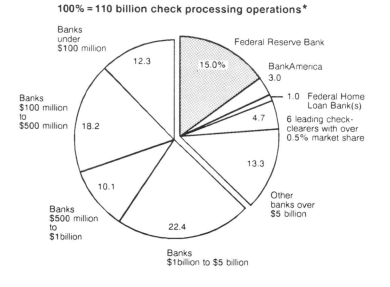

100% = 110 billion check processing operations*

* The average check is "processed" 2.2 times

share. More than 40 percent of all processing is done by banks below $1 billion in size. There is little room for outside processing. Correspondent banks play virtually no role in processing for banks over $500 million in size. In fact, even 60 percent of the very smallest banks (less than $100 million in size) do their check processing in-house. Thus, check processing remains highly fragmented but is not a disaggregated activity.

The Federal Reserve Bank plays a major role both as regulator and as direct competitor. Currently, the Fed collects approximately 33 percent of all not-on-us checks. The margins of the correspondent banks in the collection business are under severe pressure as the Federal Reserve Bank moves aggressively to capture more business. Approximately 49 percent of all check-clearing banks experienced decreasing margins between 1982 and 1987, and the rest experienced stagnant margins. In turn, the Federal Reserve Bank's revenues from check collection grew to $500 million by 1987. As a result, there is processing overcapacity and, for most correspondent banks, the outlook for the check clearing business is not particularly favorable.

Summary

In summary, the retail check processing business has not yet been very substantially transformed by technology—particularly with respect to industry structure. It is still in Stage B—front-office automation. As a result, it remains a fragmented business with thousands of players and very little concentration. Electronics may speed up the flow of funds, but we believe this impact is likely to take some time. Banks should not expect any immediate changes in this line of business.

AUTOMATED TELLER MACHINES (ATMs)

From the perspective of consumers, ATMs are very visible. They are an obvious Stage C development reaching out beyond clerks directly to banks' customers. As the first effort at self-service banking, they have come to symbolize the public "face" of electronic banking. Twenty years after their introduction on September 9, 1969, at a Long Island branch of Chemical Bank, there are more than 72,500 ATMs in the United States that have become a permanent part of the banking landscape.

Development of ATM Usage

Although the machines are now ubiquitous, banks have not been completely successful in convincing the public to use them. Approximately 40 percent of all transaction account holders use an ATM once a month or more. Although 138 million debit (i.e., ATM access) cards have been issued, one-half of them are never used. Still, the trend is positive. ATM transactions are growing at a 14 percent CAGR. ATM usage is skewed towards groups that adopt innovation faster—young, well-educated, and/or urban residents, for example. Thus, it seems logical that ATM usage will continue to expand—but gradually—as younger bank customers replace older customers.

The dual role of an ATM is to divert transactions from tellers and to conveniently extend the duration of the service window hours to times when teller service is uneconomical. To achieve this Stage C function effectively has required two parallel developments: (1) growth in machine functionality, and (2) behavioral change among customers. The evaluation is mixed. Functionality has grown and some machines offer a dozen or more types of transactions, yet the transaction mix is still limited:

- 75 percent are cash withdrawals,
- 15 percent are inquiries,
- 9 percent are deposits, and
- 1 percent are transfers/other.

The number of cash withdrawals has undoubtedly reduced the number of checks that would otherwise have been written. In fact, there are now 3.5 billion cash withdrawals from machines and only 2.5 billion checks cashed with a teller. ATMs are one of the four major ways to obtain cash, along with check cashing at supermarkets, teller checks, and getting cash back from a deposit. In this way, ATMs have helped to control and contain the rate of overall growth in the checking system. They may have also displaced some in-store check purchases to cash purchases, but reliable statistics on this point are difficult to develop.

The failure to date to convert more of the industry's nonwithdrawal transactions to ATMs is unfortunate, but may be changeable with technological evolution. The machines are not static, but are evolving. They have potential for significantly improved functionality and user-friendliness.

Development of ATM Technology

Most ATMs currently in operation are still first-generation technology. They combine on-line devices, bill dispensers, and a data entry capability. But experience is helping to make them better. New machines have features such as "swipe" or "dip" card readers (as opposed to the "eat-em" type), statement printers, touch screens, multilingual programming, voice guidance, and color displays. All these help the customers interact with the machine. According to Fujitsu, whose ATM sales are now 90 percent color, the color factor alone may increase usage by 10 to 15 percent. A capability such as statement printing attracts more usage and can reduce the cost of mailing monthly statements. First Hawaiian Bank, for example, prints approximately 3,000 statements per week, even though it charges a $1 fee. At Citizens & Southern Bank, four ATM statements per month are offered free to customers who open a no-statement, no-returned-check DDA.

Reliability, a key measure in keeping consumer interest, is also improving. Originally, machine failures were a significant source of consumer complaints. Now, however, mean time-between-failure as long as

7 months (i.e., 35,000 transactions for the average machine) is being reported. Assured uptime should have a salutary effect on consumers' willingness to trust ATMs.

Future generations of ATMs will probably offer considerable advancements. IBM has come up with a machine that counts deposit amounts, greatly simplifying the ease with which a deposit can be made. Also, the number of cartridges can be increased to dispense both coins and all denominations of bills, not just $10 and $20 bills. Moreover, with the use of OCR and image technology, deposited checks can be scanned, read, and even verified on-line to the payer's bank; then, checks could be cashed on the spot, down to the penny. Considerably improved customer interface, intelligence, and information-provision capabilities should be expected. As these improved features displace more transactions from tellers, the industry will have a better chance to achieve its cost-reduction goals.

Economic Potential Offered at ATMs

The industry's 60,000 banking locations absorb approximately 55 percent of the industry's cost base. Because consumer deposit gathering, the primary business in branches, may have only generated a 12 basis point ROA in 1988 (depending upon how an institution chooses to value its consumer deposits), cost reductions are of major importance. However, the investments in ATM technology have not yet reduced branch costs in a fundamental way. In as recent a year as 1987, for example, only 8.7 percent of all branch transactions were conducted through an ATM. This low penetration is one reason the number of banking locations and tellers (600,000) has not decreased substantially in the past 15 years. The costs of the ATM technology itself are too high relative to the cost of the teller it is displacing. Further, the pace of transaction conversion—particularly of transactions other than withdrawals—is too slow, and the needs for human interaction with the customer are still too strong.

Two further issues are the cost of ATMs themselves and the creation of incremental transactions. First, ATMs represent a significant investment: a full-function machine still costs approximately $30,000. The fully loaded operating cost of a machine is approximately $50,000 per year, resulting in an aggregate annual industry expense level of approximately $3.6 billion. Much of this cost is labor, depreciation, space, and overhead. The cost to drive all these ATMs (i.e., the actual processing of the electronic messages) is approximately $600 million per year. These significant cost levels act as a drag on branch profitability. Second, ATMs tend to *create* additional transactions. Customers who use ATMs regularly tend to withdraw cash more often, in smaller amounts (about $50 on average), whereas customers who cash checks with tellers withdraw less often, in larger amounts (about $200 on average). The DDA of an average ATM user contains approximately 30 debits/credits per month compared to a non-ATM user total of approximately 18 per month. This increase in transactions is an obvious benefit to customers, who can now get cash when and where they want it and, if the ATM is conveniently located and has no lines, as often as they want it. It is not, however, a help in cutting costs; incremental transactions drive up operating costs and inflate the supposed diversions of transactions from tellers to machines.

However, the potential benefits of ATMs are real. An average ATM transaction costs from 40 to 60 cents versus 90 cents to $1.20 for a teller transaction. That is why banks originally viewed ATMs as a one-for-one substitution for tellers. (Artists' early renditions of ATMs had them neatly lined up in the lobby at the teller line, but failed to reckon with the desires of customers. Few ATMs are actually located on teller lines because they need to be reached after teller hours. They provide a 24-hour, 7-day-a-week value to the customer that tellers never could.) Because ATMs have a higher fixed-cost component than do teller operations, their approximately 60-cent unit cost advantage ought to increase with time as ATM transaction volumes continue to grow and as the capital cost of the equipment drops. The bottom line is that ATMs still offer *potential* to reduce the cost of branch banking, and possibly to improve the profitability of retail deposit gathering, but this potential has not yet been fulfilled.

Competing with ATMs

Competition with ATMs has gone through three stages of development:

- *Proliferation.* Initially, banks stressed ownership in an effort to be distinctive and attract customers. But the same three vendors (Diebold, NCR, and IBM) sell 90 percent of the industry's machines. Within a few years, virtually every major bank had them and they all performed basically the same (with one exception, discussed below).
- *Consolidation.* Then sharing came in, and banks were faced with the choice of maintaining a proprietary network or joining the shared networks.

- *Next Stage?* Now that sharing is widespread, banks will be dealing with its implications in the future. Bank branch distinctiveness may fade if customers come to perceive all retail banking outlets as utilities.

Direct ATM ownership is still highly fragmented. The largest owners of ATMs are those banks, like Bank of America or Citibank, that have large branch networks. Bank of America owns approximately 1,700 ATMs, which is a little more than 2 percent of the country's total. Roughly 7,700 separate institutions have invested in ATMs, although 90 percent of them have less than $500 million in assets and only own, on average, one ATM per institution. Banks with more than $10 billion in assets only own about one-third of all ATMs. (See Figure 4-4.)

The practice of ATM sharing, or linking different banks' machines through an ATM network, has grown rapidly since 1980. In 1982, for example, only 11,000 machines were part of any shared network, but by 1988 that number had grown to 65,000—or 90 percent of the country's machines. Banks strongly believe that to attract checking account customers they must make the associated debit card attractive. A wide choice of machine locations is now mandatory in order to do so.

As both the number and scope of shared networks have grown, the number of transactions switched between banks has also grown. Approximately 95 percent of the switched transactions are cash withdrawals, with the rest being balance queries, transfers, and even a few deposits. Currently, regional networks (e.g., NYCE, Star) predominate over the national shared networks (e.g., Plus, Cirrus). As ATM usage has grown, these regional networks are becoming powerful competitive forces.

The Distinctive Type 1 Approach

The primary approach to seeking distinctiveness in ATM competition is to have a proprietary network. Citibank's retail network in New York City offers the classic example of this Type 1 approach. Citibank does not share its machines with The New York Cash Exchange (NYCE), the large regional network to which most other New York City banks belong. Instead, Citibank has chosen to continue to go it alone. Further, it is the only U.S. bank with its own proprietary machines made by its own subsidiary, Transaction Technology, Inc. Citibank's CAT2 second generation of machines (1,200 recently installed) are highly user-friendly and feature

FIGURE 4-4
ATM Market Shares, 1988

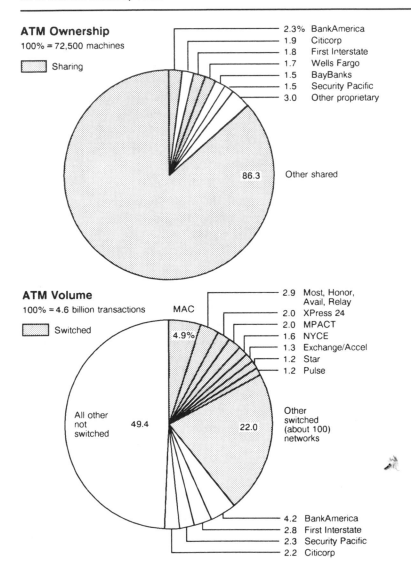

ATM Ownership

100% = 72,500 machines

▢ Sharing

2.3% BankAmerica
1.9   Citicorp
1.8   First Interstate
1.7   Wells Fargo
1.5   BayBanks
1.5   Security Pacific
3.0   Other proprietary

86.3   Other shared

ATM Volume

100% = 4.6 billion transactions

▢ Switched

MAC
4.9%

2.9   Most, Honor, Avail, Relay
2.0   XPress 24
2.0   MPACT
1.6   NYCE
1.3   Exchange/Accel
1.2   Star
1.2   Pulse

All other not switched   49.4

22.0

Other switched (about 100) networks

4.2   BankAmerica
2.8   First Interstate
2.3   Security Pacific
2.2   Citicorp

touch-screen technology, 55 choices of transactions, and three languages: English, Spanish, and Chinese.

Citibank does see benefits from its ATMs. Its customers tend to use these ATMs more than other banks' customers use theirs: 80 percent of Citibank's depositors are active machine users and a reported 50 percent never use tellers at all. Because they are so popular, Citibank's ATMs helped increase Citibank's share of New York City retail deposits from approximately 4.5 percent in 1977 to approximately 14 percent in 1987. Also, Citibank has experienced some reduction in branch staffing and teller staffing costs.

However, the costs of this proprietary approach are high. To outside observers, it appears that the cost differential between Citibank's machines and an equivalent number of IBM machines is between $50 million and $100 million. (Citibank, for example, must spread all of its development costs over a much smaller base of installed machines.) So, the Type 1 proprietary approach, in contradistinction to the Type 2 shared utility, is high risk/high-reward.

As if to illustrate this point, First Atlanta attempted a similar proprietary ATM approach in the late 1970s, but it lost out when it was forced to join the Citizens & Southern/Trust Company network. Based on our experience with clients, we believe that only players with truly deep pockets can successfully attempt the proprietary approach.

Consolidation of Networks

ATM networks are consolidating. Because an ATM network consists of a fault-tolerant computer, switching software, and telecommunications lines, cost structures are largely fixed. (The variable costs for machine purchase and maintenance are picked up by the owning bank.) As a result, "pure switching" is a volume game and will continue to be. Between 1987 and 1988 alone, the three largest networks increased their coverage of all machines from 24 percent to 31 percent. The proposed merger of four Southeast networks (Most, Relay, Avail, and Honor) may create a new super-regional ATM network with more than 9,500 machines. Plus and Cirrus, the two leading national networks, agreed in March 1989 to duality, effectively combining the networks. A cardholder will be able to use any machine displaying either logo. From the cardholder's perspective, of course, this network consolidation makes perfect sense. There is no reason not to have access to every ATM machine, in the same way that a Visa or MasterCard from any issuing bank can be used at any credit card merchant.

Further evidence of how important volume is comes from the progressive lowering of third-party switching fees. (The networks themselves tend to be marketing, not operations, organizations. For example, three of the five largest shared networks – NYCE, Star, and Most – use Deluxe Data Systems, the industry leader, to do their switching.) Fees per switched transaction were approximately 10 cents in 1987, but some renewal bids for large networks have now fallen to as low as 2 or 3 cents. Visa has reportedly offered to switch transactions free for the Most/Relay/Honor/Avail merger for three years. But as networks consolidate, the individual machines become less distinctive, and the competitive approaches to retail banking musts change.

The Competitive Effect of Networks

Sharing is making an industry-wide utility out of the functions that an ATM performs. So far, this is largely restricted to withdrawing cash, but as machine functionality expands, customers may find their traditional branch-based bank relationship increasingly irrelevant. For example, in the Pennsylvania–New Jersey area, the MAC name and logo has been widely popularized and accepted by the public. Cardholders think of the machine as a MAC machine regardless of which bank really owns it. But, the MAC logo belongs to CoreStates, which owns the network and drives many of the participating ATMs. The result is that CoreStates (and MAC) have a profitable consumer franchise. But, in some respects, their participating banks may be losing elements of control over their own customers.

With an ATM utility, servicing accounts with less investment in brick and mortar becomes more possible. Approximately 4,000 small banks, thrifts, and especially credit unions have already joined networks but do not own any ATMs. The Banc One/AARP program, to be discussed in Chapter 9, offers a national by-phone-and-mail-only credit union. By joining a shared network, the Banc One/AARP joint venture was able to give its customers a way to get cash without building a physical presence anywhere in the country.

A concomitant development is that more and more ATMs are being installed away from bank premises. Approximately 21 percent of all machines are now located at supermarkets, convenience stores, airports, and shopping malls. Ownership of machines by nonbanks is also expanding. For example, some 900 Money-Maker machines located in Texas 7–11 stores are owned by Affiliated Computer Systems, Inc., and this trend should continue. Perhaps the biggest gap between the current locations of ATMs and the locations demanded by many consumers is at the place of employment. This is really just an extension of the current situation. We believe that it is very likely that if the machines were essentially open to all cardholders and the proprietary aspect removed, customers would want machines placed at the most convenient locations.

Summary

In summary, ATMs are a lot more than just cost-cutting devices. In the hope of reducing teller labor, banks may have stumbled on a new way to disaggregate retail banking and change the competitive dynamics. There is no reason why the ATM provider, the switch, and the account provider need be the same organization. As with other customer automation developments, the transaction acquisition could be delinked from the account servicing. Banks could "pay" to "acquire" transactions from ATM owners. NYCE, for example, passes 38 cents from issuer to acquirer on each withdrawal. One founding member of NYCE already makes $1 million per year on net ATM interchange, mostly because its machines are more conveniently situated. Acquisition could become a disaggregated stand-alone business similar to credit card sales draft acquisition.

Moreover, market shares could shift. Retail banking competition is all about convenience. For many years, this translated into a battle to have the most branches in a local market. A number-one share of branches has often created a disproportionate share of the deposits. But as the functionality of shared ATMs grows, the smaller players may be able to expand at the expense of the bigger players, and the power of a large branch system may diminish. Based on our client experiences, we believe that retail banks need to watch this evolving ATM dynamic carefully.

POINT OF SALE (POS) SYSTEMS

POS systems, used with a debit card, have the potential to become a major payment method in stores. The concept has been around for a number of years (since the late 1970s, at least) and is potentially one of retail banking's biggest technological challenges. However, despite its potential, progress in implementation has been extremely slow.

Development Status

POS/debit is targeted at a subsector of the approximately 60 billion transactions made in United States retail stores. Sixty-eight percent of these transactions occur in just three sectors: supermarkets, convenience stores, and gas stations. These outlets generate high volumes of low-value payments by cash or check. This is where POS/debit has real potential.

However, despite this potential, the debut of POS/debit has been long, slow, and painful. By the end of 1988, there were only 45,000 on-line debit card terminals installed in the United States, the bulk of them by just a few enterprising merchants and networks. Ninety-two million POS/debit transactions were made, less than .2 percent of the number of checks. (To compare, there were close to 1 billion POS/debit transactions on 90,000 terminals in France. Thus, the French POS transaction rate per capita is 40 times higher than the United States rate.) The near-term estimate is that approximately 2 billion POS/debit transactions per year could be generated if terminals were widely available in these three critical sectors. Yet even if current growth rates can be sustained, this target will not be reached until 1995.

Although consumers are not clamoring for POS, the existence of 138 million ATM debit cards cannot be ignored. Approximately 70 million of these cards belong to banks whose ATM networks already have some POS terminals. And most active ATM users (approximately 40 percent of transaction account holders) claim in surveys that they "definitely" have an interest in POS. This core user group, estimated at 16 million people, presumably believes that making a POS/debit payment will be easier than writing a check or withdrawing cash. In fact, the POS/debit programs already in place have 2.2 million regular users. It seems reasonable that consumer usage will develop, despite the lack of clamor, when enough opportunity is available.

Merchants: The Real Customers

Merchants are the real customers for POS/debit systems, and the potential benefits must be sold to them. We believe that ultimately these benefits are positive and significant. In fact, POS/debit could be the least expensive of their payment options. One estimate that we have seen of the merchant's cost to handle an average cash purchase is 48 cents; for a check, 50 cents; for a credit card, 97 cents. The same estimate showed that a POS/debit payment would cost 32 cents or less. In addition, service would probably be faster. One source showed that check purchases take an average of 90 seconds in the checkout line, whereas cash and debit card purchases take an average of 20 seconds apiece.

The specific circumstances in each of the three key retail sectors will strongly influence how each approaches POS/debit systems:

- *Convenience stores*: The nation's convenience store industry grew extremely rapidly in the 1980s, reaching 50,000 outlets, and as a result, financial performance was hurt. For example, operating expenses rose from 14.6 percent of sales in 1983 to 18.3 percent in 1987. Today, the convenience industry is consolidating, and the largest chains are in a fierce struggle to attract more customers. Approximately 60 percent of convenience stores already accept credit cards for this reason, and installing debit card terminals is an additional option. Four of the top 12 chains (Circle K, Starvin Marvin, Stop-N-Go, and ARCO) already have substantial POS programs that cover 34 percent of their stores. However, these innovators may not be directly rewarded, because they incur the highest costs and make the most mistakes. Those chains who play fast-follower may do better. Southland (doing business as 7-11), the industry leader with 6,800 stores, only began testing debit cards in 1988 and will probably take another three to five years for national roll-out. These events make it likely, but not certain, that POS/debit will become a permanent convenience store feature during the 1990s.
- *Supermarkets*: The situation is similar in the supermarket industry, which was also substantially overbuilt during the 1980s. Sales per square foot, real sales per labor hour, and asset productivity have dropped. As a result, supermarket chains are now focusing on cost control. One analysis shows that a POS/debit program could fit right in, saving a typical supermarket up to $3,500 per year in check losses, deposit fees, cash handling costs, and courtesy booth expense. As a result, 3 of the top 12 chains (Lucky, Von's, and Publix) have established ongoing POS programs, and 2 more chains (Kroger and Alpha Beta) are still in the test or pilot stage.
- *Gasoline Stations*: The nation's 120,000 gasoline stations are also candidates for POS/debit. They focused on increasing productivity during the 1980s. For example, throughout per station rose from

54,000 gallons per month in 1981, to 73,000 gallons per month in 1986. Debit cards could potentially keep that productivity initiative going, either by (1) attracting more customers via increased convenience, or (2) making automated gasoline stations practical. Furthermore, gasoline retailers need to offer as many payment options as possible. Gasoline proprietary cards make up 30 percent of industry sales, and bank and T&E cards constitute 10 percent of sales. Thus, four of the top five retailers (Exxon, Chevron, Mobil, and Amoco) either have ongoing or pilot POS/debit programs. Mobil and Exxon have been the most aggressive, equipping approximately 30 percent of their outlets to accept one or more bank debit cards.

The bottom line for the banking industry, if it wants this technology to succeed, is that it must find ways to convince merchants of the benefits of POS/debit systems.

Successes and Failures

Today's experiments have shown that consumer interest can be piqued. The most successful program has been that of Lucky Stores, which only began installing terminals in 1985. Some of Lucky Stores' success factors have been an identifiable product name (EZ Checkout), heavy advertising, offers of up to $200 cash back, access by 50 percent of California's debit card base, well-trained checkers, and an extra terminal in each store for balance verification. Because Lucky Stores is so far ahead of its competitors, it does have a true (if temporary) competitive differentiation, attracting young, well-educated shoppers who enjoy using their ATM cards.

Some attempts, however, have gone poorly. Kroger installed a pilot in 15 Cincinnati stores in 1983, but five years later the terminals only handled 2 percent of the purchases in those stores. Safeway scrapped its POS/debit plans after a pilot in Washington, D.C., failed. The Honor ATM network has 5,000 POS/debit terminals in Florida that each, on average, handle less than one transaction per day.

The critical issues seem to be pricing, technical problems, and response time. POS/debit involves high initial costs for software, establishment of a back-office, and purchase of terminals. Trying to recover these costs through relatively high per-transaction prices seems to be counterproductive. Some programs, such as those tried by Honor and

Avail, charged an interchange fee to the bank on each transaction and passed it on to the merchant, thereby mimicking the pricing of an ATM transaction. Naturally, this discouraged the participating banks from promoting the service. It is more reasonable that merchants should pay for a POS/debit transaction, just as they do with any other type of purchase.

The many links required in on-line, real-time debits create technical problems. As many as 10 separate communications may be involved between store, chain headquarters, acquiring bank, network switch, and issuing bank. Each computer link can go down. Software to convert protocols and formats may be required at each interface. A lot can go wrong, which although ultimately solvable, has a dampening effort on merchants' enthusiasm. Also, response time must be fast, with 10 seconds generally considered a maximum. These implementation issues must be resolved for the technology to gain wider acceptance.

Two Technological Approaches

There are two competing approaches to establishing a POS/debit system:

- *On-line.* In the on-line scenario, the cardholder swipes a bank debit card through a reader at a checkout counter and enters his or her personal identification number (PIN) in a PIN-pad. The dollars are then debited real-time to the cardholder's account and credited to the merchant. This approach eliminates the need for paper and eliminates the merchant's risk. It has relatively high fixed costs for terminals and telecommunications, but has virtually no cost for card issuance because the cards are already in customers' wallets. This is the approach banks generally favor.
- *ACH.* The alternative is to capture transactions with no PIN verification and pass them in batch through the ACH. This approach can give a day or two of float to the cardholder, like a check, thereby resolving one perceived disadvantage with the real-time on-line option. However, the merchant still absorbs risk on the transaction. This approach avoids most of the telecommunications expense but creates a lot of card issuance expense. In fact, the cards can be issued by the merchant, and many favor this approach for reasons of exclusivity. Eventually, both approaches might become common, with the ACH approach more applicable at supermarkets where the customer's credit standing can more easily be known.

Difficult Competition Ahead

Banks may experience difficulties in competing with POS/debit. For one thing, the fledgling projects now operative are too small and too concentrated to offer a useful roadmap for the future. In 1988, only two California networks (Star and Interlink) had 42 percent of the nation's POS/debit terminals. One California merchant, Lucky Stores, was generating 22 percent of all transactions. Another merchant, ARCO, was generating 18 percent. (See Figure 4–5.) Their experiences are not necessarily indicative of what will work and what will not.

A second issue is that retailers are a major implementation force. They own approximately 50 percent of the current installations. Lucky, ARCO, Mobil, and Exxon control their POS/debit transactions up to the point where they reach the acquiring bank. Some projects are owned by Type 2 shared utilities, either dedicated to POS (e.g., Interlink and Cactus Switch) or extensions of ATM networks. But only one bank, CoreStates, seems to be well positioned today to enter POS/debit as a business. CoreStates offers comprehensive credit and debit card merchant services, and has focused so far in placing terminals at stations of gas retailers such as Sunoco, Texaco, Atlantic, and Getty.

Heavy involvement by nonbanks has a precedent in the credit card POS business. None of the top 10 draft capture networks are banks. To capture and switch an electronic transaction at the point of sale is certainly traditional bank work, but it is also a data processing function highly specific to the retailing world. Access to low-cost telecommunications capacity is a vital factor, as is integration with retailer's other needs. Some major competitors in POS/debit include EDS, Buypass the System, J.C. Penney System Services, GTE EFT Services, Deluxe Data Systems, and Visa (which processes for Interlink). Some have no direct bank affiliations, and all have other businesses that require substantive data communications capacity.

A third factor is that some substantial and costly investments may still be required to get POS/debit networks up and running. Banks are pinning some of their hopes on today's ATM networks, but it is not clear if these will suffice. POS/debit networks require merchant deposit accounting, acceptance of nonbank cards, sweep functions for cash management, and integration of many different (intelligent) terminals. None of this is typically needed on an ATM network. If new network investments are

FIGURE 4-5
POS/Debit Networks, 1988

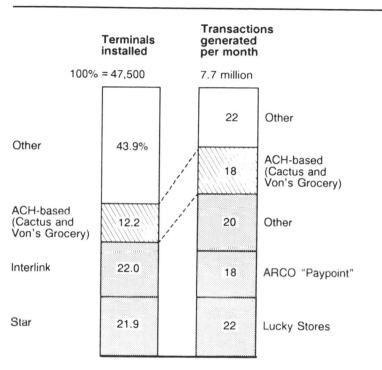

required, it will either be third-party providers or Type 2 utilities that make them. The average bank that currently accepts a retailer's checks will never be able to make these investments.

In addition, some types of retailers will want specialized features or payments. Electronic charges generated at unattended fleet refueling gas stations are a growing business dominated by Shell, Buypass, and Sears. The nation's 2.5 billion annual food stamps could be automated; the federal government has already sponsored five demonstrations of "electronic benefits transfers." Other efforts will probably rise to automate the 10 billion plus consumer goods coupons cashed every year. Banks will have less interest in offering these features, given the support nature of the payment in most banking products.

Summary

Like checking, POS/debit will almost surely evolve in time as another utility. To be accepted by retailers, the POS/debit utility must penetrate a high fraction of all customers with a limited number of debit card logos or marks. This condition has been largely absent until recently. But unlike checking, retailers or third-party processors will probably control the terminals and transactions all the way to an acquiring bank or to a switch. Banks' fees will have to be low—only pennies per purchase—to be competitive with check deposit fees. Total revenue might reach $100 million by 1995, possibly displacing 2 to 4 billion checks per year and potentially saving an incremental $300 million yearly. However, extra expenses for software, telecommunications, data center capacity, and support may end up equalling those benefits. *POS/debit will probably be a break-even development at best, even when successful. At worst, it will hurt the retail deposit gathering business by increasing the level of fixed costs and squeezing the thousands of competitors into a more consolidated structure.*

The opportunities in POS/debit will be for network and switch processors, merchant support servicers, and software/terminal vendors. Although POS/debit is banking work, and part of the payment system, we think *few banks per se can make substantial money at it.* Rather, it is another case of functional disaggregation. Winners are more likely to be focused data processors who can navigate independently of the banks.

HOME BANKING

Home banking, through PCs or dedicated video terminals, is neither an important part of retail banking nor the payments system. Despite several years of experiments and offerings by many of the largest banks, there were only approximately 100,000 subscribers at the end of 1988. Users' transactions equaled less than one-tenth of 1 percent of the number of checks.

Furthermore, some of the most well-known home banking programs have folded through lack of response. Viewtron, a Knight–Ridder videotex demonstration in Florida that included home banking, closed down after $30 million in losses; VideoFinancial Services, a seven-bank consortium offering a home banking gateway, lost money and was sold; and

Chemical Bank was the latest to fold its product—despite pouring tens of millions of dollars into its Pronto System, it had generated only approximately 20,000 subscribers nationally.

Significant Potential Benefits

The concept of home banking, loosely defined as direct consumer manipulation of accounts, has several potentially attractive features. Under certain scenarios, costs can be reduced and additional customer value created because of the on-line access. The most likely source of check displacement (and cost reduction) is the bill-paying feature. Of the 15 billion checks written at home, the vast majority are for recurring payments, for example, utilities (35 percent), rent or mortgage (15 percent), other debts (32 percent), and insurance (15 percent). These are the types of payments handled easily without checks (and without home banking) in other countries' payment systems, such as in Germany or Sweden. There is no reason to assume the same could not be done in the United States. Potential savings are more than $700 million per year.

However, home banking has the potential to be much more than just a payment initiator. Electronic reporting of account balances and transaction data is an obvious use. Combined with check truncation, the standard paper-based consumer monthly statement could be eliminated, saving the industry an additional $250 million per year. Details on account transactions could be downloaded directly into PC-based software that prepares budgets, compiles a household financial profile, reconciles with receipts, and prepares data for submission of IRS returns. Recurring bills could also be presented to home banking users (or their banks), bypassing the mails. Also, home access to financial products is not restricted to commercial banks. It has just as much applicability in accessing money market, securities, investment, or pension accounts. Of course, other financial institutions will not have the transaction-intensive accounts that banks have, but this does not negate the value of direct access.

Another obvious need is for information about security price movements. Smartvest, for example, is an on-line service from Olde Discount Corporation that offers real-time quotes, on-line order entry, portfolio management, account retrieval, and news/research summaries. Finally, reporting and payment of credit card accounts can be envisioned. American Express has offered in-home inquiry capability via PCs to Green Card holders since at least 1986.

There may even be a role in home banking for the "smart" microprocessor card (to be described in more detail in Chapter 5). Much publicized (and maligned), the smart card has, so far, found very little applicability in banking. Yet in the long run, card "intelligence" has great potential. For example, "receipts" from POS/debit transactions could be kept electronically on the card and then retrieved by inserting the card into a card reader attached to a home banking PC. It would be possible for an entire transaction account to be maintained and reported on a PC, eliminating the paper-based mess that the average upper-income household checking account has become. All that is required is enough reductions in the cost of the technology, including not only the cards, but also the readers, PCs, terminals, and bank data centers and networks. Yet, as will be described in Chapter 8, continuing order-of-magnitude decreases in the costs of core technology are virtually a certainty.

Substantial Problems

Despite the apparent potential, this technology has, to date, experienced very substantial problems in gaining effective use and acceptance. Difficulties include lack of consumer preparation, high costs, and technical inadequacies. By 1987, only 13.6 million U.S. households owned a PC and of these, only 4.1 million (i.e., 4.6 percent of U.S. households) owned a modem—the critical piece of communications hardware required to link a PC with external data. Even those who own the requisite hardware are not that interested. In general surveys, less than one-fourth of the modem owners claim to be interested in home banking; this is about 1 percent of U.S. households. So, to date, broad consumer acceptance is a very, very substantial barrier.

In addition, the investments to provide this technology have been (and continue to be) high. Banks have invested in software, telecommunications, consumer marketing, training, education, and operations. However, a substantial part of the home banking back-office is not yet electronic, but is still paper-based. This drives up labor costs, impedes operations, and hurts service. For example, it is difficult to collect payments from consumers and remit them to payees in bulk. One way is that each payment can be processed individually through the ACH, if the payee is willing. Or a payee's payments can be combined in a check and sent with a detailed advice of credit. Neither approach is perfect and both require relationship building with payees.

To recoup development costs, banks originally tried charging users up to $15 per month. But most customers did not think the extra convenience, if there was any, was worth it. For that kind of price, the consumer wanted access to other information services, such as news, weather, travel reservations, shopping, and so forth. In certain cases, to meet this apparent need, banks joined their services to those of general-purpose videotex systems, broadly defined as in-home access to remote databases.

However, videotex has also had a hard time. A major provider called Covidea recently closed down, and CNR Partners, a joint venture of NYNEX and Citicorp, has yet to introduce a product. Trintex, a joint venture of Sears and IBM, had invested more than $250 million by 1988 in developing and test-marketing Prodigy, a service which generates advertising revenues as well as subscriber fees. Manufacturer's Hanover provides account processing and transaction switching for local banks, such as Citizens & Southern, that offer home banking in Prodigy's test markets. Comp-U-Serve, one of the few commercially viable videotex services, continues to offer access to some banks, but subscriber interest is generally low. Whether videotex will eventually take off is still to be determined.

It may be that more narrowly-based services will penetrate the home market much faster than full-line services. For example, bill paying by telephone is a less complete service than video home banking, but has proven to be more resilient. Transactions are more limited, and customer reports and statements are absent. Nevertheless, telephone bill-paying has been around for a decade now. Approximately 40 percent of all large banks, as well as numerous smaller ones, offer it. For example, NBD Bancorp's service, Telephone Banking Center, received 2,645 calls per day in 1988. Recent advances in voice response technology have reduced the operational costs and somewhat improved the operation of the service. An estimated 5 million users pay approximately 500 million bills (i.e., 1 percent of current check volume) per year by phone.

Competition

The shape of the competitive structure for home banking has not yet emerged. As this industry structure forms, it may well be disaggregated in a fashion similar to POS/debit. The electronic links between homes and bank computers are likely to emerge as the key battleground. Much like POS/debit, the business will require heavy DP skills, as well as low-cost, high-volume telecommunications capacity. Third-party processors will service small banks. And there will very likely be one or more Type 2 players: a gateway or industry utility that switches transactions between transaction acquirers and account-issuing banks.

Although it is likely that home banking in a more mature form will take on a commodity aspect, it is also possible that some banks will take advantage of it. This will probably not be by reducing the cost of checks, but by designing accounts with unique features related to home use. For example, user friendliness might be a key criterion. As elsewhere, this technology will probably result in an increase in the output and value-added of banking services. *We speculate that as a result of "home services" banks' customers will benefit while the industry as a whole may not show greater returns. We also speculate that home services are likely to cause the competitive equilibrium between retail players to change-favoring successful innovations.*

New software development will be required. Banks such as Citicorp and Bank of America, which apparently intend to remain in the game, may be the long-term survivors. Home banking users can be located anywhere, just like credit card account holders. Thus, home banking may prove to be a beneficial enabler for those few players whose goal is a national presence at the retail level. In time, such a Type 1 strategy could make sense and could certainly hasten the restructuring of traditional local branches. In turn, the technology, when established, may help stimulate industry concentration for a few profitable, high-volume players. But only those with deep pockets will be able to try this approach.

SUMMARY

The retail payment system is a very, very critical component of the overall banking industry—particularly because it consumes one-half of the entire industry's resource base. We estimate that because of these high expenditures, the principal product—consumer deposits—is only marginally profitable when its funds are valued at competitive rates. In short, the consumer deposit gathering vehicle—despite enormous efforts to improve branch productivity—is still relatively inefficient.

At the same time, systems technology appears to offer very high potential for automating vast numbers of retail payments—potential that is so far largely unrealized. The retail payment system is still dominated by the check. The newer electronic substitutes, while potentially more productive (particularly if they become widely accepted), are still in an emergent state.

We believe that certain "winning banks" will try to play a role in influencing how and when each electronic substitute will evolve. Because of today's highly fragmented check processing activities, it is possible that competition with electronic substitutes will evolve in a distinctively different way. Not as many banks will be able to sustain the level of investment as the electronic substitues grow. Larger banks, nonbank payment processors, and shared Type 2 utilities are likely to be the dominant players in the future. Small banks are only likely to survive as part of a shared utility, and in this case they must find a way other than using technology to achieve market distinctiveness.

We believe that in the next 10 years (viewing the situation from an industry perspective), retail payments, currently one of the most fragmented of all banking businesses, will probably undergo profit pressures, substantial consolidation, and automation as the level of systems intensiveness increases to that of the more mature wholesale product (see Chapter 6). Although our theme of created value and destroyed profit is displayed today more completely in the wholesale payment business, where automation has advanced further, we believe that the retail payment business may well display that same pattern in the future. For this reason, it is important for retail banks to understand the changes that have affected the wholesale products.

CHAPTER 5

CREDIT/CHARGE CARDS

Credit cards are a popular and generally profitable payment/lending product that uses systems technology extensively. The card issuance side of the business does not yet really display our theme of destroyed profits, primarily because the business first developed in the 1960s, subsequent to the introduction of technology, and never went through a change of fundamental economics. Instead, issuers have enjoyed steady growth in primary demand (14 percent per year) and a relatively stable industry structure with little pressure on prices. Only on the merchant side of the business, which is much smaller than the cardholder side, has our theme been displayed. There, a substantial conversion of paper-to-electronics has already occurred, creating a chain of systems investments, overcapacity, price pressure, and unprofitability.

However, new applications of systems technology are entering the cardholder business at many different points. Examples include enhanced use of scoring models, cards integrated with other products, and cards with embedded microchips. These technologies threaten to upset the competitive equilibrium when and as they are widely accepted. Adjusting to these changes and to the ever present competitive and cyclical economic pressures will be the biggest technological challenge for those banks that remain in this business.

GOOD, IF CYCLICAL, ECONOMICS

As mentioned above, profits have not been destroyed in the credit/charge card industry—quite the contrary. In 1988, bankcards earned $2.7 billion, or approximately 10 percent of the banking industry's total earnings. These earnings equal roughly 240 basis points on $113 billion of outstandings. Roughly 128 million bankcard accounts are responsible for these earnings, which amounted to about $21 per account. American Express, the most important nonbank card issuer, earned $750 million on its roughly 20 million worldwide cardholder accounts in 1988. Earnings per account for American Express were thus about $37.50. These levels of profitability have been remarkably successful in attracting issuers and in making them willing to stimulate demand and to continue investing in the product. (See Figure 5-1.)

Bankcard Issuers Depend on Spreads

The key drivers of bankcard profitability are net interest income, fees, loan losses, and operating expenses. Credit cards have been a relatively profitable product because their net interest income (after loan losses) plus fees is quite high relative to expenses. This net interest yield in 1988 was approximately 5.7 percent, or $6.4 billion. This came from a gross yield of 14.2 percent and a cost of funds of 8.5 percent. In 1985, when the gross yield was 15.7 percent, the net yield was 6.9 percent, but competitive pressures dropped this by 120 basis points by 1988. The cardholder fees and net interchange amounted to $5.7 billion, or an additional 5 percent yield on average balances.

The nominal Annual Percentage Rate (APR) (i.e., the contractual rate on the cardholder balances) has stayed in the 17 to 19 percent range, making card portfolios essentially a fixed-rate asset. Historically, the cost of funds has been cyclical, meaning that issuers make money when rates are low and break even or lose money when rates are high. The well-known and oft-maligned stability of the nominal APR reflects both the switching barriers inherent to the product as well as consumers' general insensitivity to the cost of low-balance convenience credit. Thus, an ROA of up to 500 basis points was obtainable throughout most of the 1983 to 1986 period— when rates were low. However, when the cost of funds rises, as it did in 1988 and early 1989, the operating earnings do get squeezed.

Operating expenses on the cardholder side of the business remained in the range of 450 to 500 basis points on outstandings for most of the 1980s. Including both the cardholder and merchant servicing sides of the business, costs total 780 basis points to outstandings. Cost levels do vary fairly significantly according to the portfolio size, number of product enhancements, and amount of reinvestment in new account acquisition. The credit/charge card business displays significant economics of scale, equal to approximately 400 basis points, between a 2 million account portfolio and a 25,000 account portfolio. But most

FIGURE 5–1
Bankcard Profitability, 1988

Percent of Outstandings ($ Billions)

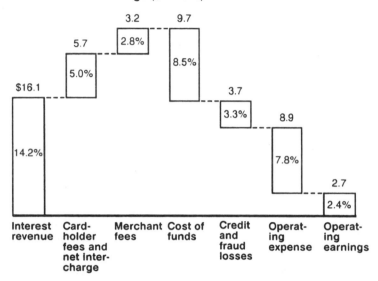

T&E Card ($ Millions)

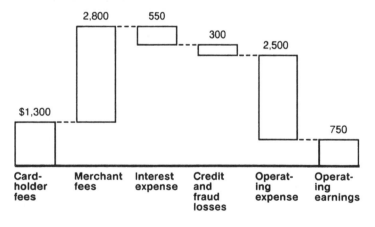

smaller issuers survive by using third-party processors, which spread the benefits of their own scale economies.

Marketing expenses—including advertising, card issuance, enhancements, and credit control—constitute a substantial 36 percent of operations costs, or about 280 basis points. Market saturation has driven up the cost of acquiring accounts so high that expanding issuers have significantly higher expense ratios than do issuers who are not trying to grow. Discontinuance of portfolio expansion might be the first action that an issuer would take if the cost of funds were to rise and the excess profits vanish. To illustrate these costs, the most sensitive variable in marketing cards today is the take rate on a direct mail solicitation. For "plain vanilla" cards, this response rate can easily be below 1.5 percent, producing a cost-to-acquire of approximately $260 per account.

Net charge-offs are a major cost item and a recurring industry concern. They grew from 1 percent of outstandings in 1977 to 3.2 percent in 1988, reflecting an extension of the card base to riskier segments of the population, legislation that liberalized the consumer bankruptcy laws, and accelerating portfolio growth. Because great variations from the 320 basis point average exist in the industry, the real question for most issuing banks is whether the losses are 200 basis points or less versus 400 to 500 basis points or higher—and on which cardholder segments they occur. Overall, commercial bank loan losses averaged only about 25 basis points throughout the late 1970s and only went up to about 50 basis points in the 1980s—excluding LDC debt write-offs. As a result, living with write-offs of 300 basis points in the credit card portfolio has been an adjustment for many bank managements. One potentially better way to look at the credit card business is to examine interest income (14.2 percent) net of both cost of funds (8.5 percent) and loan loss expense (3.2 percent). The resulting net spread is 250 basis points, which compares to, for example, a net spread on commercial loans of roughly 140 basis points (a 10.1 percent yield less 8.2 percent cost of funds and .50 percent loss loan provision). So, the net spread is still quite attractive—almost twice that of commercial and industrial loans even with very high write-offs.

Credit/charge cards have never been designed as a cost displacement device, even though they are certainly displacing other methods of making payments, especially checks. The average (fully loaded) operational cost of a bankcard transaction is approximately $3.40—far more than a check or debit card transaction. Issuers can make such healthy profits on what are more expensive transactions simply because cardholders are willing to pay for the product's value—value that is not confined to the transactional element of the business system, but that is embedded throughout the business system.

In fact, the distinction between the credit card and the less profitable check, whose (fully loaded) operational cost equals at most approximately 80 cents, is that the costs of the credit card are mostly in higher value-added activities. For example, most of a check's cost is simply in the transaction itself, but with credit cards, the actual processing cost of the transaction is roughly 35 to 40 cents. The remainder supports many value-added features, which are discussed below. In turn, this value creates consumer demand and stimulates merchants to pay the discount. If banks could transfer some of these lessons from credit cards to checking accounts (and other products), they might be considerably better off.

American Express Depends on the Merchant Discount

American Express's economics are significantly different from those of the bankcards. They depend heavily on revenues from their merchant discount, which averages from 3.5 to 4.0 percent of transaction volume. This discount rate is substantially higher than the bankcards' average of about 2.5 percent. Merchants tolerate this higher discount only because such high volumes are charged on these cards. The high discount of American Express is protected as long as it retains its "share of wallet," so to speak. Thus, many of its expanding list of extras, such as Buyers Assurance, are not targeted at attracting new cardholders so much as they are targeted at assuring usage. If the distinctiveness between American Express cards and bankcards were ever to lessen, their fundamentally different economics might be squeezed. American Express's innovative use of image processing technology to help perpetuate this distinctiveness will be elaborated on in Chapter 8.

The key to the profitability of both bankcards and charge cards is that consumers like the product and use it. American consumers hold 880 million credit/charge cards, including retailer and gas/oil cards as well as bank, travel and entertainment, and miscellaneous cards. These holding patterns result from the high value that the cards create for their holders. (See Figure 5-2.)

HIGH VALUE

Credit/charge card values break down into three parts: the credit component (present even on a charge card), the transaction component, and the

FIGURE 5–2
U.S. Credit/Charge Card Volumes, 1988

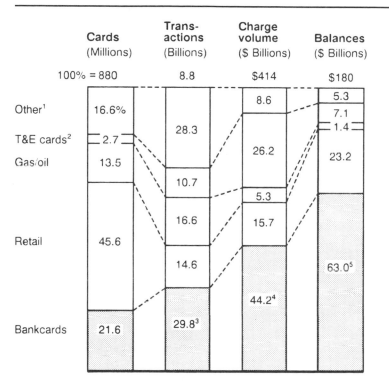

	Cards (Millions)	Trans- actions (Billions)	Charge volume ($ Billions)	Balances ($ Billions)
	100% = 880	8.8	$414	$180
Other[1]	16.6%	28.3	8.6	5.3 / 7.1 / 1.4
T&E cards[2]	2.7		26.2	23.2
Gas/oil	13.5	10.7		
		16.6	5.3	
Retail	45.6		15.7	
		14.6		63.0[5]
			44.2[4]	
Bankcards	21.6	29.8[3]		

[1]Telephone, Discover, Air Travel Card, miscellaneous
[2]Includes all American Express, Diners Club, and Carte Blance
[3]94% purchase, 6% cash advance
[4]84% purchase, 16% cash advance
[5]Excludes securitized balances

extras, or "enhancements." This is a powerful combination, little of which is present in a pure transaction product such as a check, a funds transfer, or debit card.

Convenience Credit

During the 1980s, the demand for consumer installment credit burgeoned. (See Figure 5–3.) Total outstandings grew from $313 billion to $670 billion in just eight years. Bankcards gained share from both retailer

FIGURE 5–3
U.S. Consumer Installment Credit Balances ($ Billions)

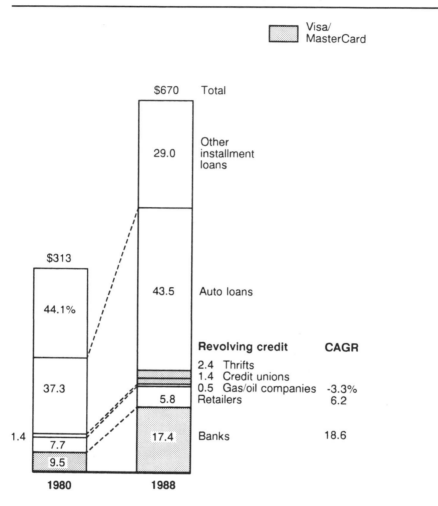

and gas/oil cards, and from other traditional financing sources, such as finance company offices or bank branches. They became the most popular way to obtain unsecured consumer credit, and banks discovered that the credit card is the least expensive way to make a small personal loan.

Cardholders view card balances as convenience credit and treat it differently than they do other forms of consumer credit. They use it less, keep it outstanding for shorter periods, and are willing to pay more for it.

For example, the average bankcard balance is only about $880 per account, small compared to the average new car loan of roughly $10,000. Furthermore, approximately 28 percent of all bankcard holders are "convenience" users: they pay their charges off each month without incurring finance charges. Despite conventional wisdom about our "profligate" society, credit/charge card balances are not particularly onerous and at the end of 1988 constituted only 4.7 percent of all household debt.

Other sources of installment debt are usually obtained for (and secured by) a specific purchase. Because consumers obtain such credit (e.g., auto loans or mortgages) only when needed, they are much more price-sensitive. But the credit/charge card credit line is really more than a loan. It is a reserve purchasing power that can be used as circumstances dictate, literally years after it is approved. Cardholders perceive this as created value. It is one of the reasons they are willing to accept APRs higher than for other forms of consumer credit. (Corporations do much the same thing, paying substantial fees for credit lines or backup letters of credit that they will not necessarily use.) The card approach is now so popular that the "all other" loan category in Figure 5–3, which contains noncard forms of unsecured credit, has been shrinking in real terms since 1980.

Superior Transactional Ability

As transaction devices, credit/charge cards have many superior features. Evaluating them against five fundamental payment product attributes, it is easy to see why they have become so popular. (See Figure 5–4.) Cards offer a level of liquidity that no other product offers, because of the convenience credit aspect and the reserve purchasing power. Cards' universality is almost on a par with cash, especially outside the United States, and is much better than that of checks. For example, cards are now widely accepted, and their acceptance at a specific location can be determined in advance. They are far more secure than either checks or cash because the cardholder has little or no liability in the event of loss or theft. Charge-backs are a unique feature that protects the cardholder in the event of an unresolved dispute with a merchant. Usage requires less effort than with a check (and a checkbook). Finally, officially accepted record keeping is automatically created.

Credit/charge cards excel when the buyer/seller are unknown to each other, the standard arrangement in United States commerce as well as in traveling over long distances. American Express's roots are not in

FIGURE 5–4

Evaluation of Alternative Payment Products

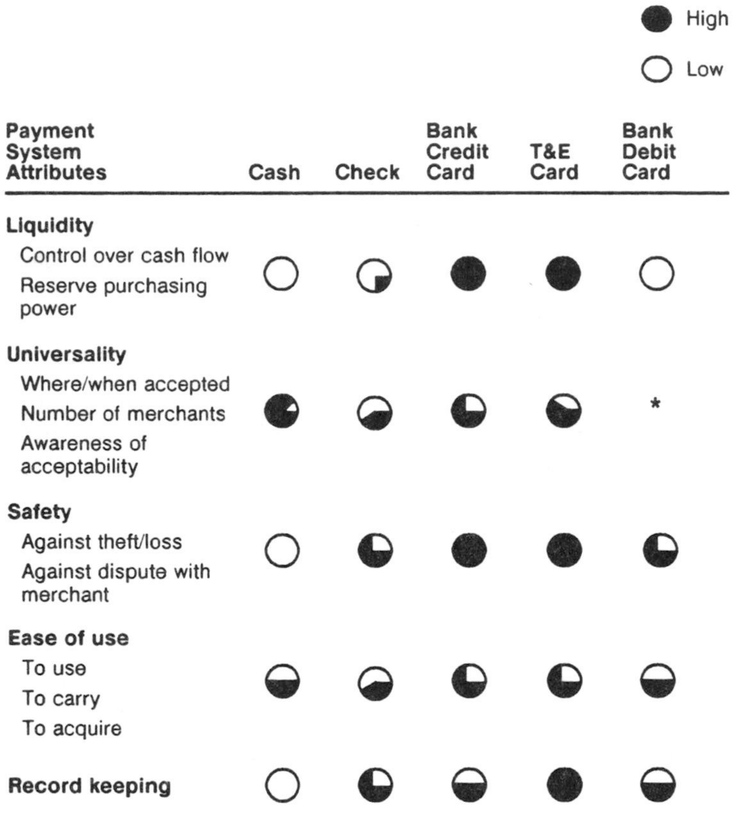

● High

○ Low

Payment System Attributes	Cash	Check	Bank Credit Card	T&E Card	Bank Debit Card
Liquidity Control over cash flow / Reserve purchasing power	○	◕	●	●	○
Universality Where/when accepted / Number of merchants / Awareness of acceptability	◕	◑	◔	◑	*
Safety Against theft/loss / Against dispute with merchant	○	◔	●	●	◔
Ease of use To use / To carry / To acquire	◒	◓	◔	◔	◒
Record keeping	○	◔	◒	●	◒

*Depends on merchant incentives and necessity of using PIN

finance and banking at all, but in the shipment of valuables or money to distant points. In fact, the travel and entertainment (T&E) card concept was originally designed to substitute for a traveler's check or a money order, not a local payment mechanism. Credit/charge card enhancements related to travel are thus superior to the older payment mechanisms: they offer speedy worldwide replacement and are currency-independent, which standard checks are not.

Because of these superior transaction features, card volumes have grown dramatically. Total charge volume on United States bankcards grew from only $14 billion in 1973, to $183 billion in 1988 — a remarkable 18.7 percent CAGR over a 15-year period. Volume on the American Express cards also experienced a high rate of growth. Cards are now so popular that one-half of all noncash purchases at a point of sale are made with a card. In certain industry sectors (e.g., airlines, hotels, and white-tablecloth restaurants), the overwhelming majority of revenues are generated on cards. For example, in 1988 approximately 30 percent of the airline industry's $54 billion in revenues was generated solely on American Express cards.

The number of cardholders and card transactions could only grow in tandem with merchant acceptance. Worldwide bankcard-honoring locations passed the 6 million mark in 1988, more than 2.4 million of which are in the United States. The worldwide total of American Express-accepting locations is about 2.5 million. Except certain merchant categories (e.g., supermarkets and fast food outlets), virtually every category of merchant has been heavily penetrated. Visa, MasterCard, and American Express have even converted most of the department stores and gas stations that still offer their own proprietary cards. Even Sears, the biggest retail holdout of all, began a 12-store Visa/MasterCard/American Express test in 1988.

Other Features, Too!

As if all this were not enough value, credit/charge cards are famous for having an abundance of extras. ATM access, card registration (in case a wallet/purse is lost), automatic airline insurance, cash advance checks, personal identification numbers (PIN), cash or merchandise rebates, guaranteed hotel reservations and express checkout features have all become standard. At American Express, which is the clear leader in the extras department, a thick booklet comes with every new card just to explain how to use it. American Express has its country club billing, flexible spending limits, year-end statement, warranty extensions, auto club, health club, discount long-distance service, luggage insurance, and so forth.

At American Express, and increasingly at commercial banks, the cardmember base is being heavily cross-sold. Although cross-selling is designed to benefit the card issuer, it also represents extra value to the cardholder. Presumably, those cardholders who buy, which is many of them, find it a worthwhile way to shop. Meanwhile, checking account customers, who also get monthly statements, do not seem to be as aggressively cross-sold. The credit/charge card has an affinity, a connection, with its holder that the check and the checkbook does not to the same extent. Perhaps the deferred payment feature really does stimulate incremental purchases.

In summary, most of these features, perhaps all, could be added to other consumer payment products, but generally are not. It is no wonder that so many people think about their cards first, not about the cash, when they lose their wallet/purse. Credit cards have been the good news in the banks' portfolio of payment business for some time now. The question is, of course: How long will it last?

THE COMPETITIVE CARDHOLDER BUSINESS

The credit/charge cardholder business has become extremely competitive as aggressive players have sought a greater share of such a profitable and expanding marketplace. Banks compete with retailers and nonbank financial companies for share of market and share of wallet. All players, including the nonbanks, are increasingly looking to segmentation and micromarketing to match their cards better with specific customer needs. These segmentation trends can be seen in the rise of affinity cards and in the introduction of the Optima and Discover cards.

Competition Expands

Commercial banks entered the credit/charge card business relatively late but have clearly become the dominant players. However, they are not alone. American Express, Sears (with its 40 million proprietary cards), J.C. Penney, the major oil/gas retailers, and more than 500 other specialized retailers remain enormous powers in this business. Many other niche players (e.g., Avis, Hilton Hotels, etc.) have their own low-volume, high-cost, limited-purpose charge cards.

Through the increasing adoption of affinity cards, large organizations such as American Airlines, the American Automobile Association (AAA), and the AFL-CIO now play a role in the credit/charge card business. During 1989, AT&T announced its intention to selectively convert its proprietary telephone cards into general purpose credit cards. As markets have globalized, cards such as JCB, Airplus, Access, and Eurocard have been started outside the United States—and offer competition to United States cards. Even General Electric Capital Corporation now issues a bankcard in addition to its industry-leading 6 million private-label accounts. Yet despite all these issuers, the product has retained its profitability.

Competition within the bankcard industry has been the toughest. Visa and MasterCard will essentially license the right to issue a bankcard to any depository institution, and in fact Visa alone has more than 20,000 members worldwide. Thousands of United States institutions still issue credit cards, although the heavy marketing and systems requirements have concentrated the business considerably. The top 5 bank issuers have approximately 40 percent of the market and the top 20 have almost 60 percent. (See Figure 5–5.) Citicorp, the bankcard leader, has approximately 17 percent of bankcard assets. Still, complete concentration is unlikely to occur and, in fact, the level of concentration remained unchanged between 1985 and 1987. Small issuers survive (and in some cases thrive) because they have a niche customer base and have their processing done by third-party vendors. For example, in 1988 approximately 3,000 different credit unions were issuing cards, some with a portfolio as low as 500 cards. They have been very successful at placing 12 million plain vanilla cards in their members' hands — all with very little investment in systems, facilities, or marketing.

Nonbank Players

New entrants in the credit/charge card business do, however, represent a threat to established players. The 700,000 or so U.S. locations that were accepting the Discover Card in 1988 probably now generate 80 percent of the bankcards' total charge volume, meaning that Sears has essentially won the battle for merchant acceptance. Discover's card base reached 27 million by early 1989. Although this card's charge volume and balances per account were still lower than those of the bankcards, the card turned profitable in the last quarter of 1988, earning $6.7 million. Greenwood Trust, the bank Sears founded for this purpose, had about $5.9 billion in receivables by the end of 1988, enough to place it among the very largest bank issuers. American Express's Optima card has also been very successful, attracting several million cardholders and generating more than $2 billion in balances by 1988, enough to rank its credit card bank 12th among bankcard issuers.

Among the large bankcard issuers, competition has focused on issuance of affinity cards, portfolio acquisition, addition of bells & whistles, and never ending efforts to reduce operating costs through technology. Affinity cards have been around for roughly a decade. The oldest pro-

FIGURE 5–5
Top 15 U.S. Bankcard Issuers, 1987

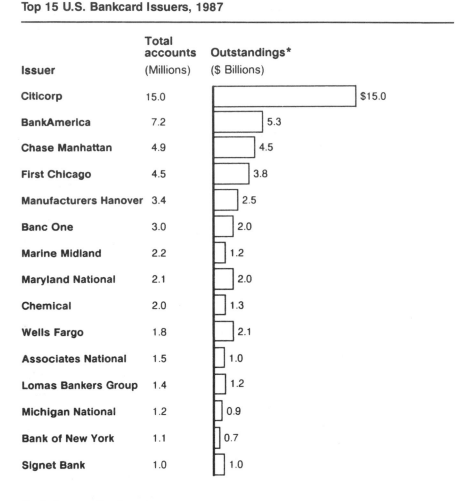

Issuer	Total accounts (Millions)	Outstandings* ($ Billions)
Citicorp	15.0	$15.0
BankAmerica	7.2	5.3
Chase Manhattan	4.9	4.5
First Chicago	4.5	3.8
Manufacturers Hanover	3.4	2.5
Banc One	3.0	2.0
Marine Midland	2.2	1.2
Maryland National	2.1	2.0
Chemical	2.0	1.3
Wells Fargo	1.8	2.1
Associates National	1.5	1.0
Lomas Bankers Group	1.4	1.2
Michigan National	1.2	0.9
Bank of New York	1.1	0.7
Signet Bank	1.0	1.0

*Includes securitized assets

gram, offered jointly by 27 banks and the AAA, has more than 3 million cardholders. The most visible recent program is the joint Citicorp–American Airlines card, which grants AAdvantage frequent flyers one free mile for every dollar charged. An estimated 1 million cardholders had signed up by 1988 and tended to use the card as a T&E card. Although yields were low (10 percent of outstandings), charge volume was very high (approximately $7,000 yearly versus $1,300 for a standard bankcard).

American Express is by far the most significant competitive threat to the bankcards. Its steady expansion of merchants, of features, and of perceived status have made it the card of choice for many cardholders. Yearly card volume – approximately $3,600 – is considerably higher than on the bankcards. American Express has expanded its cardmembers through segmentation and micromarketing, areas where systems technology plays a key role. Because it controls the business system end-to-end, American Express can do things the banks cannot, such as its recent implementation of enhanced country club billing. The issue for banks is whether they can continue their success in credit cards in the face of such substantial levels of competition.

Technology Not Focused on Transactions

Systems technology is used throughout the credit/charge card business system to control costs, to handle growing volumes, and to service new needs. But in contrast to the individual and wholesale payments business, the sources of profit in the cardholder side of the business have not yet been destroyed by technology. Neither the spreads nor the merchant discounts have been driven down by speedup or by overcapacity. Card issuers have created plenty of value and have been able to charge for it. There are several reasons for this, including switching barriers, price insensitivity, and cross-subsidization from cardholders with heavy balances. Systems technology has been used in all parts of the credit/ charge card business system. (See Figure 5-6.) The use of technology is not restricted, even primarily, to the transaction processing segment. *All segments use systems technology, and in this respect, credit/charge cards are fundamentally different from most other banking products.* Systems technology plays a major role in each of the following segments of the credit card business system.

Product Development
Product development is systems-intensive, because the product – the bundle of features that constitutes the offering – is always created with databases and with software. For example, many of the more than 600 affinity card programs require software links between the card issuer and the affinity group. Interorganizational systems may be needed to convert purchases to credits, to maintain duplicate customer bases, or to resolve billing disputes.

FIGURE 5–6
Cardholder Business System

	Product development and marketing	Credit	Process transactions	Customer service	Collections	MIS
Major functions	Purchase and manipulation of lists Marketing through affinity groups Direct extract from credit bureau files Cross-selling	Credit scoring models Behavioral scoring models Bankruptcy scoring models	Authorization system Draft capture at POS Data entry Posting of accounts Settlement	Statements Remittance processing Card issuance and control Customer service Chargebacks	Automated collection system Letter writing Charge-off accounting Credit bureau reporting	Segmentation and profitability reporting Feedback to scoring models
Major systems	Customer data base (batch)	Applications (batch) Credit bureau access (batch and on-line)	Authorization (on-line) Posting (batch) Data capture (off-line and on-line)	Statementing (batch) Issuance (batch) Customer service (on-line) Chargebacks (on-line)	Collections (on-line) Credit bureau reporting (batch)	Management information and control (batch) Decision support (on-line)
Percent of systems expense	2%	8	55	23	10	2

Marketing

The same process of technological support is evident in the marketing function. Mass marketing requires systems technology in order to control lists, to understand the customer database, and to handle fulfillment. New account acquisition costs are extremely high, and wasted marketing efforts can bankrupt an issuer. Technology is increasingly targeted at *cost-effective account generation*, not just back-office cost cutting. Large issuers such as First Chicago and Maryland National constantly test the efficacy of their direct marketing packages, a process with its roots in the consumer goods world. Scale, up-front investment, and sophisticated decision support systems are required.

Credit Control

To control credit risk effectively, card issuers have pioneered the use of credit scoring models and the use of credit bureau data. Originally, credit cards could be handled more like other consumer loans. They were made on a case-by-case basis, reflecting the applicant's current financial statement. With time, that changed to an actuarial approach in which statistical models predicted the likelihood of an applicant going bad.

Scoring models are considered more accurate than other approaches because their supporting historic data makes them objective, standardized, and consistent. Large issuers such as Citibank are constantly refining their models and using them for decisions (such as reissuance, collections, and credit limit increases) that concern their ongoing portfolio. By developing models for specialized market segments, major issuers can control the costs encountered with high-risk (but potentially profitable) groups such as college students or those with marginal credit records. These marketing and credit technologies require immense data bases to work, thus giving larger issuers an edge. They can be as important as operating economies.

Transaction Processing

Bankcard transactions are processed in two steps: the authorization and the transaction (purchase or cash advance) itself. The purpose of the authorization is to determine in advance the validity of the transaction. With an authorization, the merchant is not at risk, as it would be with a check or with its own credit program. The transaction itself occurs when the information on the (approved) purchase travels through the clearing system to the cardholder's bank. Today's authorization systems use sophisticated combinations of negative and positive files that are reached through worldwide electronic networks. Much of the authorization system (both for banks and for American Express) is completely automated. Positive files at the cardmember's bank keep track of account availability; negative files keep track of proscribed account numbers. Both are essential in controlling fraud and limiting the potential for credit losses.

Bankcard transactions generally clear through the Visa and Master-Card networks. Both accept tape or on-line transmissions of valid transactions from merchant acquirors and switch them to the appropriate cardholder's bank. (No paper passes through the banks' clearing system.) American Express, however, controls its transactions as well as authorizations end-to-end and has no clearing system.

Financial Features

Product features that affect finance are also systems-intensive. Offering a floating-rate card (e.g., American Express's Optima or First of Omaha's Visa) requires expanded functionality in the core software. Floating rates are not yet standard (despite the success of Optima) but may soon be. They are the only protection against a sustained rise in the cost of funds. If the level of interest rates were to rise again above 20 percent, as it did in the early 1980s, variable-rate cards might become as common as adjustable rate mortgages. Tiered rates, as offered by CoreStates, for example, are another (systems-intensive) option for attracting customers who want low rates without giving up too much yield. Cash rebates are offered by Discover, the Associates, and other card issuers. Citicorp offers the equivalent in merchandise. Whether in real dollars, airline credits, or merchandise credits rebates require software to track, post, and adjust those credits. Open-ended second mortgages ("home equity lines") are yet another twist. Balances are growing rapidly—reaching approximately $70 billion by 1988—and card access to those balances had been introduced by approximately 50 banks; New York's Crossland Savings is one example. Again, this linkage requires new software.

Customer Service

The same systems-intensiveness occurs on the back end of the business system, where accounts are maintained and serviced. Partly because of their complexity, credit/charge cards generate significantly more customer service activity (and cost) than either consumer loans or checking accounts. The more value the card offers, the more customer service is required. For example, American Express, with its numerous card features, must individually track more than 200 different types of customer service calls. The elaborate software system required to do this takes more than 1 million lines of code and handles approximately 23 million telephone calls per year.

Collections

Collections is another area where systems and operations expenses are high. Gross bankcard charge-offs in the United States in 1987 were $3.8 billion—up at a CAGR of 51 percent from $1.1 billion in 1984. Forty-seven percent of this total results from delinquencies, so insurers have focused their efforts on calling, writing, and monitoring the progress of all delinquent accounts. Collection systems have become a critical productivity-enhancing tool. Most banks, and American Express, now have sophisticated on-line systems that feature work scheduling, automatic monitoring of recontact dates, automatic letter writing, productivity measurement, automatic call making, and many other features. They are an essential tool for controlling charge-off rates in a reasonably cost-effective manner.

Thus, systems investments are required across the credit/charge card business system, from marketing and product development through collections. This integrated business system is consequently quite different from the deposit-based products. Much more attention is devoted to tracking and controlling each customer's behavior. There is more of a real "relationship" in place. In the process, a highly valuable product has been created that yields better profits—in stark contrast to the less profitable DDA product.

CONCENTRATED THIRD-PARTY PROCESSING

The requirements for processing credit cards are so systems-intensive that processing is itself considerably more concentrated than is card issuance. Processing, as used here, means all the back-end functions that require use of systems technology. Because processing requires such tremendous technological investments, a unique situation has arisen. Issuers of cards must either be large-scale or must use a third-party processor. Because up to 10 million accounts are required to reach optimum processing efficiency, there are very few small self-processing issuers left. This has led to a considerably different industry structure than with DDA, for example, where literally thousands of banks do their own processing.

Figure 5–7 shows how the 155 million general-purpose U.S. credit/charge accounts were processed in 1987. The three stand-alone cards—

FIGURE 5–7

U.S. Processing Market Share, 1987 (General-Purpose Credit/Charge Card Accounts

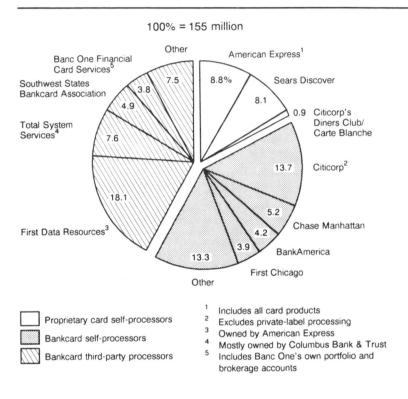

100% = 155 million

Proprietary card self-processors	1 Includes all card products
Bankcard self-processors	2 Excludes private-label processing
Bankcard third-party processors	3 Owned by American Express
	4 Mostly owned by Columbus Bank & Trust
	5 Includes Banc One's own portfolio and brokerage accounts

American Express, Discover, and Diners Club—processed for themselves, as did most of the largest bankcard issuers. Only 2 bankcard issuers in the top 10 did not process for themselves. MHC now processes at FDR (owned by American Express) and Maryland National processed at SSBA. But because concentration had not proceeded very far, 42.1 percent of the total market (and 51 percent of the bankcard market) was processed by the third-party processors.

Third-party processors perform cardholder authorization services, capture incoming transactions, and post transactions to cardholder accounts. They may also perform customer accounting, statement printing, and remittance processing. These functions are the most suitable for outside contracting. Issuers themselves have usually performed the front-end customer interface components, including credit approval, customer service, and collections—although the systems supporting these functions are usually provided by the third-party processor.

The third-party processing business is highly concentrated. For example, FDR and Total Systems, the two leaders, both grew approximately 30 percent between 1985 and 1988 and now have 43 percent and 18 percent of the third-party processing market, respectively. Meanwhile, all processors below the top three experienced negative growth. Processing remains an attractive business for the two leaders, which have approximate margins of 25 percent. New entrants in this business are unlikely because of the high entry barriers. There are significant economies of scale, high switching barriers for the customers, and a need for deep skills in the specific business. The presence of these third-part processing firms limits how far concentration can proceed among issuers. For example, both FDR and Total Systems have customers whose portfolios are as small as 10,000 accounts. Some third-party programs, such as the Banc One/CUNA program discussed in Chapter 9, are specifically targeted at issuers whose portfolios are as small as 1,000 accounts.

Among the self-processing banks, however, the pressures are intense. Constant technological reinvestment is required to stay current. Issuers must keep up with competitive product developments, new Visa/Master-Card operational requirements, and changes in core technology. The difficulty of keeping up will probably result in an increasing share for the third-party processors. These reinvestment pressures also effect the third-party processors themselves. Almost all of the cooperative processing associations started in the late 1960s have sold out, except for SSBA. Although a decent package is available (from Credit Card Software, Inc.), this is a solution targeted primarily at medium-sized players, that is, those processing less than approximately 1 million accounts.

Processing considerations will continue to have a strong influence on strategy. No actions can be taken in the card business without insuring processing support. Control over that support, or access to it, is a must. The proprietary software and features of the self-processors will remain pitted against the shared solutions of the third-parties.

THE MERCHANT SERVICING BUSINESS

Merchant servicers handle the relationship with, and process for, card-honoring merchants. Typically, they own a contract that sets the discount rate and assures provision of all required support (e.g., authorizations, hot card lists, decals, charge slips, merchant statements, chargeback processing, etc.). Players in merchant servicing include the merchant banks themselves (where the deposits are made), third-party processors, value-added networks, and retail applications providers. Typically, if the servicer is a bank, it has other relationships with the merchant, such as accepting check and cash deposits or providing financing. Historically, merchant servicing has been a fragmented business dominated by local, not-too-large banks.

Merchant servicing is rapidly shifting from paper to electronics. Authorizations are already heavily automated. Now retail locations are being penetrated by electronic draft capture (EDC) terminals and electronic cash registers (ECRs). The effects have been striking: *Merchant servicing has become a low-margin commodity business.* Competitors generated about $3.2 billion in gross fees in 1988, which meant net fees of $1 billion after accounting for the interchange and Visa/MasterCard assessment fees. On this revenue, they took a loss of about $300 million. Furthermore, "new-game" players with high fixed costs are driving down prices, competing on a national scale, and spurring many of the "old-game" players—primarily banks—to quit the business. Consolidation is accelerating and local banks find they cannot justify remaining in the business.

New-Game Players

Systems technology is changing the way merchant servicing works. Once, the paper draft acquired with each transaction had to be physically delivered, giving local banks an edge. But this is not the case anymore. EDC (discussed below) makes merchant servicing a purely transaction-oriented business that any DP-intensive company anywhere in the country can play. Many of the new-game players are not banks at all. NaBanco and National Data Processing (NDC) are two examples of third-party processors that have forward-integrated and now offer complete merchant services to their own portfolios. (See Figure 5–8.)

Although many commercial banks are still in merchant servicing, they are under increasing pressure. The new-game players have moved quickly to capitalize on the fact that merchant acquiring has arrived at Stage C (see again Figure 2–4), where the customer interface becomes automated. These players have lower operating costs with a higher fixed-cost component. NaBanco, for example, has a 45 basis point advantage relative to the industry (based on volume). It uses this to cut its price, processing for a typical discount of 166 basis points versus an industry

FIGURE 5–8

Top 10 Bankcard Merchant Servicers Ranked by Charge Volume, 1988

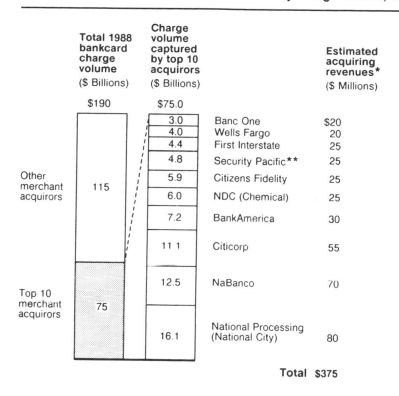

Total 1988 bankcard charge volume ($ Billions)	Charge volume captured by top 10 acquirors ($ Billions)		Estimated acquiring revenues* ($ Millions)
$190	$75.0		
	3.0	Banc One	$20
	4.0	Wells Fargo	20
	4.4	First Interstate	25
	4.8	Security Pacific**	25
Other merchant acquirors 115	5.9	Citizens Fidelity	25
	6.0	NDC (Chemical)	25
	7.2	BankAmerica	30
	11 1	Citicorp	55
	12.5	NaBanco	70
Top 10 merchant acquirors 75	16.1	National Processing (National City)	80
		Total	**$375**

*Net of interchange; excludes revenues from third party processing for other merchant acquirors
**Acquired by NaBanco 1/89

average of 210. Nevertheless, it still maintains a comfortable operating margin of approximately 30 percent. Not surprisingly, old-game players are selling out. In 1988 and 1989, MHC, Chemical Bank, and Security Pacific all sold their merchant servicing businesses.

Third-Party Processors

Third-party processors play an important competitive role in the merchant business. They generate revenues of $300 to $450 million and account for one-fourth of all merchant acquiring expense. Nearly 60 percent of all sales drafts (both electronic and paper) are processed by third parties, as are 78 percent of all electronic authorizations. As with the issuance side, the third-party players are concentrated. The top five— FDR, Total Systems, SSBA, NDC, and Credit Systems, Inc.—account for 65 percent of the third-party processing activity. NDC specializes in electronic authorizations and is so efficient that it is used for that purpose by 7 of the top 10 merchant servicers. These processors will continue to expand as the business grows, thus spurring even more disaggregation.

These pressures and trends should continue as long as the economics remain unattractive for small players. Net servicing revenues were essentially stagnant between 1985 and 1987, while operating income dropped from roughly break-even to a $300 million loss. Those that made money, such as NaBanco, will continue to expand at the expense of the smaller servicers.

Electronic Data Capture's (EDC) Rapid Expansion

Automation has affected merchant processing activities in two distinct waves. During the 1970s, electronic authorizations through a stand-alone terminal, ECR, or a CPU-CPU connection became common. The cost savings were substantial: an electronic authorization costs 5 cents compared to a voice authorization, which costs 45 cents. Today, only 12 percent of all bankcard transactions are authorized by the old method (Stage B) of calling the bank or its processor on the phone and having a clerk enter the data in a terminal. Now, the second wave of automation is occurring. Approximately 20 percent of all transactions are captured electronically and this share should grow to 70 percent by 1992. (See Figure 5–9.)

EDC offers significant cost savings to merchants, who are the customers and thus the recipients of the created value. Handling paper sales drafts is labor-intensive and expensive for a retailer. A manually read document costs 10.5 cents whereas an EDC document costs only 5.5 cents. Because many merchants, especially large ones, do the data entry themselves, these cost savings are directly passed on to the customer.

Furthermore, the time required to receive funds can be reduced from 7 to 10 days (for a chain store) to 1 to 2 days. Instead of paper sales drafts being bundled at many decentralized locations and mailed to the merchant's data center, charges can be transmitted each day via leased or dial-up lines. For example, the value of this speed-up to United States Shoe Corp., which operates 15 specialty chains, is approximately $700,000 per year on a card volume of $400 million.

FIGURE 5–9

Projected Growth in EDC Bankcard Transactions (Billions Per Year)

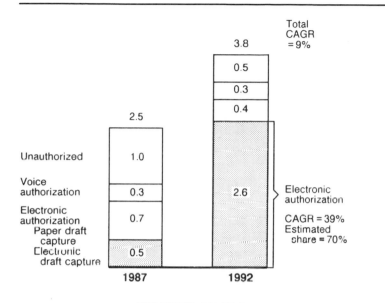

BENEFITS OF EDC

Merchant

Reduced float/quick access to funds

Reduced discount rates

Increased back office efficiency

Reduced errors

Improved information management

Faster service

Easier adoption of debit cards

Financial institution

Quicker access to discount fees

Potential for reduced processing costs

Reduction in fraud/credit losses

Reduced errors

On-line error resolution

Lower interchange fees

Potential link to debit card

Another advantage of EDC is that both Visa and MasterCard have reduced the interchange rate by nearly 50 percent. For example, Visa's normal interchange fee in 1988 for a $50 unauthorized paper draft transaction was 93 cents. But, for a qualifying EDC transaction, the fee was only 50 cents. Because most merchant discounts are set on the basis of interchange plus processing charges, these interchange reductions flow directly to the merchant.

Further benefits occur inside the store itself. EDC terminals, especially ECRs, can help merchants manage their information better. Inventory may be reduced or better linked to customer buying patterns. Many EDC terminals can accept, or be upgraded to accept, debit cards. Thus, EDC paves the way for a fourth major payment choice. With EDC, fraud and credit losses can be controlled better than before because most EDC terminals are programmed with a $0 floor limit and authorize all purchases. Finally, simple things such as reduced clerical errors and faster check-out time can enhance a merchant's labor productivity.

For all these reasons, EDC is expected to sweep through the credit/charge card industry. The number of installed EDC terminals has risen from approximately 5,000 in 1985, to an estimated 350,000 in 1989. Because terminals can now be produced in volume and because components are less expensive, the cost of an EDC terminal dropped from approximately $800 in 1985, to between $150 and $300 in 1989.

The business of providing EDC is dominated by nonbank competitors. The leading players are NDC, McDonnell Douglas, MasterCard, FDR, Envoy Corp., Sears Payment Systems, and Visa. In all cases, these firms are leveraging prior investments in value-added networks to offer these services to merchant servicers. Most offer additional applications, such as debit card processing, check guarantee, private label support, retail MIS applications, or remittance processing. The EDC business is also very concentrated because networks have such high fixed costs; the top 10 processors control 90 percent of the market.

In summary, the situation in merchant servicing is a classic illustration of how Stage C automation may destroy profits. The merchant business used to be paper-based, and local bank competitors could therefore survive. In fact, a local presence was helpful just to handle the paper. But as the customer interface became automated, concentration occurred and new-game players entered. The benefits of automation were passed to the customer. Fixed costs now predominate and are already squeezing out the smaller players. Competition may even become irrational for the big players if too much capacity is created or if leaders subsidize EDC in order to sell other services to merchants. Survival will require all players to focus on selected merchant segments and to develop carefully tailored products that meet their customers' needs.

NEW TECHNOLOGICAL DEVELOPMENTS

There are many new technological developments that promise to affect the credit/charge card business. Database technology is aiding the control of portfolios and the monitoring of consumers' credit habits; the scope of applicability of scoring models is expanding; integrated products that combine the card with other systems are appearing; and new card technology may eventually be adopted. All of these developments have the potential to significantly change how the game is played and to determine who is likely to win. (These developments involve technologies that have major applicability to the card business; technological developments that have broad applicability in many areas of banking, such as image processing, will be described in Chapter 8.)

Database Technology

The credit/charge card industry leads the way in the use of very large databases. The growth in the use of these databases has been stimulated in no small way by the recent availability of better database technology. For mass-produced products, such as credit/charge cards, control of risk through historical data is essential. Very little of today's credit card risk is controlled through personal knowledge of the cardholder. Both issuer-specific databases and industry-wide credit history databases are used extensively.

The principle credit control databases are the credit bureaus operated by TRW, Equifax Inc., and Trans Union Credit Information Company. These firms accept monthly reports from most consumer credit grantors, arrange the reports by individual, and then sell copies of the reports to credit grantors engaged in accepting or rejecting applicants. TRW, for example, has approximately 200 million separate files on individuals and issues some 100 million reports annually. Users can access the files either on-line or in batch. They can pull down an entire report into a PC in just a few seconds (as CoreStates does), or submit lengthy lists of names for preapproval or prescreening. Now the credit bureaus are expanding their businesses. They sell reports directly to consumers. Also, because the quality of the data has improved, they sell lists of credit-worthy consumers directly to credit grantors.

Card issuers are likewise keeping larger data files on their own customers. Lengthier and more complete historical records, better payment and transaction data, and expanded demographic data are enabling issuers to develop microsegmentation strategies and to apply advanced modeling technology. Segmentation will allow issuers to better match features with needs. For example, money-losing "convenience" users can be targeted with a high-fee card or a shorter grace period. Issuers such as Citibank are segmenting their cardbases by credit-worthiness and other factors. When used properly, a large database can be a significant competitive advantage.

Scoring Models

Scoring models are used to control risk. They can be used whenever a yes/no (or go/no-go) decision can be statistically correlated with known historical information. Scoring models were originally developed for use in approving or declining new credit card account applications. They are now used heavily to predict the likelihood of an applicant being a good or bad risk (e.g., a charge-off). In fact, 63 percent of all issuers above $1 billion in size use credit scoring models. Although credit scoring technology has applicability in other consumer (and small business) lending, card issuers have employed it the most.

New uses for models offer the potential to go far beyond predicting good and bad risks. More sophisticated models make an attempt to predict the profit on a new account, not just the risk. For example, an applicant might be rejected if the model predicted they would be a good risk but a low-volume purchaser or a convenience user. Mail solicitation scoring can increase response rates and ultimately boost profitability by determining whom card issuers should solicit. Behavioral scoring can help improve the performance of issuers' current accounts. For example, behavioral scoring could guide collection decisions (e.g., when to dun or to write off an account) or reissuance decisions (e.g., which cardholders to renew). Bankruptcy scoring even offers a way to predict which accounts among the current portfolio are going to go bankrupt. All scoring models depend upon having the right data and the ability to update that data frequently. Large issuers, such as Citibank, which have invested in the ability to manipulate the data can gain an advantage.

Integrated Products

An integrated product is a combination of a credit/charge card with a different system to accomplish a purpose related to payment systems. Two examples are (1) the corporate charge card, which links a card system with a travel reservation system to control employee's travel costs, and (2) the new health care cards whose goal is to reduce the costs of processing and paying health care claims.

American Express is the leader in the corporate card field, with approximately 2 million such cards in force. It has tied together its regular card system, its American Express travel agency system (the country's largest), and some special software in order to give large corporate customers a better way to control burgeoning employee travel and enter tainment expenses. American Express issues cards in bulk to its corporate customers' employees and then reports back to the customer in tailored formats. For example, the client can monitor (and even control) who rides in first class, including when, where, and why. Both MasterCard and Visa are developing competitive products but are far behind. American Express's total control of its delivery system and its ownership of a travel agency have given it a big lead in this still-developing business.

Health payment cards are a new business with high growth potential. Health care transactions are still primarily paper-based, excessively complicated, and relatively expensive to process (e.g., $5 to $10 to process a claim for a single doctor's visit). This processing cost contributes to the relatively high cost of our country's overall health care system. Health care payers — insurance companies or Health Maintenance Organizations (HMOs) — are looking for better *control* over transactions.

An example of this new product is a card from McKesson that is used to create and process payments for reimbursable drug purchases. McKesson has signed up more than one-half of the country's pharmacists and installed electronic terminals at their drugstores. Health care payers give their covered employees one of the cards; each employee then presents his or her card to the druggist instead of paying cash and later filing a paper-based claim. Aside from making payments much easier for covered employees, McKesson also controls (and can reduce) the druggists' reimbursement levels. Similar developments may well occur for hospital, doctor's office, and dentist's office claims. Eventually, there may also be other integrated products in both nonfinancial areas, such as passport issuing or airline ticketing, and financial areas such as savings accounts or CDs. The net result will be an emphasis on interorganizational systems and an advantage to players who can sustain such systems.

New Card Technology

Putting technology (i.e., intelligence) on a card is a potentially revolutionary idea. There is virtually no technology on cards today. Embossing, signatures, and holograms are nonelectronic methods of communicating information and controlling fraud. The magnetic stripe is the only part of the card related to systems technology. But it is not very secure, carries minimal information and cannot be updated once issued. Therefore, the card itself acts only as an identification device and is *not* an essential component of the product. For example, about 10 percent of all card transactions take place by mail or phone without the card's presence. Many of the remaining transactions that do occur at a point of sale do not use the magnetic stripe. All of the important control and processing functions are embedded in the worldwide credit/charge card authorization and clearing networks. The entire architecture of the system is based on a nonautomated interface with the cardholder.

However, new card technologies that allow data and processes to reside on the card itself are now technically feasible. There are several possibilities, such as the Optical Memory Card manufactured by Drexler Technology, and the supercard (with a chip, keyboard, and digital readout) that was tested by Visa in 1987. But the one that offers the most immediate appeal to the credit/charge card world is the card with an embedded programmable ROM chip, called a "smart card."

Although potentially far-reaching, an exact scenario describing how cards with intelligence will come into being is extremely difficult to predict. The technology simply offers so much potential for new approaches. Future scenarios range from the visionary idea of having one card that does everything—keeping all of our financial, medical, travel, and personal data—to the conservative idea of having no change in cards at all. The only really clear fact is that the costs of any fundamental conversion will be very high and that the worldwide credit/charge card infrastructure must, by its nature, change very slowly.

The Smart Card

Smart card technology potentially represents a real sea change in how and where information is processed. The chip can hold programs that interact with data either on the chip itself or external to the chip. These programs can be permanent and unchangeable or can be modifiable when the chip is connected to a network. Data can be stored, updated, and retrieved both when the card is issued and throughout its life as transactions occur.

First tested in France in 1974, the smart card technology has since then undergone years of demonstrations, development, and test-marketing. So far, niche uses have been found, such as in high-security installations and health record-keeping applications. The largest payment application is in France, where 20 million prepaid plastic cards with chips are used in public telephones. About half of all public phones in France do not accept coins, requiring either a chip card or a charge number.

MasterCard sponsored smart card demonstrations in the United States between 1985 and 1987 and hoped to convert its magnetic stripe cards, but it was forced to abandon the plan when adequate cost/benefit could not be demonstrated. Smart cards still cost approximately $5 per card to manufacture and encode, versus 50 cents for regular plastic cards. The cost to convert the worldwide credit card infrastructure could exceed $2 billion, much of which would be the installation of several million chip-compatible terminals.

Thus, the challenge to the industry has been to find enough benefits to compensate for these high costs. The following ideas are among those that have been suggested:

1. Placement of the PIN securely enough on the card to eliminate today's inefficient signature verification system, preclude expensive on-line PIN verifications, and reduce fraud costs in a cost-effective way.
2. Reliance on dynamic, individually determinable transaction control parameters that would help reduce fraud, curb excessive cardholder activity, and control the burgeoning cost of on-line authorizations.
3. Capture and storage of transaction data, both for control and for record-keeping purposes. (For example, paper receipts could be eliminated and detailed data stored and retrieved with the aid of personal card-reading devices.)

4. Integration of nonfinancial data such as medical history, insurance requirements, hotel and airline reservations, frequent flier numbers, tickets, product warranties, and so on.
5. Reduction of some operating costs such as frequent card reissuance, paper-based card bulletins, and data entry of paper sales drafts.

To date, none of these potential uses has been shown to be profitable or cost-effective. Putting the PIN on the card in order to reduce fraud is the most easily implementable action, but it may not be needed. Bankcard fraud costs have already been controlled with current approaches to 0.1 percent of sales volume, which was approximately $183 million in 1988. No clear quantifications of the other potential uses have as yet been put forth.

Because implementing these potential uses would mean such fundamental and sweeping changes in the card utility, conversion is very likely to take place over a long period of time. By then, the costs and storage capabilities of cards and terminals may improve tremendously. When conversion does occur, it is likely to follow our themes: (1) Significant value will be created for the cardholder, and (2) the economics and profitability of competitors will be affected, not necessarily in a positive way.

CHALLENGES IN THE FUTURE

Currently, the credit/charge card business is one of the economic bright spots for the banking industry. Overall, the products are continuing to grow because issuers are coming up with new ways to create value. Further, a segment of customers is willing to pay very attractive spreads for credit and convenience. The fact that credit card transactions cost more to process than many alternatives—particularly checks—is not entirely relevant because credit cards have carved out a niche for certain transactions. In a word, consumers prefer to use credit/charge cards for many types of transactions. Systems technology has again been the enabler. It has been used across the business system, not just in the transactions component, to create this value. This widespread use has had an impact on virtually every aspect of the credit card business.

The challenge for all players will be to maintain the credit/charge card business as a bright spot. Any number of factors could seriously erode profits, ranging from a cyclical cost-of-funds increase to a sudden shift of power to merchants, which would allow them to reduce merchant discounts substantially. Growth in primary demand must eventually subside and the costs of credit losses, enhancements, and marketing must inevitably eat into margins. Consolidative pressures may easily become worse due to downturns in margins or the pressure of new entrants.

The solutions to these problems will require new strategies that meet evolving customer needs and will, of course, depend on systems technology to do that. Cardholder segmentation and micromarketing will probably be used widely and will demand order-of-magnitude increases in the ability to track and manipulate cardholder data. The goal of American Express's ambitious Genesis project—a $300 million plus investment to rewrite all its systems—is to change from a product orientation to a customer orientation. The increased amount of data to be provided will be costly to American Express but is viewed as worth the cost. New technology—such as EDC, scoring models, and integrated products—will offer opportunities to new competitors. In the end, those who best utilize technology to meet business needs will, as in other banking businesses, emerge as the eventual winners.

CHAPTER 6

WHOLESALE PAYMENT SYSTEMS

The part of the overall payment system that has been most heavily hit by automation is wholesale payments—services offered to corporations, governments, institutions, and financial service firms. Wholesale customers usually generate and receive such a high volume of payments that the proper management of these payments has spawned many interrelated services, including funds transfer, cash management, receivables and payables management, short-term investments, recurring payments (via the ACH), and sophisticated electronic reporting methods. (See Figure 6–1.)

The wholesale payments system has two tiers: one for high-value payments and the other for low-value payments. High-value payments (or payment instructions) flow through the three major interbank funds transfer systems: the Clearing House Interbank Payments System (CHIPS), the Society for Worldwide Financial Telecommunications (SWIFT), and Fedwire. These utilities are essential for the functioning of the world economy. For example, CHIPS and Fedwire each settle more than $700 billion each day, or about $375 trillion per year—roughly 7 times the value of all the assets of all the countries in the world. Although banks compete among themselves by providing access—or "windows"—to these settlement systems and by operating the auxiliary cash management services, all players have a stake in the continued successful functioning of these settlement systems. They contain elements that transcend competition.

Low-value payments flow through the checking system and, particularly for recurring payments, through the ACH. All wholesale payments are made from liability-based transaction accounts, many of which are specially designed for high-volume services. There is also a linkage with credit, as the funds transfer systems spawn enormous intra-day overdrafts either on banks' books or at the Federal Reserve Bank. As a result, most wholesale payment customers must have credit facilities with their banks to cover these exposures.

FIGURE 6–1
Wholesale Payments

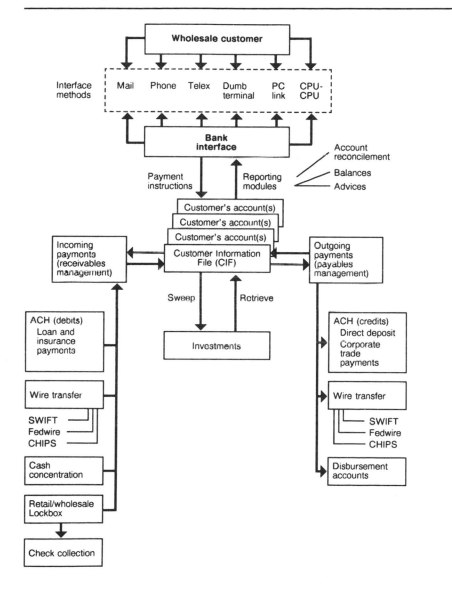

Because they are of high value, wholesale payments have become automated more quickly than have either individual payments or credit cards. SWIFT, CHIPS, and Fedwire are almost completely electronic, as is the ACH. Many cash management products, such as same-day balance reporting, are electronic. Also, the newest services, such as the treasurer's workstation, use software to integrate banking information directly with clients' internal accounting needs.

Precisely because so much automation has occurred, the economics of the wholesale payments business have deteriorated. Wholesale payments is now a marginally profitable or just breakeven business—in contrast to an earlier era when it was extremely profitable. In the cash management line of business, profits are approximately $100 million per year; in international funds transfer, losses are approximately $100 million; and domestic funds transfer is roughly breakeven. Because payment velocity has increased by an order of magnitude, float and balances have been reduced, overcapacity is rampant, and competitors' margins have come under severe pressure. Yet electronic wholesale payments do add substantial value for customers. *The story of technology in wholesale systems is truly one of value created and profit destroyed.*

FUNDS TRANSFER SYSTEMS

The banks' business of selling highly secure real-time payment services to their wholesale customers has a cost base of about $400 million. These payments, or the instructions about the payments, can travel through a number of channels. Many countries have emerging automated settlement systems—such as the United Kingdom's CHAPS, which settles sterling transactions. However, Fedwire, CHIPS, and SWIFT are the ones of greatest importance to U.S. commercial banks.

CHIPS and SWIFT are utilities that are both owned by and service their members. CHIPS is a private, "irrevocable" on-line payment network with enormous dollar volumes, but its transactions are not in fact settled until the end of the day. SWIFT is a multinational, multicurrency, interbank message system, handling more than 70 types of messages, although 80 percent of its transactions involve payments. Fedwire is owned by the Federal Reserve Bank. It not only handles messages, but it also settles for private networks, for the check clearing system, and for transfers of government book-entry securities. Only in Fedwire can final interbank dollar settlement occur.

FIGURE 6-2
Funds Transfer Networks, 1988 (millions of transactions)

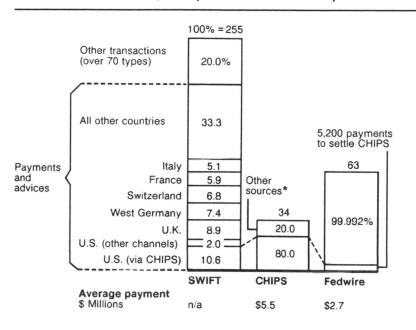

*Cable, telex, mail, etc.

A strong linkage exists between SWIFT and CHIPS, and between CHIPS and Fedwire. Approximately 80 percent of all CHIPS payments arise from instructions transmitted over SWIFT. (See Figure 6-2.) Although CHIPS handles a tremendous dollar volume, more than $700 billion per day, at the end of the day it actually settles by netting everything down on an interbank basis. Thus, CHIPS contributes only a minuscule fraction of the Fedwire transaction activity. But the dollar exposures at CHIPS are enormous and, combined with the Fedwire daylight overdrafts, have stimulated the Federal Reserve Bank to control overall cross-system risk.

The automation of these funds transfer systems has had a profound effect on global banking, the capital markets, and world trade. The speedup in the flow of money and the linking of what were once local or regional financial marketplaces were major economic trends of the 1980s and will continue in the 1990s. This technological linking process has had a profound effect in competition, pricing, and the financial interdependence of these markets. The old ways and profits of banking have been hurt because of float loss, overcapacity, and the U.S. banks' structural inability to rationalize, yet the new electronic payment systems benefit the financial markets immeasurably. This is a very clear illustration of how technology has created value for the users, while destroying profits for many of the providers.

Fedwire

Slightly more than 7,500 United States financial institutions are users of Fedwire. Each one has the power to enter or request payments, for itself or others, that are individually transmitted and settled immediately on the books of the Federal Reserve Bank. In effect, each member's reserves at the Federal Reserve Bank act as an interbank demand deposit account. In addition to specific payments (e.g., credits) for specific customer transactions, Fedwire handles requests for payments, service messages, and net settlements of private clearing systems. Fedwire also contains a separate system for settling trading in book-entry government securities.

The Federal Reserve Bank offers three levels of access to its computers, depending on transaction volume: direct CPU to CPU interface, direct access via remote terminal, and access via dial-up terminal. Naturally, the number of institutions connected electronically has grown dramatically: from approximately 700 on-line banks in 1979, to approximately 6,600 in 1988. Now that this Stage C automation (see again Figure 2–6) of the customer interface is almost complete, only the smallest, lowest-volume banks still generate written, telephoned, or telexed instructions to the Federal Reserve Bank—their volume constitutes only approximately 1 percent of all Federal Reserve Bank transactions. The main driver in the conversion to electronic transactions has been cost savings. The total price of a Fedwire to a bank customer is roughly $8.75 for an electronic transfer and $13.50 for a nonelectronic one.

How Speed-Up Creates Overdrafts

High payment volumes and electronic speeds have vastly increased the ratio of payment value to balance value, thus creating a problem unique to the electronic age: intra-day overdrafts. These can occur on the books of a sending bank when one of its customers requests that a payment be made before a covering payment comes in. In the event of customer failure, the bank is at risk. Overdrafts also occur at the Federal Reserve Bank for the same reason—only for much higher amounts. If a bank were to fail, the Federal Reserve Bank would be at risk.

Federal Reserve Bank overdrafts are exacerbated by (1) banks repaying Federal Reserve Funds loans in the morning before reborrowing the same amount at night, and (2) securities sellers building long positions during the day. The Federal Reserve Bank has never *required* United States depository institutions to maintain a positive balance during the day. In fact, banks have historically had little incentive to do so. Private payment networks such as CHIPS do not incur overdrafts per se but do incur intra-day "exposure" that in turn creates tremendous systemic risk. The network would be at risk if one participant were to fail during the day and could not settle.

By 1985, daylight overdrafts had become a major worry. One precipitating factor was the November 21, 1985, computer malfunction at the Bank of New York (BONY), which prevented it from sending out book-entry securities and effectively locked it into an enormous debit position. The Federal Reserve Bank was forced to make a $22.6 billion overnight loan to BONY—many times the size of its capital. This widely publicized event simply highlighted a particular example of the ongoing risk of exposure. The aggregate level of daylight overdrafts had reached approximately $50 billion per day for Fedwire (measured on a biweekly average), $50 billion for CHIPS, and another $35 billion for the government securities book-entry system.

Moves to Control Overdrafts

To control the level of daylight overdrafts, the Federal Reserve Bank instituted three new control policies in March, 1986:

- All private, large-dollar transfer networks (especially CHIPS) were required to establish bilateral net credit limits between each participant pair and net debit caps for each participant.
- Cross-system sender net debit caps were established for all private network or Federal Reserve Bank participants.
- A limit was placed on the size of securities transfers (currently $50 million).

To implement the cross-system net debit caps the Federal Reserve Bank developed a policy of self-assessment. Banks were allowed to set their own caps based on balance sheet strength as well as their perception of their own operational and technological capability. (With time, the Federal Reserve Bank will probably tighten its technological requirements and introduce more standardization into the assessment process.)

This policy has been relatively successful, holding the nominal value of cross-system overdrafts constant at approximately $80 billion per day as total payment values continue to climb. The ratio of Fedwire overdrafts per dollar transferred dropped from 10 percent in 1986 to 8 percent in 1987. Also, the number of banks incurring overdrafts in each two-week period dropped from 3,600 to approximately 3,100. Although the self-assessment criteria were purposely designed to accommodate each bank's existing payment patterns (e.g., banks with 84 percent of the overdraft volume assessed their capacity as "high" or "above average"), it is also true that only four institutions exceeded their cap in a recent quarter. The Federal Reserve Bank cut the caps again in 1988, but most banks had no trouble complying. Among large United States banks and United States offices of foreign banks, which together account for 80 percent of all overdrafts, cap usage averaged only 40 percent.

Future Developments

To control overdrafts in the future, the Federal Reserve Bank will probably take some or all of the following actions:

1. Encouraging some form of settlement finality for the private networks (to reduce systemic risk);
2. Supporting term or multiday Federal Reserve Bank funding as a replacement for chronic rollovers of Federal Reserve Bank funds;
3. Encouraging legally enforceable netting by novation (as is done in the London forward foreign exchange market);
4. Charging a fee for overdrafts, thus giving banks an incentive to control them; and
5. Establishing liquidity reserves at private networks.

Any or all of the above developments would raise the costs of the computer systems that are required to participate in the funds transfer business. Automated monitoring and control systems would be required so that each bank can track its own position. Large banks would develop (as some already have developed) systems to monitor their customers' overdrafts. Pricing of overdrafts and the concomitant development ("priority payments") would require new applications software to track all payments and assign them to pricing categories.

The net effect of these developments should be a gradual movement toward more concentration among the banks that are in the business of making funds transfers for institutional customers. Overcapacity would cause price drops, and netting would further exacerbate the overcapacity by reducing the volume of payments. But not enough concentration would occur to make Fedwire a particularly profitable business—as long as every bank belongs to Fedwire and the industry contains so many banks.

The bottom line is that profits can be elusive when an electronic utility, such as Fedwire, serves so many banks. Little distinctiveness is possible when a bank makes payments via Fedwire. At the same time, of course, access to Fedwire is virtually mandatory. The issues with overdrafts simply illustrate that payments flow much faster in an electronic world, reducing the level of balances that participants will choose to devote to transaction accounts. Not only does this create its own problem (i.e., systemic risk), it destroys the old economics of the business, which were very dependent on a high level of excess balances. Banks need to adjust pricing so that it reflects either transaction volumes or intra-day extensions of credit, or both.

Clearing House Interbank Payments System (CHIPS)

CHIPS is a private network opened in 1970 by the New York Clearing House Association (NYCHA). It is 100 percent on-line and real-time. CHIPS plays a unique role in international finance, handling more than 90 percent of all United States dollars transferred between countries. Because the dollar is the *lingua franca* of international finance, CHIPS is very, very important. By 1988, 139 banks, including most of the world's major banks, were participating (42 United States and 97 foreign). Each participant must have a bank or agency in New York City from which all payments are entered.

CHIPS payments arise largely from financial transactions—including loans, foreign exchange sales, Eurodollar placements, Eurosecurities settlements, and sales of short-term funds—rather than international trade. Payments can arrive at CHIPS from all over the world directly through member banks or via correspondent banks. CHIPS exchanges payments but does not settle. Once payments are released, they are irrevocable in the sense that unilateral reversal is impossible. But settlement does not occur until the end of each day on the books of the Federal Reserve Bank. Foreign banks, which cannot join the Federal Reserve Bank, settle through one of CHIP's 11 clearing house banks, which have the authority to settle for others. In essence, nothing happens during the day except bookkeeping—until settlement occurs.

Controlling Risk

Failure to settle (e.g., because of an intra-day failure of a bank) could be catastrophic. CHIPS has a three-phase plan to cope with this possibility: First, extra time would be allowed to find funds or loans to cover the exposure; second, just the transactions of the nonsettling participant would be reversed; and third, all transactions would be unwound and would be up for reconsideration. The second phase and especially the third phase could cause other banks to fail, which leads to the concern over systemic risk. To control this risk, CHIPS has put in place bilateral credit limits between each pair of banks and a net debit cap for each sender. These actions have contained CHIPS's total intra-day exposure at a constant level of approximately $45 billion, which is less than 8 percent of the payment volume. However, CHIPS is introducing further measures because the unwinding process described above is no longer considered viable and has fortunately never been needed. CHIPS wants to ensure settlement finality by creating a formula for risk-sharing in the event of a failure and by requiring participants to post adequate liquid collateral at the Federal Reserve Bank.

Competition and Economics

There has often been a concern that CHIPS volumes would concentrate in too few hands. The largest CHIPS volumes are in fact generated by the big players in international correspondent banking. (See Figure 6–3.) But the statistics on transaction share given in Figure 6–3 illustrate that concentration is not currently occurring. In 1988, niche and small players gained share, reinforcing the long-term trend for more banks to participate directly in CHIPS. The specific reasons for share changes can vary. Chemical Bank's foreign exchange trading volume was down in 1988, for example, which reduced its share, and J.P. Morgan discontinued its European securities operations, reducing its share. Some players were driven by noneconomic factors, such as a desire to be perceived as a global player, and some large players with relatively weaker balance sheets may have reduced their share to help control their exposure.

FIGURE 6–3
CHIPS Market Share

Share of Transactions, 1988

100% = 34 million

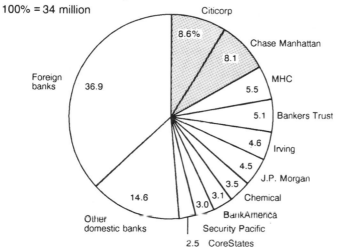

Change in Share, 1987-1988

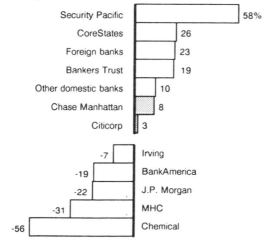

Because electronic technology is so efficient, funneling international payments through CHIPS is not, in itself, a high-revenue business. CHIPS charges only 29 cents per qualified transaction no matter how many millions are involved. A typical charge to a participating bank's customer is only a few dollars. Because stand-alone profitability is difficult to demonstrate, banks do it mostly as part of a comprehensive relationship. The benefits have traditionally been the compensating balances.

Beginning in 1980, however, compensating balances began to decline. For example, the total aggregate balances left by international banks at the top eight United States correspondent banks, which control 75 percent of the business, dropped from $7.6 billion in 1981, to $4.2 billion in 1986. This was also a period of declining interest rates, so that the value of these balances dropped by more than 70 percent—from $1.1 billion in 1981, to $250 million in 1986. Banks did not react fast enough and the operating earnings in international funds transfer went from $922 million in 1981, to a loss of $30 million in 1986. (See Figure 6–4.)

Technology was a principal causal factor in this decline. In 1981, CHIPS's systems investments enabled it to move from next-day settlement to same-day settlement. A correspondent bank could now handle more transactions with a given amount of balances or the same number of transactions with fewer balances. At the same time, electronic reporting of same-day balances was making the money center banks' correspondent customers much better informed. The result was that customers managed down their excess balances substantially. The money center banks reacted by moving to more explicit fee-based pricing, but because of poor cost accounting systems and high shared overheads, progress was slow.

By 1988, this downward trend had reversed somewhat, but is unlikely to ever regain the high levels of the early 1980s. However, the decline did cause some of the majors to rethink their approach. Some banks, such as Citibank, Chase Manhattan, and Bankers Trust, made the decision to stay in the international funds transfer game and compete aggressively. Based on their specific customer mix, pricing, and cost accounting conventions, these leaders may even view this as a profitable business. Others, such as J.P. Morgan and Chemical Bank, did not invest in additional capacity; their market share stabilized or began to decline. Still others, such as CoreStates and Security Pacific, began to compete as niche suppliers, not as high-volume producers.

The overall conclusion is that CHIPS, acting as a Type 2 (see again Figure 3–5) shared network, has equalized some of the competition, and

FIGURE 6–4
Top 8 U.S. Correspondents' Operating Earnings by Business

International Funds Transfer ($ Millions)

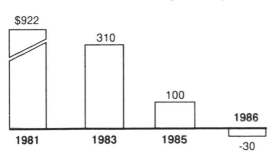

Domestic Funds Transfer ($ Millions)

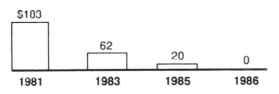

Check Collection ($ Millions)

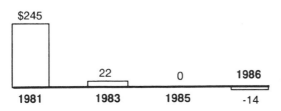

access to it may well become defensive, not distinctive. Once again, the development of an electronic payment system has hurt the profits of some banks that depended on the float and balances of the old, paper-based system.

Society for Worldwide Financial Telecommunications (SWIFT)

SWIFT is a worldwide utility that transmits messages electronically between banks. The service began in May, 1977, and volume reached 255 million messages by 1988—a 25 percent CAGR. To support continued growth, SWIFT is planning for volumes of 1.5 million or more per day in 1990. By early 1989, there were more than 1,600 members, mostly banks, with approximately 3,000 endpoints; 160 of the member banks and 350 of the endpoints were in the United States. Originally restricted to banks, approved categories of members now include securities firms, exchanges, and clearing and depository institutions.

With few exceptions, SWIFT's reach extends into all developed and newly emerging countries. Even the Soviet Union, East Germany, Czechoslovakia, Hungary, and China are included. Both Israel and Arab countries such as Iran, Egypt, and Jordan are on the network. SWIFT has a truly unifying international presence. However, traffic is concentrated among the countries with financial centers. The United States, United Kingdom, and West Germany generate 36 percent of all SWIFT traffic.

Benefits
Prior to SWIFT's implementation, interbank messages were generally sent by telex, cable, and mail or over proprietary telecommunications networks. These methods could be slow, were sometimes expensive, and offered no guarantees that the message was received correctly. Even worse, data had to be reentered whenever a message was received, and there were no standard formats for messages. SWIFT's success is due to its elimination of these problems.

The original purpose of SWIFT was to transmit payment instructions/advices, which still constitute 80 percent of all its messages. Because SWIFT carries the instructions only, the payment is always effected elsewhere—on the books of a correspondent bank, through CHIPS, or via another clearing network. Over time, SWIFT has expanded to include more than 70 message types, including foreign exchange transactions, collections, securities trades, documentary credits, statements, and netting. In addition, a SWIFT subsidiary sells terminals and software and operates a value-added network that performs services such as European Currency Unit (ECU) netting. The society also has a joint venture with software vendor I.P. Sharp that markets a global risk management system.

SWIFT message types are completely standardized, so much so that SWIFT absorbs the financial risk if a message is mistransmitted. SWIFT's standards have become the de facto standards for all international bank messages and are increasingly used within banks for internal messages. As a result, the interfaces between banks and SWIFT, and between CHIPS and SWIFT are now largely automated. In other words, SWIFT is a Stage C development in our transaction automation framework (see again Figure 2-6.) SWIFT has automated the interbank customer interface.

Competition
Unfortunately, the same set of results has occurred: the economics of some banks have been hurt, especially those competing directly with SWIFT. SWIFT's costs to transmit a message are generally low—about 50 cents to send a message anywhere in the world. Thus, it tends to draw off the bulk of the applicable traffic wherever it is available. Although proprietary networks have been hurt, they are still used by the largest global banks for internal purposes and for correspondent messages that lie outside SWIFT's domain.

SWIFT is a Type 2 (see again Figure 3-5) competitor that has changed the nature of competition in the international correspondent banking business. Its low costs and extended business initiatives have become a threat to certain money center banks. Several Type 1 U.S. money centers that had built global telecommunications networks could not use all of their capacity. Their correspondents, which are Type 4 players, increasingly opted to use SWIFT. SWIFT now has more capacity than any single bank and has concomitant economies of scale, giving it a cost advantage. Banks that continue to invest in worldwide networks for correspondent banking are playing a high-risk/high-reward game. Differentiation in services is necessary to attract business, yet the economics of competing with SWIFT are difficult. Only a few major banks may be able to do so successfully.

In summary, automation of the world's major funds transfer networks has had far-reaching effects on the business of wholesale banking. Although these networks are efficient from a cost perspective, they hurt many of the same players who depend on them. Speedup, balance reduction, and collective overcapacity have made the funds transfer business more difficult. At the same time, these electronic funds transfer networks are utilities that are, and will remain, open to many players. In the long run, with the costs of technology dropping, wide access to these utilities seems assured.

CASH MANAGEMENT

Cash management services meet customers' needs for receivables and payables management and for investment of short-term funds. An estimated 600 U.S. banks provide some or all of these services, creating a business with about $2 billion to $3 billion in yearly revenues. Along with funds transfer and checking, cash management is the major back-office service sold by banks to wholesale customers. Specific services include cash concentration, wholesale and retail lockbox, disbursement accounts, check collection, check and account reconcilement, and access to short-term investments.

Cash management customers are concentrated among the largest U.S. corporations — approximately 80 percent of the Fortune 1000 companies use one or more cash management services. They reap the benefits of the technology, as cash management services constantly improve. Because of better reporting over electronic networks and the gradual consolidation of bank regions, major customers are slowly reducing the number of banks they use for cash management. The average for a corporate customer dropped from nine to eight in the 1980s. The most attractive customers (sales over $4 billion) now use 10 banks, on average, instead of 13. Consequently, the customers are in the driver's seat as consolidative pressures squeeze the margins and cash management banks scramble to keep up.

Cash management involves a complex mixture of new electronic technology and older paper-based systems. Electronics are on the ascendancy, although the bulk of the payments is still made by check. The fastest-growing products, such as daily cash balance reporting, tend to be electronic. *As a rule, this trend toward automation has hurt providers' profits more, through speedup and reduced float, than it has helped them by cutting costs.* Banks more than doubled their explicit cash management fees between 1980 and 1987, as they attempted to compensate for their lost balances. But, at the same time, margins were declining. Overcapacity kept prices low while, on the cost side, continued systems investments were required. Some providers have consolidated, but not enough.

Approximately 50 percent of all cash management banks still view the product as a "service" that attracts lending business, rather than as a profit center. As a result, so many banks price the product incrementally or even below cost that the overall level of profitability is marginal even for the profit center competitors.

Receivables Management/Lockbox

Managing receivables requires collecting and/or concentrating a customer's funds as quickly as possible. Speedy processing of checks is needed to maximize availability. Specific products include lockboxes, preauthorized drafts, depository checks (DTCs), and preauthorized debits through the ACH. Concentration means moving a customer's funds from scattered locations to a centralized point for better control or higher returns from short-term investment.

Lockbox is the primary paper-based cash management service. Between 4 and 6 billion checks are received yearly in lockboxes, generating revenues of approximately $600 million per year. Banks pick checks up directly at special postoffice boxes—sometimes 20 times per day. Using specialized machinery and systems technologies, the lockbox operator opens the remittance envelopes as fast as possible, encodes the checks, captures the remittance data, and releases the checks into the check collection system. A lockbox can save from two to six days of float for the depositor, the value of which depends on the magnitude of deposits and the level of interest rates. For example, an insurance company receiving checks worth $300 million yearly could gain $500,000 per year with a lockbox.

The lockbox business has two very different subsegments. Retail lockbox ($200 million in revenue) is a low-margin business that many banks have exited. Wholesale lockbox ($400 million in revenue) has kept its margins higher because of the value-added tailoring required. In retail lockbox, high volumes of payments mailed by individuals need fast, standardized processing. For example, utility, loan, or mortgage checks are accompanied by a remittance coupon that explains where the funds should be credited, what time period they cover and the expected payment amount. The coupon is usually read by high-speed scanners employing optical character recognition (OCR) technology. Labor is needed for the check-encoding function and for balancing and exception handling. Because the payment amounts are low, the key criteria for competition is low unit costs. In wholesale lockbox, however, nonstandard remittances are received from corporate payers or from affiliates or branches of the payee. The check values are high, and long advices may accompany each check with details of what the check covers (and does not cover). Each payment must be individually handled, often with the aid of image processing, and the customer needs more tailored processing and reporting. Collection speed is a more important competitive weapon than unit processing cost.

Technology and Competition

Lockbox competitors have increased their overall effectiveness by moving the lockbox itself as close as possible to the point where the payer mails the check. This cuts the payee's mail float to a minimum. Depending on the volumes and locations of mail origination, a large customer could choose between multiple lockbox banks, a one-bank proprietary lockbox network or a lockbox utility.

Customers have preferred lockbox networks in recent years, and approximately 30 percent of the Fortune 1000 companies now use one. First Chicago's lockbox network, for example, has its own zip codes in Newark, Atlanta, Chicago, Dallas, and Los Angeles. National retail lockbox customers might be tempted by the U.S. Post Office's Accelerated Reply Mail (ARM) program, in which mail displaying special zip codes is held up at 220 postal centers and picked up by agent banks. Several major customers have already signed up with National Remittance Centers, a private firm that arranges for checks to be truncated by the ARM program and transmitted to the bank of deposit by wire. This is another example of a nonbank processing company biting off a piece of the payment system front end.

Despite the automation requirements and unfavorable economic pressure, the lockbox business is not yet unduly concentrated. There is still a local flavor to it because so many remittances (e.g., for a local phone company) are mailed and processed in one city. Worse, many banks process remittances for their own purposes (e.g., for credit card payments) and view lockbox, at least retail lockbox, as a low-cost source of incremental revenue. For example, the largest retail lockbox player, Mellon, has only a 3 percent share of the market.

In the long run, the lockbox business is living on borrowed time. Although checks will not disappear soon, today's volume of 50 billion checks will almost surely stop increasing and start decreasing during the 1990s. The influence of the ACH, corporate trade payments, POS/ debit, and home banking products should cause this to happen. However, all it takes is a downturn in volumes for the margins of a high fixed-cost processing business to get squeezed even worse than they already are. What are marginally profitable businesses may easily turn outright unprofitable. This is what happened to banks in the stock transfer business when stock certificates became immobilized. So the long-term prognosis for lockbox is not favorable, but receivables management will stay around — in electronic form. The challenge for banks will be to make that transition.

Payables Management

Managing payables requires a variety of disbursement products to meet the needs of wholesale customers. Controlled disbursement services make payment, generally by check, on the last day before a penalty is incurred or a discount lost. The payers are playing the float game. Remote disbursement aims at the same objective by writing checks drawn on remote clearing locations. Although remote disbursement was popular at one time, many banks no longer market this service actively. Collection has become too fast and too standardized in recent years as the Federal Reserve Bank squeezes float out of the system. Corporate treasurers now care more about the information they receive, and they find that dealing with one bank is far easier. Only 13 percent of major paying corporations now split their endpoints.

A more attractive product today is zero balance disbursement accounts. These products maximize funds control by allowing the customer to write checks on special no-balance accounts. Funds are kept centrally and each day only enough is deposited to cover that day's clearings.

Disbursement is one part of the cash management business that still enjoys higher-than-average margins. Most customers have set up more accounts than they need and have allowed a residual level of balances to stay in them. But these easy profits are diminishing, again because of automation. Electronic reporting has given the customer a better ability to understand and reduce the balance levels. For example, the aggregate level of float in the U.S. corporate check collection system dropped from $7 billion in 1980, to approximately $0.5 billion in 1985, and much of this came out of disbursement accounts.

The net result is that cash management products, like so many others, have lost much of their former profitability as they become automated. Competition is still tight, yet too many banks have stayed in the business. Some do not know their own costs and some do not have the proper incentives because cash management is not treated as a stand-alone profit center. The situation bears out the subtitle of this book: the *customers* have gained the benefit that cash management offers. Control over funds is far better and the real cost to customers of moving funds should be far less. Yet the profits of those banks that remained dependent on float and balances were hurt. Overcapacity resulted, preventing enough implementation of transaction pricing. The net result is another difficult business.

THE AUTOMATED CLEARING HOUSE (ACH)

The ACH is the first, and so far the only, electronic payment system to carry any significant number of recurring payments. In this sense, it can be called a success. Since it was begun in 1973, the ACH has increased its payment volumes approximately 20 percent each year, reaching 1.4 billion transactions in 1988 and generating approximately $40 million in sales. The national ACH system is a confederation of 42 local and regional clearinghouses (i.e., bank associations) that clear transactions in their areas. One national organization, National Association of Clearing House Associations (NACHA), sets national policy. Most processing of ACH transactions is done by the Federal Reserve Bank. Three western clearinghouses use Visa as a processor; the New York Clearing House Association does its own processing; and one bank, Chase Manhattan, operates a proprietary ACH.

The customers for ACH services are the originating institutions. More than 60 percent of the Fortune 1000 companies now use the ACH in one form or another; in fact, it is the fastest-growing cash management service. As a consequence, thousands of banks belong to the ACH system and can originate and receive payments. The largest ACH originator is Chase Manhattan, with about a 5 percent market share, closely followed by Bank of America. Chase Manhattan's proprietary ACH allows it to bypass its local clearinghouse for endpoints outside the Second Federal Reserve District. This gives Chase Manhattan a cost advantage estimated at several mills per item.

Benefits and Growth

Although ACH volumes are far lower than the volume of checks, it is undeniable that *some* checks are being displaced, and that even more will be in the next few years. For example, only 15 to 20 percent of all employees are now paid by direct deposit (through the ACH) rather than by paycheck. The Social Security Administration pioneered this application for social security payments and has been quite successful with it. It seems inevitable that the penetration of direct deposit will grow. It is obviously beneficial to employees, giving them faster availability and eliminating an unnecessary trip to the bank. In fact, 46 percent of the Fortune 1000 companies now offer direct deposit and the NACHA is planning to begin advertising the benefits of direct deposit.

Corporate customers should also see benefits from the ACH. Potential benefits include reduction of expenses such as check printing costs, postage costs, and check reconcilement costs. Exact cash disbursement schedules for personnel are possible. There is a negative (a loss of float), but, as we have already seen, float is diminishing anyway as a major factor in the corporate treasurer's world.

However, payment systems always change slowly. Even at its current 20 percent per year growth rate, the ACH volume will not reach 10 percent of the check volume level until 1995. But this is progress of a sort; no other electronic system for recurring payments even comes close.

A further stimulant to growth is that the ACH can now handle a wider variety of payment types. Originally its scope was limited to checks written or received in the home. These types of payments—paychecks, insurance premiums, loan or mortgage payments, and dividend or pension payments—still constitute approximately 90 percent of all ACH transactions. But creative new applications are constantly being added. At an ACH conference in 1988, Exxon claimed to use the ACH in 15 different ways, ranging from POS to direct deposit. In 1987, Northern Trust, the Midwest's leader in ACH volume, offered an interrailroad car leasing payment product based on the ACH. As discussed in Chapter 4, some budding POS programs use the ACH. Through such efforts, the ACH volumes should eventually reach a critical mass that will begin to reduce the volume of checks.

Limitations Keep Costs Low

The ACH does have some technical and conceptual limitations. It is a *batch* payment system designed only for recurring flows between one wholesale originator of transactions and many recipients. Settlement is next-day. Originators of debits (or credits) must know and maintain both the bank number and account number of each recipient. Originators must have some way to receive communications from recipients regarding amount or account changes and some way to resolve problems. Typically, the amount, value date, and reason for debit/credit are also passed with each item. A preauthorization (a zero-amount transaction) is required to establish the existence of each new receiving account. Transactions must be submitted in advance of the value date. The overall approach is a far cry from a realtime on-line system, such as the ATM and POS/debit systems, but is also a reason why ACH costs are so low.

For an ACH transaction the Federal Reserve Bank charges only 2 to 3 cents, and Visa charges 0.95 cents — compared to an incremental cost of approximately 10 cents for a check. Because this unit cost has a high fixed-cost component, it should decline even further as volume expands. Furthermore, the ACH system is not yet totally electronic. Returns and exceptions processing are still done manually, and many submissions still rely on mailing or physically delivering a magnetic tape. The New York ACH was one of the first to forbid paper return items and movement of physical media starting in 1990. As technological improvements occur, the costs of the ACH should come down even further.

Corporate Trade Payments (CTP and CTX)

Approximately 20 billion checks per year could be displaced by the existing ACH technology. This is the number of checks written by individuals in the home for recurring purposes (12 billion) or written by corporations to individuals on a recurring basis (8 billion). This is a significant market — about 40 percent of all checks. Another 10 billion checks are written from one wholesale customer to another and could be diverted to the ACH if its technology were modified enough to handle the different needs of corporate trade payments.

The first effort to extend the ACH in this complementary direction was a new payment format, called CTP, that was developed by the Federal Reserve Bank in the early 1980s. It could accommodate up to 5,000 semifixed message records of 94 characters each. A wholesale payer making a wholesale payment could theoretically list strings of invoice numbers or adjustments to go with the payment—the type of detailed information usually sent on a thick printout with an intercorporate check. But for technical reasons, the CTP format was not desirable. It was not in line with corporations' growing use of the ANSI X.12 standards for intercorporate exchange of electronic data.

In 1986, the Federal Reserve announced that the ill-fated CTP was being superseded by CTX, an improved technology that employed fully variable record formats and was compatible with the ANSI X.12 data content standards. The first CTX payments were processed in early 1988 for the proprietary General Motors electronic data interchange (EDI) network.

Electronic Data Interchange (EDI)

EDI is a companion development to CTP. It consists of the electronic transmission of information, such as invoices or orders, between business units. It is a fledgling concept today but holds great future potential for eliminating paper from a wide variety of transactions. The issue for banks is whether the future evolution of electronic payments can give them a role in the EDI business. Given the overwhelming volume of orders, invoices, bills, inventory listings, price quotes, request for proposals (RFPs), and other paper documents that travel back and forth between businesses, payments are only a small chunk of the pie. Already, the leading vendors of EDI have invested more than $50 million in this fledgling business and are out drumming up more business. These leading vendors are those who already control value-added telecommunications networks, such as GEISCO, McDonnell Douglas, Telenet, and IBM.

Few banks are on this list of EDI players, and for good reason. The electronic segments of the payment system are often penetrated by nonbanks, for instance in the electronic draft capture of credit card transactions described at the end of Chapter 5. It is even more reasonable that nonbanks will dominate an EDI business which is not even a direct part of the payment system. Moreover, the business demands skills and capabilities that most banks do not have. EDI will probably evolve as an industry-specific set of networks whose required skills go far beyond banking.

Yet there is a distinct overlap between EDI and the corporate trade payment business. To make these payments, information must be passed that explains the payment. If details go on other EDI channels, there must be reference information passed with the payment. Banks might do well to consider partnering with EDI providers or developing an industry-wide EDI clearing cooperative. Enough Type 2 (see again Figure 3–5) players (i.e., shared networks) have emerged in other businesses to indicate the potential for one to form here, too. One bank, CoreStates, has already begun EDI pilot projects with selected customers, although there is no obvious payoff for them yet.

The bottom line is that banks should approach EDI with caution. Like the other new technologies, corporate trade payments and EDI will probably offer great benefits for the users. Profit payoffs will only accrue to some players who have the right skills and can offer differentiated services.

AUTOMATED CUSTOMER INTERFACE

On-line networks now allow information to flow between the bank and its customer in electronic form. This automated customer interface has had a tremendous impact on the wholesale payments business. Information delivery has been speeded up and the quality and range of the products has become much greater.

Customer interfaces have three broad components: modules to *report* balance/transaction data and investment information, *decision support* packages to analyze both bank-supplied and customer-supplied data, and transaction (or instruction) *initiation*. These function as follows:

- *Reporting*: Reporting is a classic case of systems technology creating more customer value and proliferating the available services. Customers can now choose (and pay for) previous-day ledger and available balances, balance histories, previous-day debits and credits (summarized and in detail), payment advices, integration of activity from multiple accounts, current-day debit/credits and balances, DTC reports, lockbox reports, commercial paper reports, securities transaction reports, FX exposure reports, FX netting reports, domestic money market rate reports, short-term investment status reports, letter of credit status reports, and even economic investment reports. Those using disbursement accounts can receive check reconcilement reports, account reconcilement reports, and daily clearing reports. Because so many wholesale customers use multiple banks, the reporting of multibank aggregates is yet another purchasable activity. This deluge of report options has not been all bad. Many banks have been able to price their reporting services attractively enough to reflect the value provided.

- *Decision Support*: To handle this flood of information, wholesale customers need automated tools. Cash management banks now offer software packages that assist the corporate treasurer. These packages target balance analysis, cash flow projections analysis, and debt and investment analysis. They also manipulate the bank's and the customer's data, using PCs or minicomputers. They can be purchased on a stand-alone basis or integrated with the customer's other systems.

- *Initiations*: Of course, the automated customer interface supports information flow in both directions. Customers can now initiate or amend instructions for preprogrammed repetitive money transfers, random money transfers, letter of credit processing, issuance of commercial paper, purchase orders for securities, and FX transactions. In fact, this "outboarding" of data entry, wherein the customer absorbs the costs of manual effort, has been encouraged by wholesale bankers for the same reasons that retail bankers support ATMs. The results have not been too dissimilar: the customers get all the benefits and the bankers' economic margins are squeezed because too many banks build too many systems.

The Electronic Window and the Treasurer's Workstation

Naturally, most large customers—the type who use cash management—also use other bank services such as loans, leases, letters of credit, and so on. The automated interface extends into these areas as well. To accomplish this, the advanced "Electronic Window," which dates from 1986, gathers information on many products and delivers it to the customer. In addition, it provides delivery and exchange of integrated data from all of a customer's banks. The even newer, integrated "Treasury Workstation" is a microcomputer-based system that combines cash management with payroll accounting, management of accounts receivables and payables, and general ledger functions. It is geared toward the middle to upper corporate market.

MHC has been successful in selling its Treasurer's Workstation product, called Interplex, as a technology product that is not directly related to whether or not the client uses MHC for its wholesale payments. One of the remaining major vendors in a business that has rapidly shrunk, MHC has placed roughly 400 workstations globally, generating $10 to $15 million in sales. The product will support any bank's formats and allows the user to consolidate different banks' proprietary on-line terminals into one PC. Much of Interplex's utility is in intracorporate chores, such as placing general ledger codes on transactions and communicating them to corporate accounting.

The business has been tough, despite the generally believed attractiveness of the market. Even among the largest players in cash management (Bank of America, Citibank, First Chicago, Chase Manhattan, and Mellon), no more than 30 percent of the customer base has taken a treasury workstation, despite the growth of automated interactions. However, MHC has achieved a relatively high share (32 percent) of those Fortune 100 companies in New York that have a Treasurer's Workstation.

A relatively rare example of a bank successfully selling its own technology comes from Chemical Bank. Beginning in 1980, Chemical Bank licensed its own cash management product under the name BankLink. By 1989, it had 65 domestic and 15 international licensees serving approximately 13,000 corporate end-users. Holding a license enables a bank (typically in the $1 to $25 billion range) to offer cash management and reporting services to its own customers – but with very little investment. Instead, the BankLink licensee's customer dials up GEISCO, The BankLink processor, to receive daily balance and transaction data that has been culled from the licensee's DDA and funds transfer systems. GEISCO plays the role of processor because of its low-cost, high-volume, value-added network.

Chemical Bank originally built and still controls the software, and it performs the sales, product management, and customer service functions. This arrangement has been so successful that usage grew at more than 25 percent annually during the mid-1980s. However, as customers get big, they may leave. (For example, First Wachovia recently discontinued BankLink in order to develop its own, more differentiable service.) The evolving nature of the business means that Chemical Bank will need to keep adding value to retain its customers.

These two success stories illustrate that not every bank has to lose when the customer interface reaches the stage of automation. Both Chemical Bank and MHC used a fresh approach and succeeded – although it is not clear whether either institution has generated very substantial earnings for these innovative technological services. But when hundreds of banks maintain paper-based wholesale customer interfaces and the business automates, it is obvious that not all can make the requisite systems investments. Staying away from losing investments in automating and consolidating businesses is what so few banks have been able to do.

SUMMARY

The wholesale payments business has reached a higher level of automation than the retail payments businesses. As such, the wholesale payments arena is the best illustration of the two themes of this book: creation of value and destruction of profits. Wholesale customers of banks have gained immeasurably in their control of their money. They now make more payments, faster and more securely, and know more about their bank account than they ever did in the paper-based world. They have more choice, more flexibility, and more power. They have more data that may help them in other parts of their business and in gaining the upper hand against the banks.

For the banks that compete in wholesale payments, it is the opposite side of the coin. Margins are constantly under pressure because of overcapacity. Recurring rounds of investment in technology are met by too many noneconomically driven players. The loss of balances and float has hurt. Many competitors keep their heads above water, but the endemic protection of the banking industry prevents more competitors from dropping out. It is telling that some of the oldest paper-based products, such as disbursement accounts, are the most profitable. The most technologically advanced areas—such as funds transfer, the ACH, and the electronic window—are where the margins have been squeezed the most.

The bottom line is that the inevitable automation of the wholesale payments business has not been the boon to profitability banks once thought it would be. Efficiency and speed is much greater, of course, but as the experience with CHIPS and SWIFT show, *efficiencies do not automatically create profits for bank competitors.* In fact, we believe, the reverse is more likely the result. Banking business systems change with automation, and so does the industry structure. Only those who can foresee these business-related developments are going to profit from their technology-related investments.

In Chapter 10, we will set out what we think banks need to do to perform well in the new technological era. Most of our recommendations apply in spades to the wholesale payments business. Banks need to focus on a few business lines where distinctive offerings are possible. They should consider industry capacity when making investment decisions about systems and they should link business strategy more tightly with technological reality. We believe that it is good advice for banks' top management—for now and for the future.

CHAPTER 7

THE TRUST AND SECURITIES BUSINESSES

The trust and securities businesses are important factors in the operating performance of the nation's large banks. We estimate that the 35 large banks accounted for 70 percent of the industry's operating expenses for trust and securities. Thus, these businesses consume approximately 10 percent of the total operating expenses of the large banks.

These businesses exhibit a wide range of operating performance. For example, a strong performer with a high market share and a favorable cost structure, in an endemically strong industry such as dealers clearance, may earn $20 million or more a year, yielding a 50 percent pretax margin. A participant with high market share but poor cost structure in an endemically weak industry, such as institutional securities safekeeping, may lose $15 million annually. Thus, any one of these businesses may contribute to, or degrade, a bank's aggregate ROE. (See Figure 7–1.)

Trust and securities businesses fall into three broad categories: (1) personal trust, (2) investment management, and (3) a range of other processing businesses such as mutual fund processing, master trust, and stock transfer. An examination of these businesses as discrete product areas is necessary to understand their operational and profit dynamics and to see how these factors are affected by technology. Not only is the process of conversion from paper to electronic processing proceeding at a different pace across these businesses, which have apparently few back-office synergies among them, but also the competitive characteristics of each are unique. Figure 7–2 summarizes where each of these businesses stands in this conversion process.

FIGURE 7–1
Characteristics of Trust and Securities Businesses

	Strong performer		Weak performer	
Endemically strong business	Pretax earnings ($ Millions)	Pretax profit margins (Percent)	Pretax earnings ($ Millions)	Pretax profit margins (Percent)
Personal trust	$ 3	15%	B/E*	B/E
Institutional investment management	10	20	B/E	B/E
Processing-based services				
Mutual fund processing	20	30	-$5	-30%
Master Trust	20	25	B/E	B/E
Dealers clearance	20	50	15	25
Endemically weak business				
Processing-based services				
Institutional securities safekeeping	B/E	B/E	-$10	-20%
Stock transfer	$ 5	5%	- 10	-22

*B/E: Break-even

PERSONAL TRUST

The personal trust business is especially large and is highly fragmented. Mellon Bank, the market share leader, had personal trust assets of approximately $11 billion, or 2.5 percent of the market in 1988. Assets under management in 1987 totaled approximately $446 billion, yielding estimated revenues of about $2 billion and profits of about $300 million. This business is among the least systems-intensive of the trust and securities businesses, as illustrated by the fact that systems account for an estimated 10 percent (or less) of annual operating expenditures.

FIGURE 7–2
Line of Business Perspective—Trust and Securities

	Profitability	Systems intensity	Degree of concentration	Stage of conversion from paper to electronic
Personal trust	M	M	L	Mid
Institutional investment management	M	L	M	Early
Processing-based services				
Mutual fund processing	H	H	H	End
Master Trust	H	M	M	Mid
Institutional securities safekeeping	L	H	H	End
Dealers clearance	H	H	H	End
Stock transfer	L	M	M	End

L: Low   M: Medium   H: High

The personal trust business consists of six primary product lines:

1. Living Trust, where the bank acts as trustee of trusts established during a grantor's lifetime,
2. Testamentary Trust, in which the bank serves as trustee of trusts established under a will which is funded at death,
3. Estates, where the bank acts as executor of estates,
4. Investment management,
5. Custody, where the bank keeps securities safe for investors, and
6. Guardianships for minors and incompetents.

Living trusts are typically set up on a revocable basis, meaning that the beneficiary can change trustees at his or her discretion. This might be done, for example, to get better investment performance or administrative support. Nonetheless, this does not happen often because switching costs for living trusts are high. Changing trustees requires going through an accounting process that is costly and time-consuming, and must be approved by a court. Testamentary trusts typically are irrevocable, meaning that the beneficiary cannot change trustees at all. Thus, share shifts among competitors tend to be relatively slow. They are driven mainly by newly created trusts.

Systems investments in personal trust have been used to automate accounting and reporting functions. The software must reflect the numerous regulatory changes that occurred in the 1980s and that will probably continue to occur. Software also reduces clerical data entry costs by automating the entire securities movement and control from the inception of a trade order to the actual settlement of the trade. Such investments can cost $10 million to $15 million if developed on a proprietary basis. Outside packages can be purchased and installed for approximately $2 million to $3 million. However, although much of the accounting and processing in personal trust is, or can be, automated, total automation of accounting and processing will probably never come about because of the complexity of personal trust activities. Filing personal tax returns and settling estates, for example, are simply too complicated and diverse. There is also a wide diversity of assets held (e.g., real estate, unique investment vehicles, options, stripped bonds, equities, or fixed income bonds). Also, banks are increasingly providing rudimentary investment performance software for living trusts. This software compares performance with the Dow Jones or the S&P 500, for example. Investment performance software costs roughly $1 million on a proprietary basis, or $300,000 to $500,000 for a package.

Given the current fragmentation of the personal trust business, these investments are relatively high for most players and may lead to increasing concentration. Market shares are likely to shift slowly, however, given the high switching costs and the dispersed retail customer base. In the short term, some banks may withdraw from particular customer segments or product lines to concentrate on key strengths.

INSTITUTIONAL INVESTMENT MANAGEMENT

While total growth in institutional investment management advanced at a 13 percent annual pace over the 1980 to 1988 period, banks lost considerable market share. (See Table 7–1.) What used to be a 38 percent share is

TABLE 7–1
Investment Managers by Type
Total Assets Under Management

	1980 Percent	1988 Percent
Bank and Trust Companies	38.1%	33.0%
Insurance Companies	36.4	30.0
Investment Advisors	25.5	37.0
Market Size ($ Billions)	100% = $1,407	100% = $3,064

now only 33 percent. The only exception is index-based funds, which accounted for approximately 10 percent of assets in 1988, up from 2 percent in 1981. Here commercial banks do well and are investing in additional systems support.

Banks offering index funds can automate most of the investment function, thereby reducing transaction fees. Strong back-office skills are required, allowing banks to dominate this business. State Street Boston, to be discussed in Chapter 9, offers S&P 500 index funds, non-S&P stock funds, and international equities index funds.

Actively managed funds require only moderate systems support. Although actual decision making is still largely judgmental, fund managers rely on computerized data bases for securities prices, availability, performance, and other decision support services.

In the future, we believe, investment management will utilize more sophisticated decision support aids, specifically including expert systems. Investment decisions—which are problems characterized by uncertainty, incomplete data, or conflicting rules—are not adaptable to rigorous analysis with current programming techniques. By building knowledge bases that capture the logic of the best investment managers, it may be possible to generate solutions for such problems.

PROCESSING-BASED SERVICES

A broad range of trust and securities businesses involve either the issuance and record keeping of securities for issuers, or the custody and clearing of securities for investors. We have highlighted five specific businesses in this chapter: mutual fund processing, master trust, safekeeping, dealers clearance, and stock transfer. There are others, such as securities lending and trusteeship, that we have not discussed. In general, they are smaller and affect fewer banks. Collectively, all of the securities processing businesses generated revenues in 1988 of about $3 billion and pretax profits of about $470 million.

Mutual Fund Processing

Mutual funds have become a major investment vehicle in the United States. By the end of 1988 there were 2,718 different mutual funds. The growth in assets and number of accounts has been strong, propelled by higher yields and an expanding variety of fund purposes and investment strategies. (See Figure 7-3.) As a result, processing of mutual funds has become an important support activity. Much of this support activity is performed in-house by the mutual funds organizations. The remainder constitutes the third-party processing market, which is dominated by banks and a few nonbank players.

There are two sides to the mutual fund processing business:

- Shareholder record keeping and transfer agency needs result from shareholder purchase and redemption transactions. Required functions include statementing and customer service, account maintenance, and may well include an offering of access methods like checks or debit cards. In 1988, revenues and pretax profits were approximately $500 million and $100 million respectively.
- Custody handles the receipt and accounting for securities owned by the mutual funds. Specific needs include security safekeeping and settlement, portfolio accounting, cash management, general ledger accounting, and security lending services. In 1988, revenues and pretax profits were approximately $400 million and $80 million respectively.

Since the shareholders constantly purchase and redeem shares, the volume of transactions can become quite high. The accounting and record keeping requirements on both sides are very complex, and successful participation demands large investments in both hardware and software. The most popular means of performing shareholder record keeping and transfer agency for the approximately 56.1 million mutual fund accounts is in-house processing. (See Figure 7-4.) The leading third-party providers are

FIGURE 7–3
Mutual Fund Growth

Assets ($ Billions)

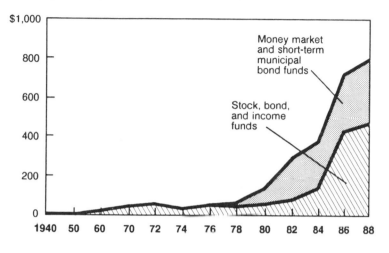

Shareholder Accounts (Millions)

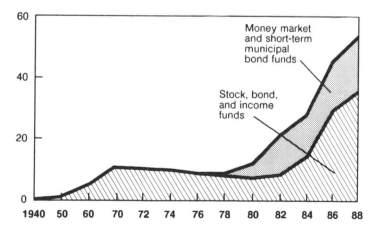

FIGURE 7–4
Mutual Fund Processing, 1988

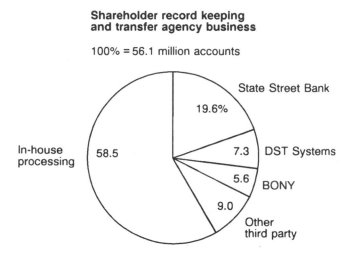

Shareholder record keeping
and transfer agency business

100% = 56.1 million accounts

- State Street Bank 19.6%
- In-house processing 58.5
- DST Systems 7.3
- BONY 5.6
- Other third party 9.0

State Street Bank and DST Systems, Inc. These providers can perform the full range of support functions for a mutual fund except account acquisition and portfolio management.

In recent years, the transfer agent role has increasingly been pulled in-house (e.g., Fidelity and Merrill Lynch). This has occurred for two reasons:

- Large mutual fund sponsors are increasingly competing on service quality and have therefore moved to exert more control over their interface with the customer. Third-party providers have traditionally had difficulty in providing sufficiently customized services to meet the special needs of large mutual fund sponsors. For example, they typically cannot develop applications for new product lines in a timely fashion.
- The business has been growing less rapidly in recent years and has become increasingly competitive. Some consolidation between funds has occurred. Funds management by small and medium-sized sponsors have increasingly been merged into larger organizations. The overall third-party transfer agent market has shrunk as large sponsors provide more of these services in-house.

In addition to the full service transfer agents, there are vendors that perform remote systems services, which are independent of any transfer agency relationship. The dominant players in this area are DST Systems and Sun Guard Shareholder Systems. Together they control over 90 percent of this market. This business has significant scale economies but is only approximately $150 million in revenues. Thus, potential entrants pose a minimal threat.

On the custodial side of the business, State Street and Bank of New York were the leading players in 1988 with estimated market shares of 41 percent and 22 percent respectively. As with the transfer agent business there are high economies of scale and only enough room for a few highly focused players. (Again, see Chapter 9 for a detailed discussion of State Street.)

Overall, the mutual funds processing business is relatively young and has been based on technology since its infancy. Thus, profits have not been impacted negatively by the type of paper-to-electronics conversion seen in other businesses, such as stock transfer or funds transfer. This business remains a solid earner for the few banks that can participate. Only on the stockholder record-keeping side of the business is the market stagnant, as large sponsors consolidate and increasingly pull their processing needs in-house.

Master Trust/Custody

Master trust had its origins in the Employee's Retirement Income Security Act (ERISA) of 1974. This landmark legislation vastly increased the record-keeping requirements for pension funds and other institutional investors. ERISA created strong incentives to consolidate investment holdings and/or the reporting on those holdings that might have previously been scattered among multiple banks. Master trust is a response to that incentive.

The master trustee delivers a package of services that includes accounting, custody, reporting, securities processing, and securities lending. In addition, because the plans are typically managed by multiple outside investment managers, status reports aggregate the separately managed portfolios and compare investment manager performances. The master trustee also makes distributions to pension fund beneficiaries.

Master custody is a very similar service that provides all the services of a master trustee without incurring legal trusteeship. It is targeted at public employee plans, endowments, or foundations where legal trustee-ship is held within the customer's institution.

Master trust/custody has undergone a highly sophisticated electronic evolution. Plan sponsors and investment managers now have terminal or personal computer access to trust systems. For example, investment managers can communicate trade information directly to their bank's security movement and control systems. The plan sponsor gains lower cost and higher quality processing.

Terminals also allow plan sponsors to directly access detailed infor-mation on their security holdings, transactions, cash flows, portfolio characteristics, and performance. They manage their cash flows tightly, can refine the portfolio analytics provided by the master trustee, and can monitor performance of investment managers very closely. These on-line systems help free plan sponsors from reliance on fixed-format, hard-copy reports.

Bankers Trust, Northern Trust, State Street, and Chase, among others of the top 30, have systems that can be accessed by terminals or PCs located in the offices of the plan sponsors and the investment managers. Most master trust competitors still rely on a mix of batch and on-line sys-tems, and we believe investments will be made to move everything to on-line processing. Additionally, because of numerous regulatory changes in the last 10 years, many banks need to invest in rewriting their master trust accounting systems. In sum, we believe that to continue playing in this game, competitors must invest in the software and telecom-munications needed to give plan sponsors and investment managers termi-nals or PCs, as well as in developing fully on-line systems and updated accounting packages.

The master trust/custody market continues to grow. For example, 80 percent of pension funds with assets over $10 million used master trustees in 1988 versus 49 percent in 1980. It is profitable: total revenues in 1988 were estimated at $650 million and pretax profits at $75 million. Never-theless, several banks, including Chemical, First Chicago, and Wells Fargo, have already dropped out as the level of technology investment has escalated. The top five industry leaders in 1988 had a combined share of 54 percent, earning pretax margins, we estimate, as high as 25 percent. These leaders continue to invest heavily—each spent $5 million to $15 mil-lion in 1988 on software development targeted primarily at the upper end of the pension fund market. An additional development is "global" systems—software capable of multicurrency accounting and providing on-line access to several different securities markets around the world.

The impact of these investments will be seen in an even more concentrated market in the future. We expect upper-end providers to fall from 15 to 10 or less during the first half of the 1990s. Pricing wars may erupt if too many players invest in duplicate capabilities, thus creating overcapacity. To date, primary demand has expanded enough to prevent much price pressure. But as market penetration gets to 80 percent, primary growth must slow. We believe profitable niche strategies also exist for those banks that target the middle and lower end of the market with products less systems-intensive, such as those with limited on-line access that are tailored to the needs of less active plan sponsors.

Institutional Securities Safekeeping

Institutional securities safekeeping encompasses custody, processing, and record-keeping services that banks perform for corporations and other financial institutions. The largest customer segments for this product are bank trust departments. In other words, a large bank, usually a money center bank, will hold securities for a small bank, usually one with which the large bank has a correspondent relationship. This business is undergoing a complicated and very expensive transformation from paper-based to electronic processing. The clerically intensive data entry and inquiry functions have been replaced by automated communications between the bank and its customers. Also, securities handling is now mostly done electronically. This process is called "immobilization": for example, the replacement of paper-based securities by purely electronic "book entry" securities.

Immobilization can be implemented in two ways:

- Existing paper securities are placed in a depository that maintains electronic records for its members.
- If legal, the original issue can be a book entry and no paper is ever issued.

The practical effect is the same. Reductions in labor cost are a major benefit. For example, transfer costs can decrease from $25 per paper item to $2 per electronic item for equities. Production speed is increased and quality control is improved. Book-entry electronic transactions now account for over 90 percent of securities transactions. We project that a large portion of the remaining paper-based trades will disappear in the 1990s because the economics of processing electronically are so advantageous.

At present, all treasury securities and certain government agency issues (e.g., Freddie Macs and Fannie Maes) are completely immobilized at the Federal Reserve. Most equities and corporate bonds traded by institutions and active retail investors are immobilized at the Depository Trust Company (DTC). The DTC has also immobilized many municipal securities. This process has been facilitated by eliminating the issuance of new coupon bonds.

Globalization is another important trend affecting securities processing. By the end of 1988, the market value of equity securities available to global investors represented almost three-quarters of the total global market capitalization of $12.9 trillion. In light of burgeoning off-shore capital markets and the rapid pace of deregulation in such key financial centers as London and Tokyo, the major trading banks have pushed back geographical boundaries as fast as regulation, technology, and investor interest have allowed. Participation in globalizing securities markets requires multicurrency systems with real-time information about an investor's holdings in an increasing number of capital markets. The future costs of electronic, integrated global clearing systems are likely to be very substantial. For example, competitors may need to upgrade their trust accounting systems to provide compatibility across markets so that customer files in various cities can be merged at one central location.

Chase Manhattan, Manufacturers Hanover, and Bank of New York are the principal banks servicing the institutional securities market with proprietary products. We estimate that they have an approximate 40 percent combined market share, largely concentrated in securities traded by domestic correspondent banks. Other banks serve smaller segments and have shares below 5 percent. We estimate total business segment revenues in 1988 to be about $270 million.

The high degree of automation, the essentially undifferentiated nature of the services, and the difficulty of maintaining proprietary relationships in this business lead us to believe that, at best, market leaders in securities safekeeping operate at break-even. Other large participants may lose up to $10 million each on this business. Moreover, immobilization and globalization continue to change the competitive environment. The substantial investments needed to remain competitive have already created strong economies of scale. Consequently, several players have already withdrawn from certain segments of the market. J.P. Morgan & Co. withdrew from certain segments of domestic bank safekeeping, for example. Most important, however, the depositories—particularly the DTC—have emerged as powerful Type 2 consortia competitors (see again Figure 3–5). For example, by expanding membership beyond the 12 founding members to over 175 participants, the DTC has gained significant market share from the traditional "piggyback" providers. The DTC's inroads have aggravated the difficulties proprietary players face in building the processing volume necessary to establish economic efficiencies.

Successful proprietary players are likely to be banking companies that target correspondent banks too small to join the depositories. They can connect these customers electronically to their own automated depository linkages in order to build volumes and reduce their cost structure. One example is MHC's Value^x, a PC-based system that allows correspondent customers to communicate electronically with MHC's securities movement and control system. Electronic access not only saves the community bank the cost of making a long distance phone call, but it also provides a higher level of service. MHC wholesales this product through its larger regional correspondents, and has found it to be a profitable way to serve this market.

Dealers Clearance

Dealers clearance involves receiving and storing securities, typically issued by government agencies, for major brokers and dealers. Unlike institutional securities safekeeping, this is a profitable business in which the banks with the largest market share may earn approximately $20 million annually. We estimate annual segment revenues of $100 million.

There are three reasons for these high profit levels:

- The customers are nonfinancial institutions that cannot become direct members of the Federal Reserve. They have to go through banks to access clearing and settling mechanisms for treasury transactions.
- The business has historically been highly concentrated. Just three players—Bank of New York, Marine Midland, and MHC—have approximately 85 percent of the market. This is because only large New York banks that were not primary dealers themselves in government securities were realistically eligible to offer the services. Also, the systems investments are particularly expensive, running approximately $5 million to $10 million a year for the leaders.
- The business is risky and this high risk acts as a deterrent against new entrants or players without a high level of commitment. The risk comes from unanticipated surges in trading volumes, which

may strain the systems capacity and create the possibility of failure on a settlement date.

For all these reasons, profits in this business are likely to remain high.

Stock Transfer

Stock transfer is by historical definition a paper-driven business. At its heart is the issuance of a registered stock certificate evincing ownership of a security. When an equity trade occurs, the paper must be collected from the old owner, destroyed, and reissued in the name of the new owner. The transfer agent also maintains shareholder records for issuing companies and updates these after each trade. However, since the advent of immobilization (e.g., keeping the paper security in a vault and trading electronically), there is less need to transfer certificates. More than 85 percent of all equity certificates have been registered in the DTC's nominee name and stored permanently. Thus, transfer agents primarily process certificates for smaller, less active, retail investors who prefer to hold paper certificates. For the New York Stock Exchange, these investors account for less than 15 percent of all issued shares. In essence, stock transfer is the "old" business of servicing the very long declining tail of equity trades requiring paper-based settlement.

Although still a fairly sizable business (1988 revenues of $375 million), some participants in this business have been losing money—possibly in the range of 15 to 30 percent of total revenues. Three major reasons are:

- Competitors generally do not understand the economics of the business and often hold prices down. Stock transfer often involves extensive services provided by other bank operating departments, such as check reconcilement, centralized data center, and so on, that are not loaded into profit calculations.
- Other competitors knowingly sell this product at a loss under the assumption that it can serve as an entree to up-tier credit relationships. Being the stock transfer agent for a large blue-chip corporation was once considered to be prestigious. However, recent market data does not support this hypothesis. Corporations have unbundled the stock transfer and credit purchase decisions. Typically, the stock transfer buying point is the corporate secretary, who shops for price and quality with little or no input from the corporate treasurer, who buys the credit.

- The advent of the DTC and equity immobilization have destroyed the dividend float upon which the profits used to depend. For example, over 85 percent of dividend payments are now made in good funds to the DTC, not mailed out as checks. As a result, float, which previously accounted for 50 percent of revenues, now accounts for less than one-third of total revenues. In addition, unit labor costs have doubled because the transaction mix shifted toward retail items—which are smaller and more difficult to process.

Not surprisingly, many competitors have dropped out. Examples include Chemical, Bankers Trust, Wells Fargo, and Security Pacific. In 1989, the three major players were First Chicago (approximately 15 percent market share), Mellon (10 percent), and Manufacturers Hanover (8 percent). First Chicago may be the only bank that makes money on this product, because it has a dominant 38 percent share of the more attractive multinationals market segment. These customers are less expensive to serve because they have relatively less certificate issuance activity per shareholder account.

Stock transfer is a business in which continued technological investments—in on-line capabilities, for example—are difficult to justify. We believe transaction volumes will continue to decline slowly: individual shareholder records will decrease by 6 percent a year and certificate issuance by 9 percent a year as the smallest investors become increasingly comfortable about leaving certificates with their broker. We foresee continued pricing and cost pressures in this business. Successful competitors are likely to be firms that manage their income statements tightly for the short term—that is, they do not invest heavily in systems, track volume declines with a commensurate decrease in clerical workers, and position themselves in less price-sensitive customer niches.

FUTURE NEEDS

In summary, many securities businesses require major technological investments. Increased electronic capability is mandatory for all but a few of these businesses, such as stock transfer. Investment needs will remain for the following purposes:

1. To complete the automation of processing flows in the full range of custody and clearing businesses.

2. To convert existing paper-based securities to electronic form.
3. To handle new types of securities, many of which will need to be book entry if they are to be traded actively in the secondary market.
4. To finish building global systems for foreign-held securities.

Technology investments will be of two types. First, competitors will invest in their own proprietary computer and telecommunications systems. Second, current or future depositories, or consortia players composed of banks and brokers, will invest the requisite capital to immobilize the remaining paper-based securities.

We predict that many niche businesses will emerge as Wall Street continues to create new instruments. These niches will tend to be small (revenues of $10 million to $50 million a year) but profitable, as long as only a few players enter them. A good example is the processing and clearing of American depository receipts. These are certificates that represent equity shares in a foreign corporation but trade and distribute dividends in dollars. Three banks compete in this business. J.P. Morgan & Co. entered early and is the transfer agent for close to 60 percent of what we estimate to be $3 billion in outstandings in 1988. Bank of New York is the number-two competitor. Unless this market grows substantially faster than it is growing today (15 percent a year), we believe that other banks will have a difficult time gaining enough volume to recover their start-up costs.

SUMMARY

The trust and securities processing businesses offer several good illustrations of the theme of this book. Clearly, customers of these businesses have received greater value from the addition of systems technology. Their ability to hold a wide range of securities, value them, trade them, and monitor performance has vastly increased. At the same time, segment profitability and industry structure have been irrevocably changed, sometimes for the worse, as electronics replace paper.

For those businesses that remain largely paper-based, and where the level of systems intensiveness is not yet high, many competitors can still survive. Personal trust is the clearest example—profitability is still at moderate levels because few competitors have had to drop out. Switching barriers are high and overcapacity is not a problem.

Those businesses that developed subsequent to automation tended to develop a fairly concentrated structure in the beginning and have generally been profitable from the start. Mutual funds processing, master trust custody, and ADR processing all fit this definition. These businesses serve newer needs and primary demand is still growing. Profitability is excellent for the few competitors who entered early and made the requisite systems investments.

Finally, old businesses that were fragmented and that are undergoing the technological conversion process are doing the worst. Stock transfer and bank safekeeping fit this definition. In this segment, competitors have been squeezed by overcapacity and operate near break-even at best. Loss of float, declining primary demand, and the presence of a Type 2 utility (e.g., the DTC) have all combined to transform these once profitable staples of banking.

The bottom line is that bank competitors in any business related to trust or securities processing need to have a perspective on the degree to which systems technology is penetrating their business. As systems intensiveness rises, the economics will change. Only those who recognize this fact and take appropriate action will be the survivors.

PART 3

USING TECHNOLOGY SUCCESSFULLY

Despite the title of this book, we do not believe that investments in technology are inherently unprofitable. Systems technology is a part of the environment for both business and society. In the long run, its use is neutral because profits are determined by relative strengths and weaknesses, not the overall level of technological development.

Our thesis has been that the banking industry has a fragmented structure that is changing. As electronic storage and transmission of data gradually replace paper-based storage and transmission, the economics of banking change. As more and more of the cost structure is devoted to M1 and M2–A, the fraction of all costs that are fixed tends to increase. Fewer competitors can exist in the resultant industry structure. The industry cost curve flattens, and a relatively small number of large players can provide economic capacity. It is particularly during the transition period, when the number of competitors must be reduced, that profits are destroyed.

There are two approaches for avoiding this negative chain of events:

- New bank products or approaches can change the game and create new primary demand that is unencumbered by a surplus of competitors — two examples are master trust and mutual funds processing. Then it becomes possible to succeed even though the product is heavily automated.
- Market leaders have the best chance of retaining some profitability during the period of consolidation and transition. This is because they can spread their development and transition costs over a larger

market, enabling them to utilize a "price leadership" strategy. They can exert pressure against smaller competitions, forcing them either to exit the business directly or to "milk down" their market share by pricing above the leader. We believe that Citibank, for example, used this strategy of price leadership in the mid-1980s in the funds transfer business.

This part of the book thus discusses the topics of successful technological competition and what actions may be useful to banks in the future. It begins with a chapter on the most important technological trends. Banks' actions should be geared toward the situation as it will exist in the future, not as it is today. Continued improvement of M1 core technology is extremely predictable. Banks will employ increased capability, lower processing costs, and higher capacity throughout their systems infrastructures. An understanding of these improvements is one key element in navigating into the future.

Chapter 9 will describe five successful examples of specific bank/market approaches that employ technology. The illustrations for State Street Bank, Banc One Corporation, and First Wachovia Corporation all demonstrate a new business approach or product— in other words, how these banks changed the game. The illustrations for Chase Manhattan and First Chicago show how leaders in traditional lines maintain profitability despite consolidative pressures. As they typically have mixes of new initiatives and older products, most banks need to consider both situations. The specific lessons from these illustrations give rise to a set of five potentially useful management guidelines.

Chapter 10 will describe these management guidelines. They can help manage, but they are not a comprehensive guide to success. No single chapter of any book could contain that. But technology does require efforts to look at things in a new light. The guidelines include linking business strategy and technology in an iterative fashion, using "simultaneous tight-loose" policies, treating "routine" system investments differently from distinctive investments, watching industry capacity, and focusing only on selected lines of business. All are worth consideration today—and will be even more so in the future—as the technological advances discussed in Chapter 8 become reality.

CHAPTER 8

OVERVIEW OF NEW TECHNOLOGIES

This chapter gives an overview of the new systems technologies that are beginning to impact the U.S. commercial banking industry. These new M1 and M2 developments are a driving force for change. They have the potential to change bank product economics, the comparative efficiency of different distribution channels, and the structure of the industry itself.

The pace of core technological change is relatively predictable, yet understanding its impact on banking is not as easy. Specific predictions may be fraught with error. We cannot say with certainty when a specific application, such as POS/debit systems, will become widely adopted. Nor can we predict how widely new generic technologies, such as image processing, will be used, even though we can foresee substantial reductions in the cost of purchasing the technology.

We do believe, however, that the competitive lessons from the past may well repeat themselves. More technology may hasten the consolidation process among old-game players while it simultaneously gives new-game players a chance. Profits in lines of business that have too many competitors may be destroyed as these new technologies spread. For this reason, it is critically important to understand the advance of new technologies. What are they and how might they be used? What are the potential economic and competitive effects? This chapter explores such questions.

PROLIFERATING DEVELOPMENTS

There are far too many technological developments to describe them all easily. There is not even a clear dividing line between "new" and "old" technologies. Much of what is important is the constant progression of vendor upgrades in equipment and introductions of new capabilities. Furthermore, there is no strict definition of *technology*. Some of the most interesting and needed events will arise solely from adoption of standards and better handling of data, even though these events are not new technology per se.

Moreover, the realm of current technology offers an abundance of problems and issues that have not been solved. Current technology is so complex, and already offers so many choices, that banks have their hands full with it. Only a portion of any bank's systems infrastructure can be state-of-the-art at any given time, so the issue of simply catching up (where it makes sense to do so) can be a full-time job. Banks would have a full plate even if there were not going to be any more technological advances.

Yet, that is decidedly not the case. Figure 8–1 shows how the relative performance of some selected M1 core technologies is increasing. Depending on the measure selected, relative performance in the year 2000 will be anywhere from 50 percent to 2,000 percent better than in 1990. The underlying capabilities, such as the capacity of on-line storage devices, help drive higher level developments such as image processing and artificial intelligence. Even in an area such as software development some improvement is expected.

Recognizing the impossibility of covering everything, we have selected five general categories of events: (1) general developments, (2) the wired desk, (3) image processing, (4) expert systems, and (5) integrated applications. After general developments, the four specific topics mentioned are not based on a prioritization, but are singled out because they will probably be widely adopted. They have the potential for major competitive impact, not just increased back-office efficiency.

GENERAL DEVELOPMENTS

The diversity of computer hardware is growing as manufacturers begin to use advanced technology to segment their products and meet special needs. The fault-tolerant boxes (from Tandem or Stratus, for example) are valuable in guaranteeing continuous uptime on real-time, on-line ATM, POS, or funds transfer networks. Teradata sells a database machine that is highly efficient at manipulating large quantities of data. Its unit cost to do applications based on large databases may be as low as 10 percent of what a general-purpose mainframe would cost. Citicorp is just one of several banks that have installed it. Their branch information management system has 128 processors and has validated the concept of using a

FIGURE 8–1
Change in Performance Characteristics

1990 index = 100

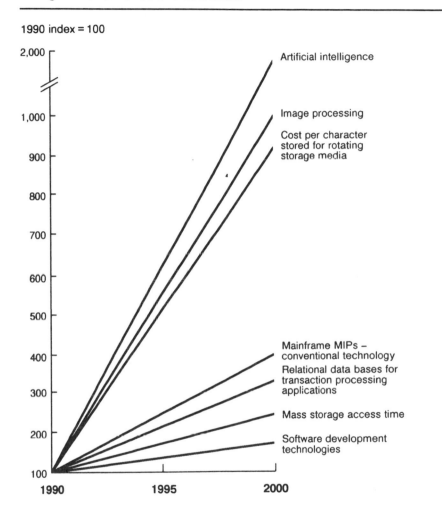

database machine instead of the more complicated approach of distribut-
ing a very large customer database across several hosts. As machines that
employ parallel processors become increasingly available in the 1990s,
manufacturers will have more opportunity to tailor their machines. By
moving functions from the systems software into the "firmware" (i.e., the
microcoded instruction set), efficiencies will be increased at the price of

specialization. Specialized mainframes, in turn, will give banks more choices in what to do and more efficiency when they purchase the specialized machines. The impact on competition may be a further focus on disaggregation with fewer competitors able to be maximally cost-effective at each separate function.

In fact, banks face an embarrassment of riches as vendors continually offer improved and targeted processors. Departmental processors, such as the DEC VAX 6000 series and the IBM AS/400 line are the latest evolution in the minicomputer product line. The AS/400 has been relatively well received in the marketplace and can replace the earlier S/36 and S/38 models. IBM's 9370 family was designed to be compatible with IBM's major family of mainframes, the S/370 group, but was not well accepted by the market. Banks are using DEC VAXes for an increasingly wide variety of purposes. They are used as nodal processors to do network management and to support funds transfer systems. Both Irving Trust and BONY use DEC equipment for their government securities clearance businesses, for example. Citicorp uses DEC VAXes to maintain customer accounts. Expansion in the usage of hardware is the natural result of improved technology, but it does create issues for banks. How long can they continue with primarily mainframe dominated architectures, thus sacrificing the effectiveness that more targeted and distributed hardware can bring?

Banks now face issues of computer connectivity, not only for the ones they own, but for those outside their organizations. Open Systems Interconnect (OSI) is slowly becoming a widely accepted architectural standard. Its seven layers address the communications issues between computers. IBM's Systems Network Architecture (SNA) and DEC's DNA are variations on OSI. Because many banks are already in the IBM environment (e.g., they have significant investments in CICS, VTAM, or IMS), SNA has been a safe choice.

Systems software is another area where important changes are constantly occurring. Over the years, IBM's large processor operating systems, which are very important for banks, have evolved from relatively unsophisticated local batch-oriented services (e.g., OS/MFT in the 1960s), to complex interactive multiprocessing services that function across the entire enterprise (e.g., MVS/ESA for the 1990s). These migrations are necessary for many banks to keep up with the growth in the demand for systems services.

The applications environment continues to advance as banks invest in teleprocessing systems, such as CICS and IMS/DC, and remote job entry systems, such as JES2 and JES3. Data management systems are constantly improving their performance. The specialized TPF/ACP is estimated to handle up to 2,000 transactions per second. An estimate for IMS/Fastpath is roughly 1,000 per second. Even transactional processing systems that support relational databases (e.g., Datacom/CICS and Adabas/CICS) can handle approximately 200 transactions per second. (These statistics are normalized to an IBM 3090-400E.) IBM has announced its Systems Applications Architecture (SAA), a master specification that is intended to promote common user access, common programming interface, common communication support, and common applications. The bottom line is that banks have a widening array of increasingly powerful systems software that is a key M1 building block for the new needs that banks face. (See again Figure 3–3.)

Many new developments are occurring that affect the applications and the data themselves. Banks' systems departments are using computer-aided software engineering (CASE) tools to do prototyping, restructuring, reverse engineering, and data design. Fourth generation languages such as query languages, statistical and graphical tools, and application/report generators are growing in popularity. And new approaches to maintaining data are now possible, especially with the aid of relational data base management systems. Distributed data base systems are potentially desirable to circumvent single machine limits and to decentralize resources. However, the complexities of security, data integrity, and disaster recovery have not been fully resolved, preventing wider adoption of true distributed processing. *Finally, data-driven approaches are now more popular than ever before.* Data can (and should) be decoupled from the application, and generic procedures can be implemented for each possible type of data and used as building blocks for more complex procedures.

Voice technologies hold great promise for banks because of the potential to reduce the cost of labor-intensive, telephone-based customer contact transactions. Automatic dialing is a simple form of the technology that has increased productivity by 20 to 40 percent in high-volume outcall situations such as telemarketing or credit card collections. By dialing the number automatically and not routing the transaction to a phone representative until the call is answered, contact rates are usually more than doubled. Voice synthesis can be used to give automatic responses to questions, and voice recognition can be used to assist in automatic data entry. The economic effects are going to be a further emphasis on telephones and a further displacement of transactions away from branches — not to mention better overall levels of customer service.

These developments and others are very likely to be very important. They mostly fall in the realm of M1 and are therefore defensive when used simply to do today's chores in a faster or less costly way. But understanding the changes that will be created in banking by these developments is critical. More power in the M1 infrastructure must inevitably translate into more opportunities, more choices and more customer value in banks' M2 and M3.

THE WIRED DESK

The "wired desk" is not a technology per se but is the embodiment of an idea: that reduced numbers of bank employees will be highly leveraged by substantial computing and communications power at their place of work. Local computing power will be connected, via networks, to the banks' data centers, mainframe computers, and shared data bases — and thereby to other wired desks. The concept potentially extends to the employees of other institutions — customers or suppliers, for example — who will have their own wired desks that can access bank databases.

The driving force behind the wired desk is the evolution of increasingly inexpensive, ever more powerful and more broadly used workstations. The IBM and DEC personal computer and workstation families have been significantly enhanced. Micros may now employ reduced instruction set computer (RISC) architectures. For example, the IBM PS/2 is a key component of IBM's SAA planning. Likewise, the "DEC windows" product integrates heterogeneous environments. Sun, Apollo, IBM, and other vendors have developed powerful (multi-MIPS) single-user and multi-user workstations using Motorola 680x0 and Intel 486 chip technology. Rich, AT&T, IBS, and others have developed user-specific terminal devices, such as trader terminals, that support both digital and analog data streams.

Although much of this is new, the banking industry has been investing in on-line technology for 20 years. Banks own an estimated 300,000 to 500,000 "dumb" terminals (e.g., an IBM 3270 or equivalent), which access mainframe applications and databases. This is the old-world structure that IBM began putting in place more than a decade ago — a large, intelligent, and centralized host driving dumb terminals. These terminals are used by customer service personnel, collectors, operations clerks, platform personnel, and systems and programming employees. Another 300,000 to 400,000 teller terminals access some of the same information. Since 1982, the industry has invested significantly in PCs, mostly for stand-alone decision support purposes. Today, we estimate that there are roughly 200,000 to 300,000 bank employees—managers, supervisors, credit analysts, lending officers, and other professionals—who have access to a PC. By 1989, specialized workstations had become particularly common among the sales and trading departments of both commercial and investment banks.

In the 1990s, it seems reasonable to anticipate three broad trends driven by the continuing improvements in desktop technology:

- The number of bank employees whose desk or other place of work has an appropriate computing device will probably increase substantially. Counting all network devices, such as local printers and file servers, the ratio of network devices to employees may well exceed 1:1.
- Devices with intelligence, such as PCs (e.g., PS/2), will increasingly replace dumb terminals (e.g., 3270) for use in selected applications, allowing considerably enhanced user-friendliness and probably employing cooperative processing.
- The concept of "interoperability," or access from any device to data or programs located at any other device, may be used where it makes economic sense to cope with the increased distribution of computing resources.

User-Friendliness

Much of the local processing power on the wired desk will be devoted to making the user interface more friendly. The paradigm of today's Apple Macintosh computer may well become much more common in banks, with the addition of screen icons, windows, menus, mouses, and so forth. Changes in application systems may well be required, too. Eventually, even more exotic technologies, such as natural language processing and voice recognition (for data entry), may be part of the user interface.

Considerably enhanced user-friendliness is a major requirement for truly making use of the wired desk. For example, most bank employees can only use a few of today's available on-line screens because the information and formats are too esoteric. The screens are stuffed so full of codes, flags, and symbols that only an experienced operator can use them easily. Even getting the right screen to begin with can be difficult. Today's screens may be efficient, but they are not effective in providing answers to problems. Each user's range of responsiveness is reduced, not to mention the limits placed on customers, who are increasingly interacting with the bank through the same on-line systems. With the continuing expansion in the amount of available information, user-friendliness is moving from the "nice to have" category to the "essential" category.

To help solve this problem, cooperative processing is a likely development. It can increase user-friendliness without increasing the amount of network traffic between the terminal and the host, or the amount of work at the host. Screen formats, for example, can be determined and formatted locally. The intelligence in the PC can be used to do edits, ask questions, prompt users, and so forth. Workstations can also store some parts of the data base that do not need to be stored centrally. Networking and interface software can be controlled centrally, and software updates can be downloaded periodically. In fact, mainframes may eventually become just data servers, storing large quantities of data but with the applications resident on distributed intelligent devices. The net results will be far more flexibility and sophistication on the part of the typical bank user—which will be needed in order to cope with the rapidly growing amount of data and programs that the typical user can access.

Other Implications

As a result of the wired desk, more of a bank's customer service and front-office work will be done with electronics, not paper. This transformation will occur faster for high-volume, less-complicated transactions. Already, departments such as consumer loan collections, DDA and credit card customer service, telemarketing, and funds transfer inquiry operate in a remarkably paper-free manner. Many of the industry's estimated 100,000 telephone customer service representatives and collectors can now do virtually all their work on-line. For many bank departments, microfiche, printouts, and other types of paper have become a thing of the past. As the power of the on-line system continues to grow, other bank departments that are still paper-based should undergo a similar transformation. Examples include the credit department of a leasing, residential mortgage, or middle-market lending operation; the work-out department; and even the typical branch of today, which is still generating many paper-based forms for other parts of the bank.

Other applications of the wired desk should include electronic communications. Many banks are now implementing electronic mail (E-mail) to communicate with wholesale customers. Credit analysts at CoreState's credit card bank use PCs to capture and store an applicant's entire credit bureau file. They then apply a proprietary credit analysis directly to the data, which results in very strong credit control.

Competitive Impact

The wired desk has great potential to improve the quality and speed of banking products, but its competitive implications are less clear. As with on-line terminals and PCs, every bank will be able to invest in this M1 technology if it wants to. The sophistication and complexity of banking services will surely grow, stimulated by the much greater access that each bank employee will have to data. But whose strategy will be favored by this development and whose will not?

It is possible that by extending so much automated capability into the hands of knowledge workers, diversity will flourish. Banks may encounter increased opportunities for focused competition. Perhaps customer service (and knowing the customer better) will become a major realm of technological competition. The wired desk may even accelerate the disaggregative trend by allowing easier communication between nonbank service providers and banks. For example, Varidyne is a small company specializing in data entry of consumer credit applications. Its efficiency, gained through workstations and electronic interfaces with the credit bureaus, allows Varidyne to offer less expensive processing with only 48-hour turnaround time. Other disaggregated approaches might occur in collections, loan approval, loan structuring, or even account origination. Disaggregation, in turn, increases the need for a focused bank— one more example of how technology is changing the industry structure.

EXPERT SYSTEMS

Artificial intelligence (AI) is a loose grouping of several related technologies, of which expert systems is the one most relevant to banking. An expert system can account for missing or conflicting information and subjective processes, and can incorporate experience. Instead of using fixed deterministic approaches, an expert system contains a *knowledge base*, which is a series of "rules" describing how a human expert might solve the problem. A rule can be viewed in simple terms as an if–then statement, although in fact, the codification of the experts' knowledge is much more complicated than that. The domain, however, is limited to areas where there are experts, whose job performance is measurably better than others, and where their knowledge is not so subjective or rapidly changing that it cannot be codified. The process of debriefing these experts is called *knowledge engineering*.

Expert systems have been in the labs for years but only reached the stage of commercialization in the 1980s as the cost of CPU cycles decreased. Expert systems can be very CPU-intensive because they are nonprocedural. Because CPU costs should continue to decline, expert systems should continue to gain in cost-effectiveness. Investments by banks may hit $200 million per year by the mid-1990s.

Vendors provide expert systems "shells" (i.e., languages) that run on either micros, mainframes, or specialized machines designed for symbolic programming. Most banks will probably build their own knowledge bases in the beginning, but packages that include a knowledge base are already available. Integration is an important issue because most production expert systems will need to be integrated with mainframe-based databases.

Production-Line Decisions

A major category of expert system applications will be "production-line" decisions, which are repetitive and high-volume but not so simple as to be automatic. There must be some element of judgment required. A well-known example is the American Express authorizer's assistant. This program advices human authorizers on charge card authorization requests that cannot be approved within the normal guidelines. This expert system has approximately 800 rules. It collects data from approximately 40 different databases in a few seconds and recommends a specific course of action to the authorizer. System benefits are an estimated $27 million per year in productivity savings, 25 percent less time for each authorization, and 30 percent fewer approval errors. For American Express, this is not a defensive investment, as the bankcards' business system employs fixed credit limits that do not require authorizers.

There are many other production-line decision processes that might be amenable to improvement via expert systems technology. Some examples are researching errors, finding the source of an unreconciled cash letter, assisting consumer loan collectors, or providing financial planning services. Both Citicorp Information Services and Cognitive Systems, Inc. (a vendor) have developed AI solutions that read telexed (and therefore unstructured) wire transfer instructions and convert them to machine-readable formats compatible with SWIFT or ISO standards. In the future, new complexities in banking products will probably arise because production-line expert systems can make them workable.

Lending

Expert systems technology has the potential to be employed in making mid-range credit decisions. One vendor, Syntelligence Inc., already sells the Lending Advisor, a package that includes a proprietary shell and a middle-market knowledge base. At a cost of approximately $1 million, this product will perform analytical analysis of the loan and recommend structuring, pricing, and approval decisions based on expertise derived from lenders. Although the Lending Advisor had not been installed at this date in a production capacity, Wells Fargo and First Wachovia have assisted in its development and were using it for training. The simple issue for banks is whether the knowledge bases in expert systems can accurately capture enough human experience to be useful and trusted — and, if they can do so, whether they can do so cost-effectively. To date, there is not enough experience to draw firm conclusions one way or the other.

If expert systems technology does come to play a role in mid-range lending, some expected competitive effects may be to create faster approvals and to allow more consistent application of lending criteria. The technology may also increase the complexity of loan structuring and allow an expansion of lending. To take advantage of these trends a loan originator might seek to use expert systems to reshape its business approach. For example, it could enter a high-risk niche lending market that could not otherwise be controlled. By a simultaneous process of introducing some new systems-based complexities, building share in that niche market, capturing experience, and *incorporating that experience in the knowledge base*, a player might construct some sustainable competitive barriers. Others, with less share, would not be able to buy or build a similar knowledge base and would thus not be as good at understanding the risk.

Other Uses

Another potential use for expert systems technology is in sifting through large quantities of data to find patterns, problems, or exceptions. Consumer goods companies are already experimenting with this approach to make sense of the million-fold increase in new data points coming from the UPC scanners now located at many checkout counters.

Banks' databases are growing at an estimated 30 to 40 percent per year and could, in fact, grow faster if banks were more capable of extracting conclusions from such masses of data. An expert system could look for errors in the flow of transactions through a corporation's transaction account, for example, and report only on the exception conditions. The technology may also be used in monitoring the day-to-day functions of ATM networks, telecommunication networks, or POS networks. The inchoate executive information system (EIS), which is partially based on AI technology, may become a commonplace on the desks of bank managers. An EIS does exception reporting and information extraction in a highly tailored way for each executive, drawing not only on the bank's databases but on outside sources as well.

In summary, expert systems have the potential for a variety of uses in banking. The overall affects are likely to range from productivity improvements to more targeted, niche approaches in middle-market lending. How fast this new technology will spread is difficult to assess, but the economic and competitive impacts could be large in those application areas where distinctive business approaches are possible.

IMAGE PROCESSING

Image processing began to catch hold in the banking industry in the late 1980s and has the potential to become a significant applications technology during the 1990s. Sales in 1990 of integrated image management systems are estimated to be $200 million for U.S. financial institutions, and are growing at more than 40 percent per year. By 1989, an estimated 50 U.S. banks had already planned or implemented systems employing this technology.

Vendor activity also picked up markedly in the late 1980s. IBM announced a "Statement of Direction" in 1989 for its ImagePlus High Performance Transaction System (HPTS). Its first target will be item processing applications. The IBM 3890 reader/sorter is planned to become image capable. TRW Financial Systems, Inc., a leading systems integrator for high-volume transaction processing, has installed approximately 25 lockbox, or remittance processing, operations that incorporate image technology. Filenet, a leading vendor of optical "jukeboxes" (write-once, read-many storage devices), has approximately 225 customers worldwide, of whom about 70 are banks. Traditional vendors of OCR equipment are now offering equipment that combines OCR and image technology. In fact, OCR/image technology is projected to replace most dedicated OCR scanners during the 1990s.

The technology itself consists of scanning anything on paper (including photographs) and digitizing the information. Shades of light and dark are represented in the image by 1s and 0s. The level of resolution can begin at 100 bits per inch (or pixels) and go up to more than 300 pixels. At a rate of 200 pixels, 40,000 bits are needed to describe one square inch of a document. Compression techniques are used to reduce the overall amount of storage. Even so, the distinguishing characteristic of this technology is the need for vast amounts of affordable storage. The compressed image of one 8½ × 11 text page typically requires 50,000 bytes.

There are three major classes of application for image processing in banking. Folder management systems maintain and process customer forms and correspondence, thus eliminating paper files. Data entry from payment or remittance documents reduces manual key-entry. Finally, document transmission replaces the clearing of paper documents with the clearing of images. Each is a fundamentally different use of the technology for unique purposes.

Folder Management

The application class experiencing the most growth is folder management. Users foresee benefits from no lost files, faster access to files, faster processing of files, and a reduction of paper archives and file clerks. Once a workflow management system is implemented, work on the files can be tracked and assigned automatically. Productivity can be improved and work queues monitored more effectively.

Examples of banks that have implemented systems like this include:

1. Citicorp, which has a credit card customer correspondence system;

2. Bankers Trust, which keeps mortgage documents required as backup collateral for CMO issues;
3. US Trust, which maintains personal trust documents—wills, probates, legal rulings, and so on—on such a system;
4. First Wachovia, which maintains signatures of valid corporate account signers on such a system and uses it for signature verification of checks;
5. Bank of New York, Barclays, and Mellon, which all maintain customer correspondence on such systems;
6. Chase Manhattan, Citicorp, and Exchange National, which all maintain loan applications on such systems; and
7. Security Pacific, which keeps its investigation correspondence and documents for its International Money Transfer Department on such a system.

During the 1990s, these systems may well become common wherever there are significant volumes of customer-created paper. The productivity gains will almost surely improve consumer service and decrease processing time for inquiries, applications, and so on. Many processes that are slowed by the need to have different people in different places review the same paper file could be substantially speeded up.

Data Entry

Data entry of characters from payment documents (e.g., credit card sales drafts or checks) can be improved by the addition of image processing. These documents contain numbers that cannot be read by conventional OCR or MICR technology, such as handwritten numeric amounts or illegible OCR/MICR characters. The new technological approach first takes an image of the document, cleans it up (i.e., removes smudges, blemishes, etc.), and then sends it to an OCR-reading algorithm. What cannot be read there is then sent to an image character recognition (ICR) engine, which can use one of several approaches to "read" the characters.

Success rates depend upon the type of document, degree of success in standardizing the documents, and whether or not the algorithm has some guidance in interpreting the document. For example, in remittance processing for bank credit cards, approximately 30 percent of the checks are written for either the total balance or the minimum amount due. By reading these amounts off the remittance coupon, the software will display a higher degree of accuracy when it finds a match for this amount on a check.

Error rates for reading block-printed, hand-made letters on forms with boxes can now be kept reasonably low. Current technology can get reject rates of approximately 5 percent with a substitution error rate of only 2 percent. IBM believes that its new HPTS will be able to read the courtesy amount from 50 percent of all handwritten checks with a substitution error rate of only 2 errors per 10,000 characters.

The final step in the new technological approach is to key-enter all characters unreadable by either the OCR or the ICR. This will be done from an on-screen image instead of from the actual document. Following this step, software would help in balancing and in power encoding. Such data entry systems are either already in use or planned at many locations. Examples include Amoco (for remittance processing), NaBanco (for credit card sales drafts), and Banc One (for credit card remittance processing). As this technology spreads, it should be adopted at most banks as a defensive maneuver. Because data entry is such a back-office function, however, there may not be any noticeable effects. Cost savings of perhaps $200 million yearly are possible if one-half of all check-encoding data entry labor can be saved.

Document Transmission

The document transmission application means to substitute an image for a piece of paper (typically a payment document). The paper is truncated and the image transmitted, stored, and, if needed, printed out. There are several examples of this application already, but the application itself is not likely to see wide adoption soon because the costs of transmitting images are still very high. For example, a compressed image of a check (front and back) takes approximately 20,000 bytes. To transmit the compressed images of 1 million checks (a reasonable number of checks for a major bank) would require 29 hours on a high capacity T1 transmission line. Until higher capacity fiber optic technology is generally available, the cost of transmitting large numbers of images in a multipoint network will probably remain prohibitive.

The examples that have been implemented to date either are low-volume or avoid multipoint clearing at all. MasterCard has a system called MasterCom, which retrieves images of credit card sales drafts in response to inquiry requests. First Interstate of Washington returns an image of each check instead of the actual check itself to 52 percent of its checking customers. The Federal Reserve Bank is soliciting vendor prototypes to assess whether returned check processing could be improved with image processing. And American Express now returns an image of the receipt of charge (ROC) to its cardholders instead of the ROC itself.

American Express's Enhanced Country Club Billing (ECCB)

American Express's application, called ECCB, began in 1987. It is one of the best examples of a distinctive use of technology. Previously, American Express incurred substantial costs in storing, sorting, and returning an estimated 30 million paper ROCs every month. Although these processes were expensive, the reduction of costs was not the primary objective. For one thing, the new system was also very expensive (in the 10s of millions of dollars), and much of the paper processing is still required. Rather, American Express's objective was to reinforce the uniqueness of its card products by cleaning up the statements and leaving a better impression with the customer.

Because American Express is completely alone it is use of ECCB, this enhancement appears to the world as a competitive strike, not a defensive move. In the bankcard world, the sales draft has always been truncated at its point of entry into the settlement system. Thus, banks lack the similar opportunity to replace the paper. But the following issue still remains: If ECCB is a better approach, should the banks start returning images of charges too?

On the one hand, maybe they should. Many might argue that the new American Express statement is superior to a standard bankcard descriptive statement. It contains more information and makes it easier for the cardholder to positively identify the purchase. On the other hand, it would cost the banking industry substantially more to create this feature than it cost American Express. The nonbank giant has only two processing facilities—at Ft. Lauderdale and at Phoenix, where all ROCs are centralized—thus avoiding the crippling cost of clearing images in a multipoint network. But the banks' drafts are captured, and statements printed, at thousands of locations. American Express's statements will probably remain distinctive—*a classic example of using technology distinctively instead of in a routine way.*

The bottom line on image processing is that it will probably play a major role in the future in controlling paper, cutting the costs of data entry, and improving customer service. One implication is that the passage of information through the banking system will be speeded up, exactly as it has been with other technologies. Second, larger, centralized players should have an initial advantage. Finally, winners are more likely to be those that, like American Express, emphasize value-added applications, not just cost-cutting.

INTEGRATED SOFTWARE

Most banks' systems contain hundreds, even thousands, of separate applications, broken down by function, product, and geography. Commonly, banks began developing application programs almost 30 years ago. Programs were later replicated, with changes, for other products. Over time, these programs (and their data) got to be redundant. A typical bank might have one set of programs for installment loans, another for overdrafts, a third for auto loans, a fourth for auto leases, a fifth for home equity loans, and so on. In fact, there might be dozens of such programs. Much of the code, however, is, or should be, the same. Each application might have an interest calculation module, for example. When variable rates become popular in consumer loans, each interest module has to be rewritten and maintained separately. Even worse, data gets duplicated between programs. The income and address file will be repeated for each application, but when the customer moves, not every file is updated correctly.

It is understandable how this problem evolved. In the beginning, no one could imagine the vast extent and growth of banking software. An architecture dating from the 1960s could not be expected to meet today's volumes, applications, and specific data needs. They could not reflect the astounding proliferation of products and the growth in complexity. *Even worse, in many cases the bank has no architecture at all, just a collection of programs that grew up over the years in a makeshift way.*

Thus, the development of integrated software is a major trend among banks. Many are going through a generational change to install their first integrated system. Whether purchased or built internally, the risks are very, very high. Since integration is very expensive, even the largest banks are considering buying a package for the core customer, asset, and liability functions. Major vendors are Hogan, Systematics, and Computer Associates. EDS is also developing a package. We estimate that total expenditures on integrated packages by this industry may be above

$1 billion in the next five years. Usually some tailoring is required to install the package, and the installation and conversion process can be risky. A few banks are rebuilding in-house, but the costs, time frame, and difficulty of assembling needed skills are major barriers. There are no easy solutions in this realm.

Integration means that the traditional interfaces and cumbersome bridges between modules are eliminated. The key is a common database that contains all customer and account information. It may well be implemented using relational database technology. Typically, there will be modules that access the common database. Customer, asset and liability modules might be a minimum set. Each module contains different components and features that are combined to create products. So, for example, savings accounts will be defined by what transactions are allowed and what the parameters are, rather than by having a separate set of code.

Asset and liability modules in integrated systems perform many functions. On the asset side, the modules provide processing and billing procedures, as well as collateral and delinquency components. Liability modules need pricing, insufficient funds, and electronic banking components. Hundreds of specific features are required. The following are a few examples, from the Cullinet Banking System: pending entry, effective backdating, stops and holds, payment allocations, maturity and renewals, reversals, fee assessments, escheats, memo-posting, rate flexibility, and so forth. The list is endless—a vivid testimonial to the power of systems technology to segment processing operations and create entirely new procedures from simple variations in information. But the point about integration is that each of these features is now in its own box and only needs to be reached once when a change is required. Given the growth of complexity that has resulted from technology's power, integration seems like a logical, indeed inevitable, development.

What effects will long-term adoption of integrated systems have on competition? To some extent, it may be defensive. The ultimate products, no matter how modular, are still going to be perceived primarily as commodities. But there could be trends, such as the following, that would affect the competitive balance:

- Large banks that implement integrated systems the soonest should be better equipped for a cross-product, full-service customer relationship. These banks can then market to the segment of the customer base that wants to deal with only one bank.

- There will be more product complexity than ever before, given the capability of integrated software to handle data. In turn, complexity will lead to more product features and more customer segmentation, thus allowing more opportunity for banks to find niches and to focus their efforts.
- Integration should allow more rapid changes in products and features.

In summary, integration is a logical development. But like so many of the other technological developments, its competitive benefit on a stand-alone basis may be neutral and very likely quite negative in particular cases. To make it pay off, banks will have to develop new business approaches. Simply using it to clean up the old, creaking systems is laudable, but is not enough for competitive success.

SUMMARY

The banks of the future will very likely be substantially different from the banks of today. They will contain much more technology than do today's banks, and that technology will look different from today's technology. Banks thus face two overwhelming issues: (1) deciding what business moves to make in the face of all that technology, and (2) designing a workable plan to migrate from today's world into the future. Neither is going to be easy.

Understanding the business implications is up to the general manager. It should be done first, as it will determine the overall sequence of technological investment. The next two chapters will deal with the issue of finding good business approaches in the new era of technology. Following an illustration of five banks that are coping successfully with the arrival of technology, we discuss some relevant implications for management.

Migration is more of a technical issue and is one where easy answers are not available. Yet the average bank could certainly do a better job in this regard. Too often migration is the result of vendor advice, monolithic thinking, or is just a continuation of current trends. How to cope with new technology is a subject that does not get enough attention from top management. As will be pointed out in the next chapter, this is one feature of a successful overall approach.

CHAPTER 9

ILLUSTRATIONS OF SUCCESS

Despite the difficulties of competing with technology, many banks have done it successfully. This chapter contains five illustrations of such success:

1. State Street Boston Corporation, in trust and custodial businesses;
2. Banc One Corporation, processing retail banking products for nonbanks;
3. First Chicago Corporation, in cash management;
4. Chase Manhattan Corporation, in the wholesale payments businesses; and
5. First Wachovia Corporation, in retail branch operations.

These five illustrations were selected because they clearly reveal, for a variety of institutions and business lines, the links between competition and technology. But they are not unique. Other well-known examples of success with technology could have been chosen: Security Pacific, for its automation company; Mellon Bank, for its correspondent data processing; CoreStates, for its proprietary ATM network MAC; Bankers Trust, for its trading and securities processing business; Citicorp, for its consumer credit, ATM, and mortgage processing operations; Bank of America, in merchant processing; and Bank of New York, for its trust and custodial businesses. In fact, virtually every large bank has *some* area in which it has used technology more effectively than its competition.

STATE STREET BOSTON CORPORATION

State Street is a medium-sized regional bank headquartered in Boston, Massachusetts, with approximately $7 billion in assets. The word *bank* is a bit of a misnomer, however. State Street has sold or closed 90 percent of its branches, has no LDC debt, will not make loans for leveraged buy outs, and has very few home mortgages, auto loans, and student loans. Sixty-four percent of its assets are in cash or investments. State Street has metamorphosed into a data processing company with a portfolio of trust and custodial businesses. A trustee or custodian is defined as an entity that is responsible for keeping possession of a securities portfolio and for tracking changes in its value. State Street's customers are large institutions (e.g., insurance companies or pension and mutual funds) that own many types of securities and are constantly changing their positions. State Street today is essentially a computerized record-keeping and accounting business. Physical possession of the security is no longer required in most cases.

When an institution that owns a portfolio (e.g., a mutual fund) has many owners, a second major processing need arises. The ownership portions in the securities portfolio must also be tracked. This activity of shareholder accounting has become incredibly complicated in modern times. For shared portfolios—mutual funds, 401(K) plans, or pension funds—State Street must track who owns what, and at what value, and must reflect all of each shareholder's buy/sell instructions. Complexities in shareholder accounting provide a classic illustration of how systems technology increases the output of products. State Street has seen this complexity coming, and has leaped to take advantage of it.

Financial Success

State Street has been remarkably successful. It has more than $625 billion under custody—far more than any of its competitors, and approximately 10 percent of all securities in the world. It is number one in its two major businesses: mutual funds and master trust/custody. (See Figure 9-1.) It is also doing well in several emerging businesses. Financial results have been outstanding. Earnings per share grew at a 17 percent CAGR between 1983 and 1988. ROE remained more than 18 percent during the entire 1980s. In 1986, the market-to-book ratio of its stock hit 246 percent—higher than any money center or large regional bank. Between 1977 and 1987, the stock returned 36.2 percent per year to investors. The driver behind this performance is State Street's fiduciary revenues, which went from $33 million in 1980, to $293 million in 1988—a 31.4 percent CAGR!

Of course, State Street was helped considerably by the buoyant markets of the 1980s. Its assets under custody have grown because of primary growth in the capital markets. But State Street is also a competitor,

FIGURE 9–1
Assets Under Custody by Line of Business

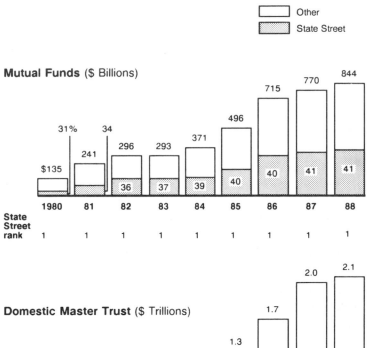

continuing to increase its market share. State Street's competitive advantage lies not only in the systems barriers surrounding the existing businesses, but also in its ability to transfer technology, operational procedures, and management mind-set from one business to the next. State Street's recent moves into global custody, indexed fund management, and trusteeship of securitized bonds are examples. *State Street has profited by cooperating with, not resisting, the industry trend toward disaggregation.*

Mutual Fund Processing

State Street provided custody for the assets of 1,411 mutual funds, totaling more than $346 billion at year-end 1988. It is the clear leader in servicing this now-critical part of the financial world. It had a 41 percent share of all mutual fund assets and a 53 percent share of all mutual funds. The Bank of New York is the number-two player, with an estimated 12 percent share of assets. Other players, such as First Jersey and PNC Financial, are far behind and have difficulty keeping up with State Street's constant reinvestment in systems technology because they have neither the needed features nor the low-cost position. In 1988, one of these small players, Shawmut Bank, sold out to State Street. More consolidation can probably be expected for the future.

Although State Street provided fund accounting and record keeping to the country's first mutual fund in 1924, it has never been a money center bank with unlimited resources. In 1973, to help it support its technological investments, it invested in a subsidiary that provides the shareholder accounting and customer service functions. This subsidiary, Boston Financial Data Services, Inc. (BFDS), is 50 percent owned by DST, a data processing and software company. BFDS is a high-volume processing operation that sets up new shareholder accounts, handles purchases and redemptions, answers telephone calls, and creates and mails customer statements. The moral is that active cooperation with nonbanks can pay off. Too few banks are willing to explore such joint ventures, even for their less-proprietary products. In contrast, State Street has entered into a partnership for a very key part of its business, and has reaped the rewards.

Master Trust/Custody

Master trust/custody is a business that serves institutional clients, such as pension funds or endowments, that need custody and portfolio accounting for their securities. As such, the core skills and systems requirements for this business are related to those of mutual funds processing. Traditionally, however, master trust/custody was a highly fragmented business populated by many regional players that, as often as not, would use an offshoot of a personal trust system to satisfy the very different needs of an institution. But in 1974, with the passage of the Employees Retirement Income Security Act (ERISA), the reporting and record-keeping requirements for institutions were greatly expanded.

Sensing a market opportunity, State Street entered the master trust/custody business with a service that emphasized more complex, sophisticated record-keeping abilities. For example, it could do daily pricing, swift month-end reporting, and GNMA pay-down reporting. The timing was good, as pension funds, with considerably more complex needs, were increasing their dominance of the capital markets. State Street's master trust assets under custody have grown at a 27 percent CAGR since then, reaching $244 billion in domestic assets by year-end 1988. It is now the number one player in this still-fragmented business; its 7 percent market share has surpassed other, and earlier, players such as Bankers Trust, Chase Manhattan, and Northern Trust.

Other Businesses/Products

State Street makes a point of moving aggressively into new businesses related to its core DP and custody skills. These new markets promise to augment, possibly even replace, the core mutual funds business that has long been rumored to be in danger of peaking out, although it has not happened yet—total mutual fund assets grew another $35 billion in 1988. Also, institutional customers' needs are growing in diversity and complexity. By expanding its offerings, State Street tries to lock up the customer. Here are some examples:

- Asset management is a business traditionally requiring high-paid entrepreneurial professionals. But with the rise of indexing, State Street again saw an opportunity. Indexed fund management combines DP-based skills with a certain amount of market judgment, such as how to "tilt" portfolios. By 1989, State Street had approximately $35 billion under management for many of the same customers for whom it does custodial work. It offers a Standard &

Poor's 500 indexed fund, as well as an international indexed fund, where it is the industry leader with a 40 percent share.

- Global custody is the business of holding securities issued in one country for an investor from another country. It is growing rapidly as U.S. investors buy more non-U.S. securities. U.S. pension funds, for example, still have only 3 to 5 percent of their assets invested overseas, but may have up to 20 percent so invested by the year 2000. Also, international investors have rapidly increased their holdings of U.S. securities. State Street has increased its international assets under custody at a 66 percent annual rate, from $3.3 billion in 1983 to $42.1 billion in 1988. Many of the non-U.S. securities are still paper-based, so State Street employs banks around the world as subcustodians to handle the paper. State Street focuses on the DP aspect—doing the data transmission, integration, and reporting and producing complete portfolio accounting services for the client. Of course, global custody requires significant systems investments. All of State Street's systems have been made multicurrency and can accommodate the significant reporting, regulatory, and legal differences between countries. Also, customer cross-selling is evident. International indexed funds, for example, are an easy way for pension fund customers to begin their overseas diversification. But being able to offer that product required State Street to have both indexing capability and global custody.

- State Street does 401(K) plan participant accounting for 375,000 people—a number growing at a 38 percent annual clip because of complexities introduced by the 1986 Tax Reform Act.

- State Street has a retained asset product for life insurance companies. This product takes a benefit payment and converts it to a checkable deposit account at the insurer.

- State Street offers custody for Nuclear Decommissioning Trusts—money set aside for replacement of aging nuclear reactors. Normally, pension funds never invest in tax-free municipals, so most of State Street's master trust competitors do not have software that handles them. But State Street does, and so it was able to capture the Nuclear Decommissioning business.

- Finally, State Street sees a growing business in trusteeship of debt securities based on securitized assets, such as mortgages or credit card loans. In 1988, based on this approach, State Street became the third largest trustee for new bond issues.

Synergy and Focus

All of the above-listed business lines and products did not happen by accident. Instead, they are part of a carefully crafted business strategy that has systems technology at its core. State Street has only one major system, called Horizon, which services all of its custody products. It is modular, table-driven, and employs up-to-date architecture. It contains thousands of highly structured program modules that perform the processing. Data held externally determines the logic of what code is executed for each product and each customer. Widely different accounting policies, such as how to accrue a variable-rate CD, can be accommodated. State Street has continued to invest an estimated 20 to 25 percent of its expenses in its systems, amounting to more than $400 million during the 1980s. State Street's equipment expense alone is 8.5 percent of its total budget—more than some banks' spending on all facets of DP. In contradistinction to many other banks, State Street does use its technology as an offensive weapon, not just as a "ticket to play."

To augment Horizon, State Street has focused and tailored its entire organization. Six of the top seven executives have industrial, data processing, or service bureau backgrounds, rather than lending or banking backgrounds. Even some of State Street's commercial lending activities support the processing business; for example, it lends to mutual funds that need liquidity. Approximately 25 percent of State Street's sources of funds in 1987 were interest-free deposits. This was not corporate DDA, but float money that "sticks" to State Street's fingers as mutual fund and pension purchases and redemptions pass in and out of its hands. Its foreign exchange trading capability complements its global custody functions. Even its credit card division is used to offer debit card access to some of Fidelity's mutual fund customers.

Summary: State Street

In summary, State Street's business really is technology. It has invested particularly in proprietary M2 that supports wise market decisions in M3 (see again Figure 3–3). Most of State Street's businesses have no overcapacity (unlike other automated bank businesses) because the core demand has a healthy growth rate. Last, but not least, it has focused on just this one successful approach. Clearly, not every bank can copy its strategy, but the principles behind State Street's approach are good, and others would do well to study them.

BANC ONE CORPORATION

Banc One Corporation, headquartered in Columbus, Ohio, is one of the nation's fastest growing super-regionals. From a $480-million country bank in 1968, Banc One grew at a 21.9 percent CAGR steadily, through technology-based businesses and acquisitions, to having assets of $25.3 billion at the end of 1988. Banc One was one of the top-performing regional banks between 1982 and 1986 based on return on average assets, return on average equity, and market-to-book ratio. Its net income per share increased at a 26.4 percent compound annual rate between 1981 and 1986—a claim few other banks can match. Banc One's technologically related success is in back-office processing for nonbanks. In essence, Banc One is a manufacturer or wholesaler of bank services, utilizing the distribution channels of nonbanks in unique and profitable ways. Banc One's mid-1989 acquisition of M Corp will allow it to play in two adjacent regions—the Midwest and the Southwest.

Credit Card Processing

Banc One was one of the first banks to enter the credit card processing business. It received a license for the original BankAmericard in 1966, making a momentous decision to develop its own credit card processing capability. Then it sought out other banks as customers for that capability. During the 1960s and 1970s, Banc One became one of a number of regionally based credit card processors serving commercial bank customers. Credit card processing was so much more profitable than credit card issuing (at least in the beginning) that by 1980 Banc One had approximately 1 million processing accounts, but only 90,000 issuance accounts.

Beginning in 1977, Banc One made national headlines when it agreed to be the bank servicer of the much heralded, and widely publicized, Merrill Lynch Cash Management Account (CMA). The CMA held a customer's cash and securities and gave him or her a high yield on the credit balance along with debit card and check access. Merrill Lynch was, in effect, offering a high-yield checking account that banks at the time could not match.

This is one of the first examples of a commercial bank willingly giving a nonbank access to both the check and the credit card payment systems. Despite some initial criticism, it was a wise decision. The payment system continues to disaggregate and today many nonbanks have access to it. In return, Banc One achieved a very profitable business with a high market share. It performed the check-clearing and plastic card account maintenance functions for what ultimately became 1 million CMA customers.

By 1982, every major retail brokerage house had developed a similar type of asset account (e.g., the Dean Witter Active Asset Account). Banc One had more than an 80 percent market share for the processing of these accounts. In fact, 12 years after its product's first introduction, Banc One is still the primary third-party processor for such accounts. Its only competition comes from in-house processing, which Merrill Lynch now does, since it owns a bank and has direct access to the check and bankcard clearing systems. This reinforces one important lesson: being first and dominant with an innovative product will usually establish a profitable, enduring lead in technology businesses.

Processing the CMA account required a joint investment in systems and technology. The checks were written on Bank One, Columbus, N.A. Then they were captured, authorized, and transmitted to the broker for posting to the customer's account. The card that came with the account was a hybrid debit card. Transactions that arrived through the Visa clearing system were transmitted to the broker for posting. Each account contained a variable credit limit that was redefined daily, based on the value of the securities and other events in the customer's brokerage account. For example, if the customer's equity securities dropped in value by $10,000 in one day, a lower credit limit would be transmitted from Merrill Lynch to Banc One that night.

This arrangement was not only innovative, but it also generated significant entry barriers. Extensive software investment was required to integrate the checks with the credit card system, to build the daily credit limit update feature, and to handle numerous other specific requirements of the product. As a result, when other brokers, such as Advest or Thomson-McKinnon, began to offer similar products, there was virtually no other place for them to go except to Banc One. Banc One's strategy for credit card processing has been to focus on unique programs that are tailored specifically for its customers. It has successfully differentiated itself from other processors, such as First Data Resources or Total Systems. Banc One is good at servicing a relatively unique customer need, and it sticks to that capability.

Credit Unions

The nation's 16,000 credit unions form a rapidly growing sector of the financial industry. They do not have the onerous capital requirements of a commercial bank and they gain access to customers through the point of employment. They have significantly lower costs than do commercial banks in providing standard banking products, such as CDs, checking accounts, savings accounts, and retail consumer credit. Some have become quite large; the Navy Federal Credit Union has approximately 800,000 accounts and several billion dollars in assets. Credit unions typically offer interest rates 300 to 400 basis points lower than banks on loans and can offer deposit rates similarly higher than banks. Because most credit unions are so small, however, they have formed industry associations such as the Credit Union National Association (CUNA) to help them gain access to third-party processors.

In 1978, Banc One and CUNA began a program to process credit cards in a standardized fashion. Traditionally, an issuer needed a minimum efficient scale of approximately 5,000 accounts in order to enter into a third-party credit card processing contract. Then, the issuer defined how its card would work, picking its features, parameters, options, and so on. Under the CUNA arrangement, however, the credit card features are limited. The minimum scale has been reduced close to zero so that even a very small credit union can play. CUNA provides the back-office servicing not done by Banc One, such as customer service and credit approval. The result is that as long as a credit union has an easily reachable source of customers, it can offer an attractive, low-cost credit card despite a lack of scale. As a result of this program and a similar one at Telecredit sponsored by Payment Systems for Credit Unions, another industry group, credit card outstandings at credit unions grew from $1.5 billion in 1985, to $9.4 billion in 1988—an 84 percent CAGR!

Like the CMA arrangement, this program required an investment in specially developed software. Banc One's financial results with the CUNA program have been impressive. By 1988, it had approximately 1.7 million accounts, spread over 1,650 different credit unions, with growth projected to reach approximately 4 million accounts by 1992. The margins are believed to be healthy. *Again, the bank has taken advantage of, instead of resisted, industry disaggregation.*

Affinity Programs

Banc One was also one of the first to develop an affinity credit card. In 1982 it signed a contract with Comp-U-Card, the nation's first large scale electronic shopping service. For a moderate price, a Comp-U-Card member is entitled to call an 800 number to get a low price quote on more than 100,000 branded items. Members then either order from Comp-U-Card or use the price as a guide for local shopping.

To sell the membership, Comp-U-Card resorted to an affinity card—a combination of membership and a credit card from Banc One. During the 1983 to 1985 period, this card was extensively marketed via preapproved direct mail. The product achieved very good response rates and increased Banc One's credit card portfolio from 90,000 accounts to approximately 1.5 million accounts. Again, an extensive amount of cooperative tailoring of software and processing procedures was required. In essence, Banc One found a low-cost way to disaggregate the marketing function, but the ability and willingness to link its systems with those of another corporation was essential to get this done.

Other issuers were also expanding their credit card portfolios during the 1980s. The key to cost-effective account solicitation has been, and continues to be, market distinction; the Comp-U-Card was just such a unique card. The experience gained later enabled Banc One to develop other affinity offshoots, such as cards for Northwest Airlines, Holiday Inns, and the Independent Tire Dealers Association. Because Banc One is both an issuer and a processor, it can control the entire product. Given its smaller balance sheet, relative to larger card issuers like Citibank and First Chicago, it has placed a higher fraction of its assets in credit card accounts. *In 1988, Banc One's net interest revenue was 486 basis points, the highest of the 35 large banks.*

American Association of Retired Persons (AARP)

The AARP is one of the nation's largest and strongest lobby groups with more than 15 million members. It has gained its strength partially because it provides its members with a wide range of services that reflect the unique needs of the over-55 group. For example, it offers personal insurance products through a variety of insurers. It also realized that a credit union would be an effective way to offer bank services.

In 1987, Banc One and AARP agreed to build a national credit union that would be marketed and accessed strictly through mail and telephone. The arrangement calls for Banc One to do all of the processing and servicing of the accounts, although the credit union itself is controlled by AARP. Current products include a credit card, a share account, CDs, and access to a national ATM network. Future products will include a checking account and installment loans. The deposits and loans appear on the books of the AARP Credit Union. Because of AARP's size and reputation, the credit union has the potential to become one of the country's largest. Although the program is still in its preliminary stages, potential revenues range from $10 million to $50 million per year. Margins may well be generous.

Other financial services firms have demonstrated how technology and telecommunications can successfully substitute for bricks and mortar. For example, the United Services Automobile Association (USAA), a reciprocal insurance company, markets auto and homeowner's insurance to several million active and retired military officers and families worldwide—completely by mail and phone. USAA is a standout insurer widely admired for its heavy use of technology, high degree of customer satisfaction, and far-above-average profitability. It has the largest single inbound WATS facility in the country, employing more than 9,200 employees to service 150,000 calls on a busy day. This high volume centralization has allowed USAA to automate many functions that remain paper-bound at other insurance companies.

At both USAA and the AARP/Banc One program, the customer service representatives can access virtually any account or transaction data through on-line screens. This requires an integrated software approach and a strong customer data base. Banc One invested several million dollars in relatively specialized systems technology for the AARP program. The bank built a dedicated data center, bought and tailored the applications software, and developed specialized credit scoring tools to reflect the needs of retired people. For example, approval can be based on net worth even if income is lacking. By heavily centralizing the operations, new technologies such as image processing become more feasible. Technology is truly the enabler for these two successful business approaches.

Summary: Banc One

The Banc One experience is exemplary. Higher margin fee-based businesses have been achieved by selling core banking skills to other financial institutions that have competitive advantages in reaching the ultimate customer. Banc One has cooperated with, not resisted, the trend toward disaggregation, which is in turn caused by the rise of systems technology. The unique twisting of the service delivery system that occurred in the CMA, Comp-U-Card, and AARP programs would never have occurred in the old, paper-based world.

Banc One's achievements are not based on core technology, per se. As noted in Chapter 3, its M1 infrastructure contains the same components as everyone else's. It has no proprietary computers, operating systems, or languages. However, much of the M2 software and attendant processing procedures is unique and does serve as a barrier; in most cases, the software has been built specifically to meet the customer's needs, once a program has been developed. Others could have built the software, too, if they had had a similar opportunity. But the real key to Banc One's ability, we believe, lies in M3. Repeatedly, Banc One has had the foresight to recognize changing customer needs and to develop better ways of delivering the product. As will be recommended in Chapter 10, it has tried to do things differently in the new technological world, and not just automate the old way of doing things.

Along the way, Banc One has developed a mind-set and a reputation that give it some advantage whenever new programs come along. Senior management is comfortable with technology and with the concept of serving nonbank competitors. Having been through the experience with Merrill Lynch, it had no qualms about cooperating with the AARP. The bank has a reservoir of experience in dealing with one-shot, custom-made programs that can be transferred from deal to deal. In short, a synergistic approach to technological competition has occurred, and Banc One's tremendous financial success is ample proof of the rewards.

FIRST CHICAGO CORPORATION

First Chicago Corporation is the 11th largest U.S. commercial bank holding company, with assets of approximately $48 billion. Headquartered in Chicago, it is the largest bank in the Midwest. More than 70 percent of its revenues derive from the Global Corporate Bank, which includes a variety of credit and noncredit products sold to major industrial, financial, and governmental institutions.

First Chicago employs a philosophy of relationship banking for its major corporate customers. It views the noncredit cash management services as an essential element in that relationship, combined with credit services, trading products, securities services and capital markets activities. Cash management is run as a profit center, although it is not regarded as truly stand-alone. But the revenues are very important. In 1989, cash management and securities services were projected to be the largest product family in the Global Corporate Bank. First Chicago is among the top five cash management banks in the United States, along with Citicorp, Chase Manhattan, Mellon, and First Wachovia. The cash management business at First Chicago employs approximately 2,000 people and includes more than 48 specific products. Although First Chicago has 15,000 cash management customers, 92 percent of its cash management revenue comes from corporations that exceed $100 million in sales.

The cash management business is tough to compete in. The products are mostly viewed as commodities, and there is always steady pressure on the margins. First Chicago's overall approach begins with being market-driven. Its goes after being the low-cost producer, primarily through efficient data processing operations, low labor costs, and a central location in the middle of the country. In addition, it has an elaborate system to measure, control, and improve its performance on many key operational statistics, resulting in service quality and performance far above industry norms. For example, its prime pass reject rate was 0.87 percent in 1987, compared to a national average of 1.4 percent.

Its technology strategy is to be on the trailing edge of the leading edge. First Chicago focuses on *appropriate technology* melded with superior people control in what is still a highly labor-intensive business. The result has been a successful "anchor" for First Chicago's Global Corporate Bank. First Chicago has maintained its prestige and many of its corporate relationships, while adding independently to the bottom line.

First Chicago's major cash management businesses are:

1. Wholesale lockbox (receiving checks from institutional payers),
2. Funds transfer (to other institutions for large amounts),
3. Check collection (for a lockbox service, deposits, or correspondent banks), and
4. Disbursements (from a controlled, or zero-balance account).

Of course, this list is not complete. First Chicago offers many other services, such as letters of credit and depository transfer checks (DTCs), which are needed to round out its full service philosophy. And it is the lead bank in an evolving proprietary corporate trade payments network sponsored by General Motors.

Wholesale Lockbox and Collections

First Chicago developed the country's first lockbox in 1947. Today, it is still a leader, operating approximately 2,500 lockboxes that serve 2,000 customers. It processes more than 1 million arriving remittances per week, using five wholly-owned processing centers scattered around the country.

Wholesale lockbox is a job shop business. The data to be captured, the handling of transactions, and the reporting requirements must be tailored for each customer. The typical customer is a large corporation that receives payments from a wide variety of customers, subsidiaries, franchises, or branches. The information passed with the payment must be recorded, as well as payer, date, amount, invoice(s) covered, discounts taken, and so on. Such information is usually nonstandard.

First Chicago is known as the leader in wholesale lockbox because of its high quality, central location, and fast collections. Because the checks are usually of high value, the key to the business is *fast collection, not just low operating costs*. Thus, First Chicago's location at the country's premier air hub, O'Hare Airport, supports both its extensive check collection business and the wholesale lockbox business. In fact, First Chicago's competition tends to be other banks with easy access to air hubs, for example, Continental Bank, also in Chicago, or First Tennessee's First Express overnight check-clearing service, located in Memphis.

First Chicago uses automated workstations to perform the entire remittance processing procedure. Reporting of balances and concentration of funds to an investment account or central account is also performed automatically. Image processing workstations have been adopted slowly, in keeping with its philosophy of appropriate technology.

Wholesale lockbox does have economies of scale, but not enough to prevent medium-size players from staying in the game — approximately 3 million remittances per year are required. But First Chicago's volume does give it an edge in developing the procedures and technology to handle its large customers' unique reporting requirements. Because each customer usually has different electronic format, protocol, and timing standards, First Chicago is adept at interfacing with a wide variety of environments. For example, in 1988 it reduced its time to install an electronic interface to a customer by 50 percent—to approximately six weeks. Sometimes, the customer is less automated than First Chicago, and data has to be reconverted back from electronics to paper before customer reporting.

First Chicago processes a large number of checks, due to its lockbox business and its clearing business with 300 correspondent banks. In fact, it is believed to be the largest third-party clearer of checks in the country, with a volume exceeding 300 million per year. However, the check processing business is very fragmented, and First Chicago has less than 1 percent national share (see again Figure 4–3). First Chicago's position in wholesale lockbox and correspondent clearing is strong, yet these two businesses will always be under pressure, because industry capacity grows so much faster than does the check volume and potential revenues. First Chicago's successful approach illustrates how to stay ahead in a difficult business.

Money Transfer

First Chicago has a segmented approach to money transfer services. It offers four different access methods to customers: (1) telephone, (2) time-sharing with a dumb terminal, (3) PC link, and (4) CPU-to-CPU. Selection is based on the customer's volume and level of sophistication in its payments. The highest-volume access methods are targeted toward securities firms, commodity dealers, and finance and leasing companies (e.g., sellers of commercial paper). First Chicago is one of only a few banks that compete for these specific customers.

By making its payments services modular, First Chicago can tailor the services closely to the needs of its customers. For example, customers with a large volume of incoming wire transfer activity can have the advices transmitted directly to their computer mainframes. These batch transmissions can come in as often as every 15 minutes. For another example, nonrepetitive transfers of less than $50,000 can be initiated by a clerk, requiring only the use of a personal identification number. Because First Chicago offers worldwide payments services, the customer can initiate payments that need to be translated into foreign currencies. There are protections against wire fraud and controls on the amount of

intra-day credit extended to each customer. Still, First Chicago is not one
of the leaders in CHIPS volume; it has a 2 percent share and cannot clear
for other banks. Money transfer can only be viewed s a contributory function, not as a method of distinction. Within the overall context of wholesale payments, however, money transfer is a valuable resource.

Disbursements

First Chicago operates a disbursement service under which corporate
customers write checks from controlled disbursement points. First
Chicago performs check and statement reconciliation for the cleared
checks as well as balance reporting. It has a totally automated sweep
product that invests balances overnight in an offshore high yield account.
Because of overcapacity, the market prices for disbursements dropped
significantly in the mid-1980s—from approximately 25 cents per cleared
item to approximately 10 cents. Customers are getting smarter and
are reducing the aggregate number of disbursement accounts that they
hold. This has reduced the overall profitability of this business significantly, but because there are economies of scale, First Chicago has
remained in the game.

Electronic Data Interchange (EDI)

First Chicago is the lead bank for the General Motors (GM) proprietary corporate trade network. Begun in 1986, this innovation is still
being rolled out. The network seeks to automate the invoicing and
and billing procedures between GM and its 40,000 suppliers. Traditionally, this information has been transmitted by paper. GM's paper
processing costs in receivables and payables are estimated at $800 mil-
lion per year. The private network will combine payments and advice
information from GM, as well as invoice information in the other direction. Six other banks are involved with First Chicago in this proprietary network.

With time, EDI will probably become a very big business. First
Chicago has the potential to be a major player in that business, precisely
because of its involvement with GM. The outcome depends on whether
entry barriers can be constructed with the software, or whether EDI will
become a typical banking utility where everybody must be able to play the

game for it to work at all. If the latter, the customers – not the banks – will reap the benefits. The savings in displaced paper will be absorbed in providing better information and in more complex reporting.

Quality Performance

First Chicago has attempted to differentiate itself in wholesale payments through a major commitment to quality, as measured by specific standards in the performance of work. High quality is achieved through two levers: automation and control of employees. It is interesting to note that systems technology is not just part of the solution, but also creates much of the need. For example, many of the performance measures that First Chicago emphasizes involve not just accuracy (e.g., low error rates), but also delivery of information as fast as possible to allow overnight investing, early morning borrowing, and so on. *Such finely tuned control over the cash flow is a direct result of the monetary speedup engendered by systems technology.*

Manual processing of paper is the most laborious and error-prone function, but First Chicago handles paper very well. With some new procedures, it reduced its error rate on check encoding from 1.5 errors per 100,000 checks in 1986, to 0.39 per 100,000 in 1988. Returned checks are processed accurately 99.98 percent of the time. Controllable errors in international dollar clearances occur at a 0.41 per 1,000 rate. Nonrepetitive money transfer errors occur at a 2 per 10,000 rate. And, the error rate in handling paper currency is 1 error per 250,000 bills handled. Finally, improvements in wholesale lockbox processing have been dramatic; error rates dropped from approximately 1 error per 3,000 remittances in 1982, to approximately 1 in 8,500 in early 1988.

The statistics for electronic transactions are even more striking. First Chicago processed EDI payment transactions for six straight months in 1988 without an error. Only two errors were committed in processing 330,000 repetitive money transfers between November 1987 and April 1988. ACH errors do occur, but in 87 percent of all weeks, First Chicago now hits 100 percent accuracy. This virtual elimination of errors in automated transactions is important not so much because it reduces costs, but because it changes the perception and expectations of the customer. With perfect processing (and perfect information), new business approaches, such as micromanagement of the cash position, become possible. In turn, the business requirements and performance expectations change for the bank. *Perhaps inaccuracy more than cost will be what ultimately kills the more error-prone paper-based payment methods.*

Many of First Chicago's performance standards measure *when* information is transmitted to the customer. For example, a balanced DDA deposit file is posted every night, usually around 9:00 P.M. The goal is 10:15 P.M., and First Chicago missed it only once in a six-month period. The daily requirements for controlled disbursement accounts must be transmitted as early as possible to allow the corporate treasurer to raise funds. First Chicago missed the 9:30 A.M. deadline (at its Woodbridge, Illinois, endpoint) only twice in six months. Previous-day balance reporting occurs at latest by 5:00 A.M., always well in advance of the 6:30 A.M. goal. Intraday transaction information is updated every 30 minutes between 6:30 A.M. and 10:00 P.M., with approximately 99 percent consistency.

A final element of performance is response to customer service calls, especially for balance and other simple information. Like so many others, First Chicago has started to use voice response technology to accommodate easily answered requests. By automating approximately one-half of its customer service calls—the most routine half—First Chicago decreased its discontinuance rate from about 4 percent to 0.5 percent, and decreased the number of required outbound calls.

First Chicago really does create value for the customer through its many performance dimensions. In all probability, only major players in cash management services can match this record of high accuracy, timeliness, flexibility, and comprehensiveness. The lesson is that for large corporate customers, the basis upon which the service is evaluated has expanded and speeded up—precisely because of systems technology. These customer demands will probably continue to rise as time passes. Meeting them requires a constant effort to mix technology in appropriate measure with control of human effort.

Summary: First Chicago

First Chicago has developed an extensive set of cash management products that generate fee revenue and balances, and support the relationships with corporate customers for its Global Corporate Bank. Without its systems investments in these products, First Chicago's position among its corporate customers would undoubtedly be harder to maintain. Going forward, the challenge for First Chicago is to continue to differentiate itself from the competition, take advantage of economies of scale, and offer information on a flexible basis.

CHASE MANHATTAN

Chase Manhattan is the country's second largest commercial bank, with assets of approximately $100 billion. It is a well-known competitor in wholesale noncredit activities, providing a broad range of cash management services, check-clearing and collection services, funds transfer, ACH, lockbox, disbursement, and information-based services. It has an extensive international presence, evidenced by its more than 100 overseas operations and 16,000 overseas employees.

Chase has provided funds transfer services for a long time, but always within the context of an overall customer relationship. Beginning in 1988, it aggregated many of its institutional transaction processing products into a new profit center, called InfoServ International, which is designed to be a major contributor to Chase's bottom line. In 1988, InfoServ earned $55 million after-tax (on a fully allocated cost basis) by processing approximately $290 trillion in informational and transactional services. Because payment businesses require lower equity than do balance sheet businesses, Chase's return on equity is between 30 percent and 40 percent. Chase believes that InfoServ will contribute at least 10 percent of Chase's core after-tax earnings in future years.

Although InfoServ offers many products — including cash management, securities processing, and trade payments — it has been particularly successful in the international and domestic funds transfer businesses. Because these products are highly automated, they have been subject to the forces of overcapacity, escalating investments, and deteriorating pricing discussed in earlier parts of this book. But despite these forces, Chase has found ways to survive and to maintain its profitability. Its experience is a useful illustration of competition in the new technological era.

International Money Transfer (IMT)

IMT is the part of InfoServ that offers international money transfers to correspondent banks located throughout the world. Typically, these transfers arrive at Chase via the SWIFT network and are either settled by Chase directly on their books or sent to CHIPS for settlement with other banks. IMT's profits are healthy despite the economic pressures that both technology and environmental forces have placed on this business. In 1988, IMT returned more than 20 percent on equity and enjoyed an earnings growth rate of between 10 and 12 percent.

Money transfers are almost completely electronic. Substantial investments are required in systems technology, both to create the transactions and to ensure enough capacity for daily and peak volumes. In 1988, IMT handled approximately 37,000 transfers per day, together worth $280 billion to $300 billion. Of these, approximately 22,000 went on to CHIPS. Payment volumes have definite peaking patterns, especially on the day after a holiday. A peak day may require Chase to process up to 65,000 transactions, together worth $600 billion.

Variances in transaction volumes have increased over time as the major source of transactions has shifted from trade related payments to foreign exchange, money market, and securities transactions. In fact, approximately 70 percent of IMT's transactions do not result from trade at all. Thus, if the dollar is particularly active in the foreign exchange market, Chase, as well as other competitors, sees a surge in its payment volume. This has increased the scale economies, as to be a creditable player now requires an additional investment just to pay for this peak capacity.

Because of the fixed cost element and the required systems investments (estimated at $30 million to $50 million), IMT's costs are considerably lower than those of many international banks, which cannot hope to equal Chase's volume. As was illustrated in Figure 6–3, Chase is the second leading bank at CHIPS, with an 8.1 percent share. To illustrate this cost advantage, IMT charges slightly more than $4 for a typical transaction, even though it might cost a nonscale international bank $35 to $50 to perform the same transaction itself. Thus, some consolidation has already occurred among international payment providers. But, consolidation moves more slowly than it might because this function, like so many others in banking, cannot be treated entirely on rational economic grounds. Some banks do transactions in-house despite the higher cost, either because of ignorance or because of prestige, control, and security reasons.

Competitive Approach

There is considerable overcapacity in the international money transfer business because of its recent conversion to electronics. Just to maintain price levels has been a struggle. Because the transaction per se is a commodity, the players have moved beyond technology to differentiate themselves. They recognize that the overall account relationship is not a commodity, so they compete on the basis of their people, their service, and their balance sheets. IMT's specific approaches to differentiation include the following:

- *Global reach*: This means not only a physical presence throughout the globe, but a culture, collective mind-set, and body of working experience that is attuned to the international community. IMT has multilanguage and multicurrency capability and an understanding of foreign cultures. It also has localized service centers for inquiry resolution and access.
- *Balance Sheet Strength*: International transfers always create daylight overdrafts. Given the size of Chase's customers, this creates significant exposure. For example, IMT's three largest customers, each of which generates 40,000 payments per month, run a peak intra-day overdraft level from *$3 billion to $6 billion*. By comparison, this is approximately six to eight times the legal maximum amount that Chase could lend to any given customer. Because intra-day overdrafts are not always covered, liquidity to absorb potential overnight overdrafts is another key factor. In addition, Chase must have the necessary credit evaluation skills to understand its customers. Each IMT customer has a credit line varying from $500,000 to $500 million.
- *Customer service*: Finally and most important, IMT competes on its level of customer service. Tracking down errors and adjustments, fixing them quickly, finding payments that went astray, handling miscodings, and providing personal customer contact from worldwide regional centers are all important. The process is also costly and time consuming. *The quality of the people and the customer service is really the basis on which the large customer chooses.*

In summary, IMT has been successful in a business that has totally converted from paper to electronics. IMT has realized that despite the conversion, *the key to success is not simply the technology.* Systems technology is the key to entry, has reduced the number of players, and has squeezed the margins. Many fewer banks can now compete in international payments compared to the past. But the fact is that the true competitive levers continue to be the people and the balance sheet, not the technology.

Domestic Payments

Chase uses both Fedwire and CHIPS to make domestic payments. Chase is one of the Fedwire leaders, generating approximately 19,000 transactions per day and holding about a 7.5 percent national market share. Its target market is the largest corporations; it handles wire transfers for approximately one-third of the Fortune 100 companies.

The domestic payments business has been automated considerably longer than the international payments business. The first electric funds transfer system in the United States, a forerunner of Fedwire, began about 1925. As a consequence, Chase's own computer systems for handling domestic transfers really began in the 1960s with the advent of the System/360 and were more than 20 years old by the mid-1980s. Over time, this business became subject to the same overcapacity, pricing pressures, and surfeit of competitors that so many other automated businesses now face.

In addition, the Federal Reserve Bank itself began to compete more aggressively in the 1980s to serve correspondent banks directly. The arrival of PC technology allowed the Federal Reserve Bank to install relatively low-cost terminals in small banks, bypassing the need for a money center correspondent. The Federal Reserve Bank does have some competitive advantage in piping the transactions, although it cannot offer the entire package of back-office correspondent services that Chase can.

In response to these heightened competitive pressures, in 1984 Chase began an ambitious reinvestment in its systems technology architecture. Chase handles both IMT and domestic payments from a common data center and common set of applications programs. By 1989, it had invested tens of millions of dollars. In the process, a new, "second generation" of domestic and international wire transfer technology was created. This system, known as Dollar Funds Transfer System (DFTS), not only modernized the underlying core technology (M1), but also added proprietary features. It was both a defensive and offensive investment. Not only did it keep Chase in the game relative to noninvestors, but it also helped guarantee sustained profits in IMT.

DFTS's features include the following:

1. Electronic connections with customers and with the payment utilities;
2. Conversion of corporate formats to Chase or standard formats, and preparation and verification of instructions;

3. High capacity geared to peak demands, with incremental expansion capability;
4. Dollar risk controls for daylight overdrafts (e.g., payment instructions that would take the customer's overdraft below a certain level are held up and kicked out for review by an officer); and
5. A sophisticated ability to read, scan, interpret, and make decisions on payment instructions.

DFTS is a classic example of a strategic reinvestment in a consolidating business. The new system's specific features can not be matched by the remaining small and niche players, but only by the other large players that also reinvested.

Summary: Chase Manhattan

The increase in industry capacity has not yet worked to Chase's disadvantage. It may never. As long as Chase continues to compete on the features that go beyond the technology, it has a good competitive shot. Also, capacity increments can now be added in much smaller quantities, reducing the penalty from excess capacity. It is possible that this evolution also reflects a gradual diminishment of overcapacity because the underlying demand for the business has been growing approximately 7 percent a year.

As a linchpin of Chase's services to corporations, technological investments in supporting wholesale funds transfer are mandatory. Making them pay is the challenge that InfoServ has been successful at so far. As these transaction businesses grow, Chase will need to continue its efforts to keep them profitable.

FIRST WACHOVIA CORPORATION

First Wachovia is a super-regional bank holding company located in North Carolina and Georgia. It had 1988 year-end assets of $21.8 billion and has consistently been one of the country's premier bank holding companies. For five of the six years between 1983 and 1988, its ROA was above 1.1 percent and ROE was above 17 percent. Net income per share increased from $2.53 to $4.22 in the same period.

First Wachovia is known for its effective management and a pragmatic, down-to-earth philosophy about technology. Its management works hard at handling technology and uses it in support of many banking services, especially operations. Yet, technology is never placed in the driver's seat. First Wachovia believes that technology is a tool and a means to an end, not an end in itself. This philosophy was articulated by Chief Executive Officer John G. Medlin, Jr., in a 1988 speech, part of which went as follows:

> A balance must be struck between what technology is available and what is truly needed to serve customers properly. Plans and capital expenditures should not be based on faulty assumptions: that newer is always better than older or that earlier is always better than later. It is important to be the low-cost provider of high-quality service, which is a goal seldom achieved by the laggard or the trailblazer.
>
> Banking is a trendy business with a herd instinct and a keep-up-with-the-neighbors mentality. It is important to pursue one's own strategies and to avoid following others blindly into the fashionable and superficial, while neglecting the sensible and fundamental. You want to be near the leading edge, but you want to avoid being on the bleeding edge.
>
> No single viewpoint should be allowed to dominate the design of bank systems and services, especially those of technicians and equipment vendors. The best and most successful ideas come from customers; are developed by teams of operations, technical, and marketing people; and are customer-tested before being set in concrete. The test of technology is not how well it works in the lab, but its utility and practicality for the user.

Personal Banker Program

In keeping with this philosophy, First Wachovia has built a distinctive approach for providing sales and service in branch-based retail products, called the Personal Banker program. It was originally developed in 1972 for the North Carolina bank and is now being extended to other banks that became part of the First Wachovia Corporation through merger or acquisition. The Georgia bank plans to adopt it during 1990.

The Personal Banker program assigns each consumer relationship to one of approximately 600 Personal Bankers located throughout the North Carolina branch system. Retail customers are encouraged to use their Personal Banker to establish new accounts, borrow money, and conduct the more complex types of transactions. The Personal Banker can handle virtually any new service for a given customer, with a few exceptions—for example, personal trust, indirect loans (through an auto dealer), and some types of mortgages. Routine services (e.g., safe deposits, check orders, and traveler's checks) are normally handled by assistants to the Personal Banker called service representatives. To implement this approach, customers are continually reminded of who their Personal Banker is. For example, their monthly checking account statement contains the Personal Banker's name and telephone number.

The Personal Bankers constitute the major branch-based customer service and sales force for both business and individual banking. There are four categories of Personal Banker, which reflect customer segmentations. Most Personal Bankers handle from 1,500 to 2,500 mass-market type customers. Executive Bankers generally handle from 200 to 500 "better" customers. Business Bankers handle from 75 to 100 customers who are small businessmen and may have both personal and small business accounts. Finally, the Branch Managers handle a variety of upper-scale consumer, professional, and small-to-medium-sized commercial accounts.

First Wachovia does have some centralized operational functions (e.g., credit card and consumer loan collections), but *the Personal Banker participates in, and in most cases controls, all phases of the customer relationship.* The Personal Banker decides how and where accounts are handled when something goes wrong. For example, Personal Bankers begin their day by reviewing their past-due loans and checks for which there are insufficient funds (NSFs). If credit card or auto loans are delinquent, Personal Bankers decide what to do: they can collect the loans themselves or refer them to central collections and monitor the progress. Because of First Wachovia's integrated systems, Personal Bankers can review the actions, comments, and follow-up dates entered on the collection system by the central collectors. For NSF items, they must decide whether to pay or to return the item. If a customer has a $10,000 CD, for example, the Persona Banker might pay the check and incur the overdraft without much worry.

The major justification for this approach, in an age of mass-market service, is to maintain a personal link with, and knowledge of, the customer. First Wachovia's contention is that no customer should have to introduce himself or herself in the branch. Each Personal Banker should be able to refer immediately to information covering the totality of that customer's product usage. Each branch staff member's desk is equipped with an on-line terminal that can access information on every product a customer might have. All data is current as of the previous night.

Finally, one person should have an ongoing relationship with the customer. The Personal Banker program is First Wachovia's attempt to answer those needs.

Marketing

Personal Bankers can cross-sell better because they have access to information covering the entire relationship. First Wachovia has approximately 2.5 services per relationship (e.g., a checking account, a loan, and an IRA for the same customer). When a Personal Banker sees a customer in the branch he or she knows what products that person does not have. Personal Bankers can open any transaction or savings account on-line. They take the required information for a loan and make the loan decision themselves, up to their approval limit. Personal Bankers are also involved in mail marketing campaigns. For example, their names were recently used in the text of a direct mail piece advertising the new home equity product. In an era when banks are searching for ways that technology can convert their platform people to salespeople, First Wachovia seems to be several steps ahead in finding an answer.

Management

The Personal Banker program is also a philosophy of management. Every Personal Banker is managed through a set of exhaustive monthly reports that describe his or her entire portfolio across all his or her customers. The reports measure both assets and liabilities by product, yield, delinquency rates, growth factors, penetration of prearranged transfers, and many other features. Personal Bankers' salary grades are based on the performance of their portfolio, not on production alone. This gives them an incentive not only to get business, but also to maintain and replenish it, to service it, and to have good credit quality. In fact, it is reminiscent of how insurance agents handle their customers. Over time, some Wachovia Personal Bankers have built portfolios as high as $25 million, and their compensation reflects it.

The three keys to implementing the Personal Banker program have been management commitment, industrial engineering, and systems technology. Management commitment is essential because the Personal Banker program is a unique way to operate a branch; no other major bank has adopted this approach, partly because benefits are impossible to quantify. First Wachovia has extensively reengineered its branch workflows over a 15-year time span to fine-tune the Personal Banker program. For example, Personal Bankers must work a high number of on-line systems. They actually have access to every system, but do not necessarily use all of them. Thus, training has been a critical and ongoing investment. Finally, the program requires tailor-made proprietary software for a customer information file (CIF) to extract information from the different application systems and combine them in the management reports.

Customer Information File (CIF)

The major technology behind the Personal Banker program is a proprietary, in-house CIF, which Wachovia began developing in 1975, years before the concept of a CIF became such a "hot" technological development. Even by the late 1980s, CIFs were still not found at many banks, although industry observers tout them as a key to better marketing, better customer service, and better control of operations costs.

A CIF is a data base that links all accounts or products purchased by one customer. The CIF will contain the customer data (e.g., the customer's address) so that it does not have to be duplicated in each separate application system. Typically, a CIF contains pointers to each separate product and allows a quick understanding of the overall relationship.

At First Wachovia, many of the Personal Bankers' activities and the monthly reports that measure the productivity of the Personal Bankers depend on the CIF. In addition, the CIF enables Personal Bankers to open accounts on-line with a minimum of work. A typical new account set-up has 78 separate data items but the Personal Banker enters relatively few of them. Edits in the CIF help assure the integrity of the data base. Another benefit is that a combined quarterly statement can be mailed, listing a customer's total assets, loan balances, and interest accrued year-to-date.

The CIF helped First Wachovia when it introduced ATMs in North Carolina during the early 1970s. It was not the first bank to install these machines, but when it did the CIF allowed one ATM card to access not just checking and savings accounts but also line of credit and credit card accounts. As a result of this higher utility, within six months Wachovia's ATM usage had surpassed that of its competitors.

Quick Access 24

Another illustration of the CIF's value is First Wachovia's new telephone access inquiry service. Dubbed Quick Access 24, the service allows customers to query the computer about their checking, savings, credit card, and line-of-credit accounts. The customer is required to enter only his or her social security number and PIN number for identification before starting to ask questions. The CIF provides the actual account number, relieving the customers of this easily forgotten burden. Customers can obtain balances, last five paid items, and data on a specific check number.

Customers can use either a touch-tone phone or a rotary phone. With a touch-tone phone, data is entered by touching the keys. For the 25 percent of the callers who use rotary phones, the information can be spoken and does not have to be dialed. Using a voice recognition package from Intervoice, a vendor, First Wachovia's system translates the speaker's voice into data. Through software tweaking, the system even accommodates the region's heavy Southern accents.

Although this dial-in service is only supportive to the Personal Banker program and not a substitute, it is another example of First Wachovia's technological approach. The CIF makes it easy for customers to dial in, and initial response has been heavy. The feature adds value, and is expected to cut branch costs. It also creates a competitive differentiation and shores up the overall level of service—clearly an important objective for First Wachovia.

SUMMARY

Several lessons emerge from these illustrations. The first is that systems must be linked with a good business strategy. None of our illustrations are about technology per se. They do not, for example, describe how Bank XYZ used a new software application to eliminate a clerical position (as is so often reported in the trade press). Rather, we see Banc One creatively servicing competitors of banks who have new ways of reaching a customer with a bank-like product. We see them working with customers to develop distinctive applications. We see State Street profiting from steady growth in the underlying demand for mutual funds and from its disaggregation of the shareholder accounting function to BFDS. We see First Wachovia developing a distinctive way of operating its branch net-

FIGURE 9–2
Lessons Learned From Illustrations

	State Street	Banc One	First Chicago	Chase Manhattan	First Wachovia
Link strategy to systems					
Use "new game approach"	√	√		√	
Maintain high share in consolidating business			√	√	
Early mover gains advantage	√	√	√	√	
"Tight-loose" approach					
Emphasize nontechnical quality			√	√	√
Treat 90/10 differently					
Develop proprietary M2 with distinctive features	√	√	√	√	√
Don't compete on M1 technology	√	√	√	√	√
Watch capacity					
Maintain high share leadership	√	√	√	√	
Focus					
Transfer skills between businesses	√	√		√	
Separate group within bank to achieve focus			√	√	
Management involvement is essential	√	√			

work. And we see First Chicago and Chase consciously stressing non-technological attributes in highly automated payment businesses. The lesson is that the conception of value added (M3 in our framework) is the place to start, either with new-game approaches or staying ahead in a consolidating business.

Second, we see a concern for economics, for the forces of competition, and for industry structure. Chase is very aware of which other banks are investing in more funds transfer capacity. First Chicago is deliberately seeking to be the low-cost provider. And State Street seems adept at developing related products where it can transfer systems experience and be a market leader. All of these banks are directing their technological expenditures in support of business considerations, not just technical elegance. These banks have done as good a job as is reasonably possible to create *profits* in addition to creating value.

Third, we see the value of focus, especially in the light of the industry's trend to disaggregation. State Street is highly focused and has demonstrated great leadership in its chosen lines of business. Chase's formation of InfoServ International has been seconded in recent years by other money center banks; for example, Manufacturers Hanover's creation of a division for processing businesses called Geoserve. The stock market is more aware of the annuity value of processing business and organizational isolation may help boost banks' stock prices.

These lessons, and more, are summarized in Figure 9–2. In the next chapter we will discuss five specific management guidelines that draw on these illustrations, as well as on information from preceding chapters.

CHAPTER 10

MANAGEMENT GUIDELINES

As information technology increasingly penetrates the banking industry, banks need to focus on wringing more profits from their technological investments. Based on our experiences in client engagements and on the lessons of Chapter 9, we have developed five key management guidelines that we believe are sometimes neglected. These guidelines are specific to the management of technology, and can help a bank *as a whole* achieve better financial performance. But they not a substitute for following best practices in the technical aspects of data processing, such as project management, data center management, and optimal systems design. In a word, they are business guidelines, not technical recommendations.

Our five guidelines:

- Link business strategy more effectively with technological reality.
- Adopt simultaneous tight–loose policies to manage systems investments.
- Treat routine automation differently from distinctive automation.
- Consider industry systems capacity when making product decisions.
- Focus, focus, focus: Get rid of those huge shared cost structures.

LINK BUSINESS STRATEGY TO TECHNOLOGICAL REALITY

Our first guideline may sound obvious, but is actually pretty difficult to do. Most bankers think they do a pretty good job of it already. One client said to us, "We have a business strategy (in a given product) that is 'such and such.' It is based on competitive analysis, market needs, and corporate strengths. Our users are in the driver's seat. Their needs determine the (appropriate) technology which MIS then supplies."

This approach is good, but it does not go far enough. A different client invested heavily in a piece of software that worked beautifully. But the underlying business was being immobilized as the paper-based securities on which it depended were being replaced by electronic tracking of ownership. The result? The bank in question continued losing money in this line of business.

Automating the Wrong Channel

Here is another case: A bank was interested in further automating its branch network. It felt that its competitors were investing in advanced teller terminals and sophisticated PCs for platform officers so that most inquiries and transactions could be handled on-line. So this bank designed a new branch information delivery system that could do almost anything. Every product could be sold and every data base accessed. Insurance and investments were available, as well as cash management and credit card products. Any type of question could be answered. Local processing, office automation, and image processing filled out the picture. Even remote databases such as D&B business reports could be accessed. (See Figure 10–1.)

Yet it is possible to question this approach, even if it is technically feasible. One justification given by the bank was that having all that information at the fingertips of the branch employees would help bring customers back into the branches. Our issue was: Did it make sense? Was the evolving role of the teller and the branch appropriate for the addition of so much technology?

At this bank, for example, only 20 percent of the noncredit-card consumer loan balances (and almost none of the credit cards) had been generated through the branch network. In line with the national trend to disaggregation, the bank was generating auto loans and leases through indirect dealer programs, mortgages through real estate agents, and student loans through referrals on college campuses. Partly as a consequence, the customers were spread out all over the country, not just in the one state where the branches were located. The question is: Why would these people go to (or telephone) a branch for questions or transactions?

Sale of bank products is not the only function being diverted away from the branches. Customer service functions are also being diverted. For instance, Wells Fargo opened a 24-hour telephone-based customer service feature in 1988. Customers calling in can speak to a representative

FIGURE 10–1
New Branch Information Delivery System

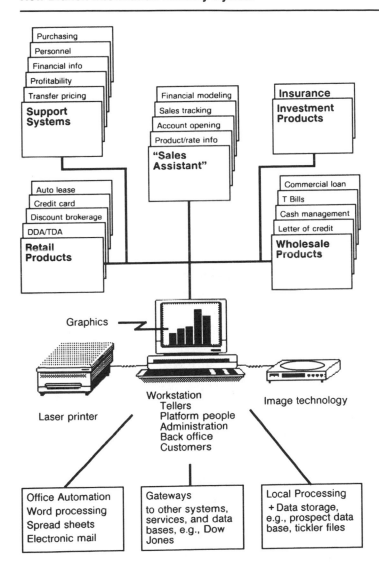

who can handle more than 100 different transactions for virtually any retail product. This capability depends on the customer service representatives having access to advanced on-line technology. Wells Fargo is receiving approximately 75,000 calls per day and may well experience a concomitant reduction in routine branch traffic. Citizens & Southern's version of the same thing handles approximately 50,000 transactions per day.

But the bank with the new branch information delivery system had failed to think through all the implications. Who in the branch was going to learn those systems? Answering customers' questions requires a high level of proficiency in order to find the right on-line screen and interpret the data correctly, and changing an item in the customer data base really requires some skill. It is reasonable that branch people should know how to adjust retail deposit accounts and possibly installment loans. But cash management, insurance, and letter-of-credit products?

Efforts to automate the wrong channel are not new. Should the horse-drawn milk wagon, popular in American cities at the end of the last century, have been automated? Trucks might have been used instead, and home delivery made more productive, but it did not work out that way. Home delivery of perishable goods died out entirely because the automobile spurred low-density suburban developments and high-volume supermarkets that could be reached easily by shoppers. So the right move for a milk wagon company might have been to change its business system entirely, not just automate its wagons.

The same dilemma faces property-casualty insurance companies today as they consider investing hundreds of millions to automate the offices of, and the communication links with, their independent agents. No one knows for sure how the independent agency system will change under the weight of automation or whether its economic viability can be sustained in the long run. At least in personal lines, direct writers such as Allstate and direct marketers such as USAA seem to be having an easier time in making technology fit their business objectives.

The moral for banks: Take a comprehensive view of the service delivery system and how it is changing; do not just reflexively automate branches—or anything else. Integrating business and technology is a lot more complicated than it sounds. In fact, it entails an iterative consideration of the three levels of technology management (M1–M2–M3) introduced in Chapter 3.

The Iterative Process

To prevent reflexive automation that may not achieve the desired purpose, we suggest using the M1–M2–M3 framework in an iterative way. In theory, the three levels of technology management are laid out linearly. But in practice, the business needs level, the applied technology level, and the core technology level are all related to each other in a circular way. There is no single starting place, and the ultimate balance between the three is found through repetition and iteration. (See Figure 10–2.)

In the typical process espoused by most banks, M3 business needs, as determined by users, determine the M2–A applications and the M2–B processing activities (see again Figure 3–3.) Of course, this approach is helpful in putting the users in command. In turn, the M2–A characteristics (software capacity, response time, configuration, etc.) determine the need for core technology (M1). To close the circle, new developments in core technology (M1) should be part of the thinking about the business. It is tough to juggle these three factors all at once, but it can be very rewarding. It requires integrating what the technology can do (a moving target, if ever there was one) with what might (or might not) work in the marketplace.

Evaluating a New Technology

For example, relational databases are just one of numerous technological developments. They are practical for maintaining customer data bases, and their performance for high-volume transaction processing applications is improving. By mid-1988, for example, IBM's flagship product DB2 Version 2 could handle system-enforced referential integrity and had increased both its on-line transaction and batch processing rates by more than 50 percent. The question is this: Does this growing feasibility—at this time—invite some new product or business approach? (See Figure 10–3.)

One possible answer: Relational technology makes it easier to keep track of greater amounts of data. Much more information on customer payment patterns will be available and potentially usable. American Express is already moving to take advantage of what it knows about its cardholders' patterns of purchases. Could banks do the same? For example, by extracting payee data from checks, could a bank begin to sell the

FIGURE 10–2
Iterative Business/Technology Linkage

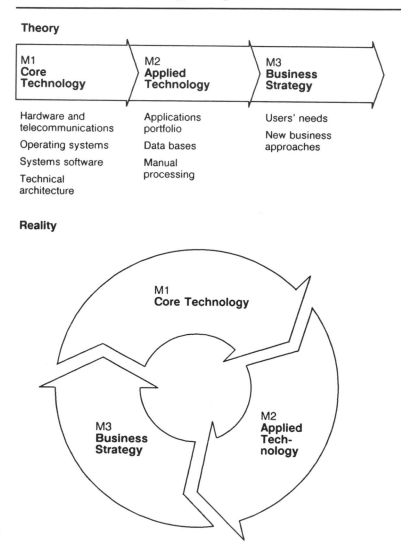

Theory

M1 Core Technology	M2 Applied Technology	M3 Business Strategy
Hardware and telecommunications	Applications portfolio	Users' needs
Operating systems	Data bases	New business approaches
Systems software	Manual processing	
Technical architecture		

Reality

names of customers who buy certain types of products? Could it segment its customers by balance levels, purpose of purchases, or volume of transactions? Could a retail bank maintain a small database on every customer and assist customers in making payments and handling their cash flow? Although these concepts have hardly ever been explored in banking,

FIGURE 10–3
Evaluating a New Technology

Business Needs Drive Applied Technology Needs

Business need	Impact on applied technology
New retail products offering more consumer choice, value, and return	Applications to support processing of individual deposit and loan products
	PC software to help platform personnel illustrate new products

Applied Technology Needs Dictate Core Technology Capabilities

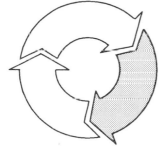

Applied technology need	Impact on core technology
Extra data for additional product parameters, e.g., variable rate consumer loans	Additional capacity for processing transactions and on-line storage
	On-line terminals for customer service

New Core Technologies Create Potential Business Threats/ Opportunities

Core technology developments	Potential opportunity/ threat for business strategy
Relational data bases	Customer data base allows more cross-selling, favoring direct marketing and integrated products
Expert systems	Specialized knowledge will allow targeted focus on high-risk lending business
Image processing	Increased cost advantage of centralized, high-volume processor

current technology is now making it more feasible to do so. Now is the time for banks to ask themselves these types of questions.

The technology-to-business linkage is different from the standard approach for employing new technologies. Many systems people might think about using a relational database just to end the redundancies in their existing databases. That is a typical intra-M1 data processing decision and very probably a wise use of the technology. But if it works, every bank will do it, and the effect will be defensive, not competitive. Automation is most profitable when it makes possible new, value-creating activities. It is less so when it streamlines old activities.

Unfortunately, it is this linkage—changing the business system—that so often gets shortchanged. Of course, it is very difficult to understand the risks of changing a business system and to know whether they are acceptable. Figuring out the risks is what managers get paid to do. *But implementing new technology without thinking about new business approaches will probably produce average results at best.*

MANAGE WITH SIMULTANEOUS TIGHT–LOOSE POLICIES

Once strategies adequately reflect technological reality, attention must be turned to managing the enterprise-wide systems infrastructure. Traditionally, banks have relied most on organization as a lever for management control. Typically, they have centralized the core DP resources—data centers and systems programmers, for example—to promote efficiency and ensure adequate control. To solve problems arising from centralization, such as unresponsiveness, some banks have decentralized resources such as applications development groups or departmental minicomputers. To create better communications, banks have organized committees that include both users and developers. The reporting lines of the DP department have often been shuffled—first reporting to accounting, then to operations, then to a CFO, possibly even to the CEO. Multibank holding companies have experimented with completely separate DP departments for subsidiary banks.

But all of these ideas are simply rearrangements of organizational boxes. Little has usually occurred in how things fundamentally get done. There has usually been a lack of explicit policy that guides (and determines) the actions that various actors can take. This lack of policy helps to explain why organizational changes occur so frequently. They are

FIGURE 10–4
Systems Policy—Architecture Choices

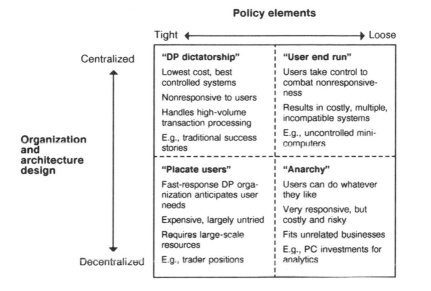

Policy elements

	Tight ⟵——————————————⟶ Loose	
Centralized	**"DP dictatorship"**	**"User end run"**
	Lowest cost, best controlled systems	Users take control to combat nonresponsive-ness
	Nonresponsive to users	
	Handles high-volume transaction processing	Results in costly, multiple, incompatible systems
Organization and architecture design	E.g., traditional success stories	E.g., uncontrolled mini-computers
	"Placate users"	**"Anarchy"**
	Fast-response DP organization anticipates user needs	Users can do whatever they like
	Expensive, largely untried	Very responsive, but costly and risky
	Requires large-scale resources	Fits unrelated businesses
Decentralized	E.g., trader positions	E.g., PC investments for analytics

ineffective, do not solve the problem, and simply invite more change because management has not yet learned to operate in other dimensions.

With the development of technology and the far greater number of business lines that depend on technology, the need for a second management lever has become much greater. This lever is policy. A good definition of the word *policy* can be found in Marvin Bower's book, *The Will to Manage.** It is "a plan for action in prescribed circumstances." A policy defines how people can act when they must act on their own. Policies help control the actions of employees so that they support the corporate objectives in consistent and predictable ways. Because bank DP departments have so often had centralized organizations, policy elements that determine how people can act have usually not been developed. Instead, DP departments have just made decisions based on their perception of the world outside the DP department—decisions that may or may not be correct.

An improvement to this situation is to implement what we call simultaneous tight–loose policy elements, adding a second dimension to how systems infrastructure can be managed. The result is a two-dimensional,

---

*McGraw-Hill Book Co., 1966.

four-box matrix. (See Figure 10–4.) Each box is a generalized abstraction of an approach that a bank might take to a part of a specific DP project. Because there are always dozens, even hundreds, of projects being implemented at any given time, a bank should find itself using all four quadrants at once. This approach can give a bank more flexibility and increase the extent to which its management of technology is in sync with the expanded scope and functionality of newer technology.

The meaning of the phrase *tight–loose* is that a new corporate systems policy cannot (and should not) specify how actions are carried out *in all cases*. Rather a policy should set some standards and procedures but also allow users the latitude to make their own choices when applications do not need to adhere to bankwide standards. For example, a bank's policy for its traders might be that they can develop their own applications as long as bankwide information exists to manage risk and fund positions. Standards to implement this policy could include:

1. one network for all trading desks,
2. common database management software,
3. standard formats for position data, and
4. limits on which application packages can be employed.

To elaborate on this approach, let us look separately at each box in the tight–loose policy matrix.

- *DP dictatorship*. This has been the traditional road to success for banks. Particularly for high-volume transaction processing, this approach will probably continue to be applicable. Even for more distributed applications, some projects need to be placed here. Networks and network interface are a good example. A bankwide network needs to be rigorously consistent and its operation must be centralized. At the same time, it must be under tight policy control. There is no room for looseness in defining interfaces.
- *User End Run*. How users accomplish that interface is another story. They usually get impatient if the purchase of PCs or workstations, for example, is too tightly controlled. User End Run is a better way to give users the flexibility to choose which equipment to install – provided it can handle the interface. If abused, this approach can result in costly, multiple or incompatible systems. But, unresponsiveness on the part of centralized DP groups is a form of abuse, too. It should be up to user groups to pay for, and benefit from, the loose policy elements.

- *Anarchy.* When banks attempt too much decentralization too fast, there is usually no policy at all and the users end up doing whatever they please—in ignorance of each others' actions. The approach is very responsive, but is also very costly. An appropriate example is the development of position analytics by bank traders. Another example could be spreadsheets for credit analysis of wholesale loan applications. What would be inappropriate would be laissez-faire investments in computers or systems software that could not be networked to other parts of the bank.
- *Placate Users.* A final option is to have tight policy elements in a decentralized organization. Position reporting would be one example. It must be done by each user (in a trading department, for example), yet must meet a tight definition. Were this not done, the data could not be combined with other positions to create accurate bankwide reports. This approach placates users by giving them autonomy of action within a framework of bankwide definitions and standards.

An understanding of this matrix and the rich increase in management options that use of *two* levers can provide should help banks manage their increasingly complex systems infrastructures even better. Even one development project may have some elements that fall in all four quadrants. To ensure success, banks will also need to publish standards and procedures to implement their chosen policy. They will need to audit their users to ascertain that they are, indeed, adhering to established policy standards. Most banks have never done this—simply because they had no policies designed to control individual actions. Yet, with a possibility of loose policy elements, some users will inevitably violate policy through ignorance or design. Enforcement will be necessary in monitoring compliance.

We believe this simultaneous tight–loose policy approach is a new and needed aspect of bank systems management. As infrastructure and business dependence grows, new approaches must reflect the diversity of needs. This approach can help banks do just that.

TREAT ROUTINE VERSUS DISTINCTIVE
AUTOMATION DIFFERENTLY

In Chapter 2, we stated that 90 percent of all systems investments support "routine" functions. These include not only true overhead—such as a payroll, general ledger, or accounting system—but also product systems, such as transaction accounts, which simply aren't distinctive. Only 10 percent of systems investments support distinctive tasks, which are tasks that others can not easily equal or duplicate.

We are not trying to suggest that investing in routine functions is unnecessary. On the contrary, routine programs and functions create the data upon which value-added distinctive applications depend. Routine data is as necessary as is the foundation of a building. Marble-walled lobbies and plush interior decorations may sell office buildings, but if the foundation is deficient the entire building is probably at risk. The same principal applies to information systems.

Some banks have erred in exactly the opposite direction by putting too little emphasis on the foundation. In one case we know, a major bank developed a sophisticated corporate customer relationship system. Its laudable objective was to take data from different accounting systems throughout the bank and create a true and comprehensive picture of the total customer relationship. Unfortunately, the project never worked very well. Because the new system could not be truly integrated with the underlying systems, it was layered on top. A series of "pipes" carried data up into the relationship management system. But, some of the needed data was not in the underlying systems to begin with. The data feeds in the pipes became ever more tenuous as some of the underlying data was massaged to create the relationship data. The steady stream of day-to-day changes in the underlying systems were generally not reflected in the pipes. The result was a system that was not trusted, was not used much, and did not help its owner's competitive position very much.

The key is to know whether a systems project is routine or differentiable and to tailor the strategy accordingly—minimizing costs for routine investments, and increasing systems allocations for distinctive initiatives. Most banks fail to make enough distinction between the two. They end up *overspending on basic functions that will never show a return, and underspending on high-value activities that could have yielded a better return if properly funded.*

Handling Routine Functions

We have two basic suggestions for handling routine systems investments: (1) use appropriate, not leading, technology, and (2) use shared solutions as much as is reasonable. Both suggestions work toward the same goal of reducing costs. After all, if the function is routine, there will be no competitive impact unless the bank screws up. The investment should be treated defensively, and that means minimizing costs consistent with safety, not leading in technology. Becoming state-of-the-art should not be considered unless there are specific and visible benefits. Yet many banks with state-of-the-art data centers and thousands of new PCs have worn-out, "me-too" renditions of the same old products.

Having accepted this lesson on state-of-the-art solutions, shared solutions make more sense. Unfortunately, too many banks have neglected this approach. IBM's Don Long, a long-time observer of banking and technology, tells the story of the S/360 introduction in 1964. It was a huge success and all the New York banks lined up to buy one. They were all interested in using it to process transaction accounts, but there was no applications software to do so. According to Long, IBM sponsored a meeting for the banks to band together and write the software cooperatively. We understand that, unfortunately, the meeting disintegrated in a welter of arguments and the cooperative software effort didn't occur. Whether or not such circumstances of this ill-fated meeting really occurred, the fact is that 25 years later many New York banks have proprietary deposit systems that all do mostly the same thing.

Banks are, however, using packages considerably more than in the past. They are increasingly determining that the integrated packages now on the market have the potential to be more powerful and cost-effective than writing a new proprietary system. We estimate that one-third of the top 300 banks have installed at least one module of Hogan's IBA package (marketed by IBM), even if few of them have installed the whole thing. Even Citicorp, the epitome of proprietary technology, uses the Hogan system for some of its savings and loan acquisitions.

The Expansion of Shared Solutions

Another way to think about shared solutions is as standard technology. *Over time, the capability and functionality available in the standard technology expands.* That is, the bank user gets pushed farther away from the core technology all the time.

The advancements over the past 30 years in computer languages are a good illustration of this. In the beginning, computers were coded in machine language, and programmers actually had to know it. Then Assembler language came in and programmers learned that. Assembler was not only fast, but it also used CPU resources sparingly, because they were then very expensive. Some shops or packages still use Assembler in places, but it is inflexible and requires painstaking work by experts when changes are needed. Then came higher level languages, such as COBOL, and operating systems that did a lot of work that bank programmers used to do. There was a time when banks wrote their own systems software. One mid-South institution we know still uses a proprietary telecommunications monitor, written in the 1960s before CICS became available. Now, however, off-the-shelf operating systems handle the interface with the peripheral devices, and banks' programmers can worry about real user needs instead of, for example, disk queuing or blocking and deblocking of records. The result has been a terrific expansion in the amount of production code, and a higher level of functionality.

Today, the standard technology is the integrated application package for core banking functions. When McKinsey helped a new private bank, Banco Commercial Portuguese (BCP), to begin operations in 1986, integrated packages were selected for all core retail and wholesale functions. BCP quickly turned profitable and achieved a leading market position in three years. Although no large bank is likely to start up in the United States, it would probably rely on packages if it did. The cost advantage is just too strong.

In fact, the growth of integrated package offerings from vendors has been dramatic. In 1988, the Branch Banking Division of MHC, with 221 branches and $15 billion in retail deposits, became the largest bank at that time to buy the Systematics package. Although Banc One and Norwest decided not to build a proprietary system when they found existing packages inadequate, they agreed to partner with EDS to develop a totally new integrated system. Currently, EDS, Banc One, and Norwest are moving forward in developing the Strategic Banking System, which is reputed to be one of the first CASE-based "open systems." Institutions facing the issue of core systems replacement or evaluating new options in enterprise architecture are obviously watching the outcome of developments like the Strategic Banking System project.

Yet some banks are still taking the risk of creating their own software, especially with the newer technologies. They might not think, for example, that any of the current expert system shells are up to the task, so they enter into special arrangements with vendors to develop new ones. But within a decade, it is likely that standard expert system shells will have improved greatly, bypassing any that banks try to build their own.

Based on our client experience, we believe that, on balance, banks ought to bet on the vendors (and their standard products) for the technology, not on themselves.

WATCH INDUSTRY CAPACITY

Our fourth guideline is to watch industry capacity when making product decisions. This capacity is constantly increasing and therefore has the constant potential to be a threat. These capacity increases result from the large banks' increased levels of systems expenditures and the concomitant upsurge in the availability of processing power.

Most of this added processing power gets converted into capacity. Thus, banks need to look carefully at industry capacity before they invest in increased output. Simply put, if demand for the new service is not significantly greater than current capacity, the investment may be unwise. The issue of industry capacity is especially crucial for large banks, because they tend to compete in the most concentrated businesses. But banks have traditionally not thought much about capacity. The word is not well-defined and there are not many measurements of it. Capacity in banking is a concept crying for development.

In the old paper-based world, when transaction processing was done by people, capacity was less of an issue. Processing was a variable cost, not a fixed one. A bank did not have to "invest in" (i.e., hire) several hundred programmers before the customers could be signed up. It could hire them slowly as the number of transactions grew. The tradition of locally protected markets also made capacity concerns less relevant. Banks could watch local market share (i.e., their percent of deposits or branches) and know where they stood.

But the industry has changed. Capacity is highly relevant when a bank must reinvest tens or even hundreds of millions of dollars to keep its core systems up-to-date. Because competition now has more of a global character, the actions of a competitor anywhere in the world can have repercussions. Watching what the competition does is essential.

When bank competitors invest tens of millions of dollars in a new system, they build new capacity and new features that deliver more and better products. They support what the customer wants today, but can not get. If the customer is a corporate treasurer, for example, and the product is lockbox, the new system may offer better reporting, faster availability, and higher accuracy. Lockbox competitors who can not meet those features will shortly find themselves losing business. So it makes sense that the capacity of others to produce the same product and sell it, possibly at a lower price, ought to be carefully considered. *Unfortunately, banks rarely keep their antennae out for these competitive events.* Too often, they only look at what is right in front of them: their own costs, for example, and how they can be reduced. But thinking about (and measuring) industry capacity, especially given the lead in systems that the large banks are opening up, is too often an alien concept.

FOCUS, FOCUS, FOCUS

Our final rule is to focus on a more limited set of business lines, and in so doing, break up shared cost structures. Commercial banks tend to have higher shared cost structures than do other types of companies. In a typical manufacturing corporation, for instance, direct costs (parts, raw material, and labor) might be 80 percent or more of total cost. Because shared costs are low, a large industrial corporation can separate its strategic business units (SBUs) so that each controls its own destiny. Synergy comes through sharing common distribution channels, for example, or through common usage of R&D facilities. But the costs to produce each specific product can be isolated and identified, allowing effective control over the products.

With banking products, however, the 80/20 split is almost reversed. In each engagement in which McKinsey has looked carefully at the costs to produce banking products, as a general rule we have come away convinced that 50 to 80 percent of the total costs of each bank product come from *shared* cost structures. From 15 to 20 percent is in the real overhead (personnel, administration, etc.), 20 to 40 percent is in the distribution system and centralized operations, and 15 to 20 percent is in the cost of data processing. Figure 10–5 illustrates the organizational difference between a typical bank and a typical industrial corporation.

These high shared costs are a significant problem because they make it difficult to pin down product (and customer) economics. Many assumptions and allocations must be made to account for all of the costs. Some product or SBU inevitably looks worse than others and its sponsors question the allocative process, which then loses credibility and political support. Even when product economics are accepted, the relevant business

FIGURE 10–5
Complexities in Bank Cost Structures

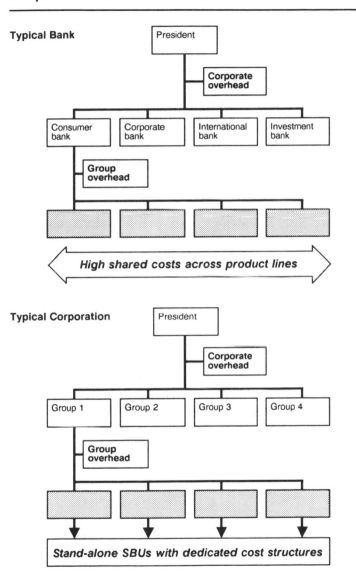

Typical Bank

President

Corporate
overhead

Consumer bank | Corporate bank | International bank | Investment bank

Group
overhead

High shared costs across product lines

Typical Corporation

President

Corporate
overhead

Group 1 | Group 2 | Group 3 | Group 4

Group
overhead

Stand-alone SBUs with dedicated cost structures

managers can not control those costs. How are product managers supposed to reduce the 25 percent of their costs that come from the branch network? They cannot. It is that simple. Despite the advancement of management science in banking, little has been done to free managers from the tyranny of shared costs, and the resultant obscurity has made it next to impossible to focus on the most important investments.

The Tyranny of Shared Costs

Examples of banks' shared costs abound. Check processing is a major cost element of virtually every wholesale and retail banking product and is almost always done centrally. Securities processing operations are usually shared, regardless of whether the customer is a correspondent bank, a broker/dealer, or an institutional investor. Many loan processing functions share the same back-office support, such as applications processing or records retention. And the typical branch facility offers dozens of products and services that cannot be accurately disaggregated.

The arrival of systems technology has only made this problem worse. The massive, centralized data centers that service every single product are obscuring accountability in the name of productivity. Despite the existence of DP charge-back systems, few managers either believe their charge-back costs or *take steps to control them.* Many users have told us that they can not even understand their DP charges. They request functional support but get charged for more CPU cycles.

Likewise, the product proliferation resulting from systems technology's capabilities has contributed to the problem. Today's typical consumer bank may have 40 or so consumer loan products, 30 or so deposit products, 3 or 4 credit cards, small commercial loans, cash management services, fee-based services, foreign exchange, commercial deposit services, and on and on. And of course each product has variations, options, parameters, choices, and bells and whistles. Many customers get special treatment—in essence receiving their own unique proprietary product. This is good for the customer, of course, but it makes cost accounting a real nightmare.

Two historical reasons have contributed to this confusing state of affairs: First, customers traditionally maintained a bundled relationship with their bank, paying for a variety of services in just one way (e.g., by leaving noninterest-bearing deposits). Second, customers were unsophisticated about managing down the excess balances that came about through the normal ebb and flow of activity, so banks made a lot of money on float.

As a result, the industry has never had a strong culture of stand-alone product profitability. If it had, more banks might have resisted the continued development of such huge shared cost structures. Instead, non-credit services were offered as loss leaders to get the credit business. Or commodity products such as commercial paper issuance were offered to garner advisory services.

Paradoxically, the high shared cost structure of a typical bank makes it harder to delegate real decision making. If all 150 products use the same DP facilities, communicate on the same telecommunications network, and use the services of the same operations department, who is really in a position to say what gets done? Only the executive who is high enough in the hierarchy to control *both* the SBUs (and their products) and the many and varied support structures. All too often this means the chief executive officer himself, the president, or a similar high-level executive. Decision making just can not get pushed down in the organization.

But these indirect business approaches are being broken up by technology and by the disaggregation of the industry. As more products chase more sophisticated consumers, the deposits and float that used to pay for everything are going away for good. This is why the issue of shared costs is getting more critical. As noninterest expense rises, and as banks increasingly compete in businesses that do not generate revenue through the balance sheet, *the ability to understand costs is more critical.*

Banking's high shared cost structure is partially encouraged by the particular regulatory protections that continue to isolate banks from full contact with an unconstrained and highly competitive market. The Bank of New York consummated the industry's first major hostile takeover in 1988, and similar deals are likely to follow. Some major banks have breakup values far in excess of their market values—a sure stimulus to takeover activity. Eventually, these high shared cost structures should be replaced by more responsive and flexible structures.

How Focus Is Successful

No more dramatic example of focus could be set forth than American Express and its credit cards. The market value of the Green Card alone (valued on earnings) is worth more to the stock market than all of Chemical Bank, Chase, and MHC combined. If we could look at what the president of American Express Travel Related Services Division does all day, we would probably see a lot of just one thing: credit cards. But if we looked at what the president of a major bank does all day, we would see a much different, less focused day. The president's breakfast might be spent reviewing LDC debt, lunch allotted for discussing retail deposit shares, and the afternoon devoted to a particular cash management customer's problems. We do not believe any one executive can get his or her hands around the problems when his or her time is so fragmented.

Many successful banks have already chosen their area of focus. Bankers Trust and J.P. Morgan are well-known for curtailing retail banking and focusing on merchant banking, investment banking, and securities processing. Morgan illustrated real focus in 1988 when it sold its historic (and share-leading) stock transfer business to First Chicago. Its announced reason: a lack of fit with its focus on investment banking.

In like fashion, Republic New York is focusing successfully on private banking; United States Trust and Northern Trust focus on personal and corporate trust; Bank of Boston and Fleet Financial focus on middle-market and corporate lending in the New England region; and Bank of New York focuses on securities processing, dealers clearance, and other wholesale banking businesses. Even Citicorp has a focus, in a sense: to be the nation's only really large, truly full-service bank.

Focus can mean dropping out of business lines, which some banks have done. Chase quit retail lockbox. First Chicago sold its freight rating and payments business (and took a book loss of $13 million). Wells Fargo dropped out of the CHIPS clearing business. Citicorp quit stock transfer. Bank of America, at one time the eighth-largest player, dropped out of master trust/custody. Sometimes, the need for focus means subcontracting a function instead of doing it internally. In 1989, a major Canadian bank, which originates approximately 25,000 CHIPS payments per month, discontinued its internal funds transfer system and switched to one of the major CHIPS clearers. It saved approximately $9 million per year.

However focus is accomplished, the need to focus will increase as the dependence on systems technology multiples. Each successive round of systems investment, caused by better and better price performance in core technology, seems to become more and more expensive. As computer systems replace manual and paper-based work, the fixed cost component rises — making it even more imperative to shrug off the shared cost albatross.

A focused bank, with considerably fewer products and business lines, could be a great success in the evolving banking world of tomorrow. Yet becoming focused may require the bank of today to make some hard choices. Any bank with 150 products and below-average returns—which includes about one-half of all banks—has got to be achieving a substandard ROE on a significant portion of its product/market segments. Culling out the losers is essential for future success.

SUMMARY

No amount of advice on the subject of technology in banking is going to guarantee success. Both technology and banking are complicated subjects, leading to great difficulties in determining the correct action in specific cases. Nevertheless, we have described these five guidelines simply because we believe they are neglected and are becoming more relevant with time. They are no panacea for poor business strategy, bad management, or sloppy handling of system development projects. Our hope is to help management think more creatively and act more purposefully about systems.

Linking technology with strategy is sound advice, assuming the strategy is a good one. But knowing how to create this linkage is another issue. We believe that the long-term trend of disaggregation is related to the presence of systems technology. As more technology inevitably enters banking, more disaggregation will occur. Maximizing returns will require doing things differently—not simply automating current methods.

More than good strategy is required. Managing successfully will mean adopting management practices that reflect an automated age. Our tight–loose policy guideline is one such practice. Another is the need to handle routine investments differently from value-added ones. And the imperative for greater organizational focus will require more management attention to the issue of where (and when) to place resources. Managing differently and doing different things is a key requirement for coping successfully with technology.

The future promises to be challenging for the banking industry. While being buffeted by regulatory problems and change, serving an ever more demanding worldwide customer base, and grappling with the forces of consolidation, bankers must also cope with unprecedented technological change. Although great value will be created by this technology, not every bank will enjoy the transformative process. In many cases, profits will be destroyed—despite the value created. In the end, those that do the best job of coping with the impact of technology on the business are those that will be the banking powers in the future.

INDEX